POLITICAL POWER AND WOMEN'S REPRESENTATION IN LATIN AMERICA

POLITICAL POWER AND WOMEN'S REPRESENTATION IN LATIN AMERICA

Leslie A. Schwindt-Bayer

OXFORD
UNIVERSITY PRESS

OXFORD
UNIVERSITY PRESS

Oxford University Press is a department of the University of Oxford.
It furthers the University's objective of excellence in research, scholarship,
and education by publishing worldwide.

Oxford New York
Auckland Cape Town Dar es Salaam Hong Kong Karachi
Kuala Lumpur Madrid Melbourne Mexico City Nairobi
New Delhi Shanghai Taipei Toronto

With offices in
Argentina Austria Brazil Chile Czech Republic France Greece
Guatemala Hungary Italy Japan Poland Portugal Singapore
South Korea Switzerland Thailand Turkey Ukraine Vietnam

Published in the United States of America by
Oxford University Press
198 Madison Avenue, New York, NY 10016

First issued as an Oxford University Press paperback, 2012.

Library of Congress Cataloging-in-Publication Data
Schwindt-Bayer, Leslie A.
Political power and women's representation in Latin America / Leslie A. Schwindt-Bayer.
p. cm.
Includes bibliographical references and index.
ISBN 978-0-19-973195-4 (hardcover); 978-0-19-993866-7 (paperback)
1. Women legislators—Latin America. 2. Women in politics—Latin America. I. Title.
HQ1236.5.L37S39 2010
328.80082—dc22 2009044072

Printed in the United States of America
on acid-free paper

For Ethan

Acknowledgments

This book is long in coming and never would have been achieved without the support of a wide array of friends, colleagues, and institutions. I am sure I have forgotten someone in this list, and for that I apologize, but I would like to thank several people for reading and commenting on various versions of the chapters in this book (or the entire manuscript), giving me advice on where to publish it, and offering suggestions on the book prospectus: Moises Arce, Lisa Baldez, Bob Brown, John Bruce, Brian Crisp, Mala Htun, Miki Kittilson, Scott Mainwaring, Bill Mishler, Barbara Norrander, Pippa Norris, Michelle Taylor-Robinson, Sue Thomas, and Nina Wiesehomeier. I also am indebted to those who helped me at various stages of the data collection for this project: numerous staffers in the Costa Rican and Colombian legislative archives, the Argentine research assistants who conducted the survey of legislators in Argentina, Felipe Botero, Brian Crisp, Bagel Johnson, Mark Jones, Erika Moreno, and Salvador Peralta.

This book would not have been possible without institutional and financial support from several places: the Fulbright Student Grant Program that funded my fieldwork in Colombia in 2002; a Tinker Foundation Grant for fieldwork in Costa Rica in 1999; the Croft Institute for International Studies at the University of Mississippi, which supported fieldwork in Argentina (2006); the University of Missouri Summer Research Fellowship Program for funding that allowed me to work on the book in the summer of 2008; and perhaps most important, the Kellogg Institute for International Studies at the University of Notre Dame, which gave me a semester away as a visiting fellow in fall 2008 to focus solely on completing this book.

Many thanks also to the anonymous reviewers of this manuscript who generously pointed out the contributions they thought this book could make and the deficiencies that were preventing it from making them. Although still far from perfect, the end product is better than it would have been without their careful reading and pointed critiques. In addition, I greatly appreciate the positive response that my editor, Angela Chnapko, gave to this manuscript from the first time she saw it and her continued support and assistance with making it into the book it is now.

Finally, I thank my husband, Jeff Bayer, for letting me escape my responsibilities at home to go to Notre Dame, put my head down, and finish this project. It would not have happened otherwise. His ongoing support lets me balance work and family and be successful at both. I am also grateful for his graphic design skills, which he used to design the book cover.

Despite my current feeling of immense accomplishment having completed this book, I know that it is in many ways still incomplete. Our efforts to write the "perfect" book are always flawed, and for those flaws I take full responsibility. I do hope, at the very least, however, that this book offers some insight into the nature of women's representation in Latin America, triggers discussion and critique, and generates interest in gender issues in the region among new scholars. If it manages these tasks, I will know that my efforts, however flawed, have been a success.

Contents

POLITICAL POWER AND WOMEN'S REPRESENTATION IN LATIN AMERICA

1

Introduction

A Theory of Women's Political Representation

Since the democratic transitions of the 1980s, women have gained unprecedented access to governments in Latin America. Four women have been elected president of Latin American democracies—Violeta Barrios de Chamorro in Nicaragua (1990–1997), Mireya Moscoso de Arias in Panama (1999–2004), Michelle Bachelet in Chile (2006–2010), and Cristina Fernández de Kirchner in Argentina (2007–2011)—and many others have run for, and seriously contended, executive office. In 2006, the average percentage of presidential cabinet posts that were held by women was 17%, up from 9% in 1990 (Htun 2000; UNDP 2008), and women have been appointed to ministries with high prestige, such as defense, foreign relations, economics, finance, and agriculture (Escobar-Lemmon and Taylor-Robinson 2005).

Women also have gained access to many national legislatures in growing numbers (see table 1.1). In the region as a whole, the average percentage of Latin American lower houses that were female in 2008 was 20%, second only to the Nordic region's exceptionally large average of 41%. This is a dramatic increase from 12% in 1995 (IPU 1995). The growth in women's representation in several countries has been particularly notable. In Argentina, for example, the first election of the current democratic period in 1983 resulted in only 4% of those in the Chamber of Deputies being female. By 2001, women comprised 31% of the lower house of congress. Costa Rica, one of Latin America's longest standing democracies, had only 3 female deputies (5%) in the 1974–1978 Legislative Assembly but witnessed a jump from 19% in 1998 to 35% in the 2002 election. Argentina and Costa Rica have been among the top 10 countries in the world in terms of the numbers of women in parliament for several years, currently ranking fifth and eighth, respectively (IPU 2008).[1] Not far behind them are Peru, Ecuador, Honduras, and Mexico with more than 20% of their national congresses being female. Other Latin American countries, however, have not witnessed such substantial gains in women's representation. Brazil and Colombia have the lowest representation of women in Latin America, averaging around 10% across both chambers of their national legislatures. Paraguay, Uruguay, and Guatemala also are near the bottom of the list with only 12% of their lower houses being female. The representation of women in all Latin American countries has increased in the past 30 years but to a much smaller degree in some countries than in others.

The growing number of women in politics in Latin America and the continued wide variation across countries augurs some important questions about women's representation in the region. Why has women's access to politics increased in Latin America, and why does it vary so widely across countries? How does having women in office affect politics? And what are the consequences of women's representation in politics for representative democracy? I answer these questions in this book with a comprehensive study of women's representation in Latin American legislatures. In this chapter, I present a theoretical framework that links all of these questions together and explains why women get elected; what they do in office and why women's representation varies across legislative activities,

TABLE 1.1. Percentage of Legislature that Is Female, as of 2008

Country	Lower House	Upper House	Congress Average
Argentina	40.0	38.9	39.5
Costa Rica	36.8	–	36.8
Peru	29.2	–	29.2
Ecuador	25.0	–	25.0
Honduras	23.4	–	23.4
Mexico	23.2	18.0	20.6
Dominican Republic	19.7	3.1	11.4
Venezuela	18.6	–	18.6
Nicaragua	18.5	–	18.5
Bolivia	16.9	3.7	10.3
El Salvador	16.7	–	16.7
Panama	16.7	–	16.7
Chile	15.0	5.3	10.2
Paraguay	12.5	15.6	14.1
Uruguay	12.1	12.9	12.5
Guatemala	12.0	–	12.0
Brazil	9.0	12.3	10.7
Colombia	8.4	11.8	10.1
Regional Average	**19.7**	**13.5**	**16.6**

Source: IPU (2008).

issue areas, and countries; and what symbolic consequences women's representation has for the electorate. This theory of women's representation applies to a wide range of political settings, but in this book, I test it with an extensive set of original data on Latin American legislatures.

To date, the majority of research on women's representation has focused on industrialized democracies of the West (Thomas 1994; Duerst-Lahti and Kelly 1995; Rosenthal 1998; Carroll 2001; Rosenthal 2002; Swers 2002; Lovenduski and Norris 2003; Childs 2004; Thomas and Wilcox 2005; Dodson 2006; Kittilson 2006; Childs 2008). Ironically, however, some of these countries have elected only small numbers of women to national legislatures (e.g., the United States, Great Britain). Over the past 30 years, the countries of Latin America have transitioned to democracy, undergone notable cultural and socioeconomic changes in regard to gender equality, and witnessed some of the largest increases in the participation of women in national politics around the world. Despite this, we have little information on just what the influx of women means for political representation in Latin America and what the example of Latin American countries may mean for new democracies and developing countries in other regions of the world.

Research on women and politics in Latin America is not sparse, but most studies have focused on women's participation *outside* of the political system rather than *inside* of it. During the transitions to democracy of the 1970s and 1980s, women's political participation occurred almost entirely outside of political institutions as women's movements pressed for democratic openings and greater participation in political decision making. As a result, most research has focused on women's movements and their role in bringing about democratization in Latin America (Jaquette and Wolchik 1998; Baldez 2002), what has happened to those women and movements in the postdemocratic era (Kampwirth 1998; Bayard de Volo 2001), and how women's groups continue to pressure democratic governments from outside the formal structures of government (Banaszak et al. 2003; Waylen 2007).

Research on women *inside* Latin American political systems has emerged only in recent years. Most work has centered on explaining the growing number of women elected to office in Latin America (Jones 1996; Matland and Taylor 1997; Jones 1998; Htun and Jones 2002; Jones 2004b; Schmidt and Saunders 2004; Escobar-Lemmon and Taylor-Robinson 2005; Marx et al. 2007; Archenti and Tula 2008b; Ríos Tobar 2008a). Some studies have examined what female elected officials do in office, but most of them have done so by looking at women only, rather than comparing women *and* men, and have been based on qualitative rather than quantitative analyses (Chaney 1979; Marx 1992; Rivera-Cira 1993; Franceschet 2005; Macaulay 2006; Marx et al. 2007; Saint-Germain and Chavez Metoyer 2008). Those studies that have offered systematic empirical tests for gender differences in substantive representation focus predominantly on the policy priorities of legislators or their committee assignments and often have been country-specific (Jones 1997; Taylor-Robinson and Heath 2003; Schwindt-Bayer 2006; Franceschet and Piscopo 2008). Finally, only a few studies have examined the effects of women's representation in office on citizens' attitudes toward engagement in politics (Desposato and Norrander 2009; Zetterberg 2009).

Because women are increasingly participating in formal institutions in the new democratic era, it is imperative to understand why women are more represented in some Latin American legislatures than others, what role women play in Latin American legislatures, and what changes for representative democracy, if any, are brought about by their presence. With its focus on all three of these questions in Latin America, this book offers a comprehensive study of women's representation in a region that has undergone significant changes in gender equality in many of its countries but has received only limited attention. It shows that even in poorer and younger democracies, institutional mechanisms such as gender quotas and proportional electoral rules help to increase women's access to legislative politics (sometimes in larger numbers than in the developed world) but that women in legislatures face many challenges to doing their jobs as representatives once in government. Both their presence and the work they do in office, however, have positive effects on constituents. Citizens view representative democracy more favorably when women and women's issues are represented. Women in Latin America are gaining a voice in politics and positively shaping the way citizens view still-fragile representative democracies. Yet, they are a long way from equality with men inside the legislative arena. Women's representation in Latin America is incomplete.

An Integrated Model of Women's Representation

The questions that this book asks about women in legislatures in Latin America are inherently about political representation. One of the foremost representation theorists, Hanna Pitkin (1967), conceptualized political representation as being composed of four interrelated dimensions—formal, descriptive, substantive, and symbolic representation. *Formal* representation refers to the rules that authorize representatives to act and the rules by which constituents hold representatives accountable, specifically elections. *Descriptive* representation focuses on the composition of the legislature and the extent to which its diversity mirrors diversity in society. *Substantive* representation deals with the way those elected "act for" their constituents through the activities of representing and their responsiveness to the political concerns of their constituents. Finally, *symbolic* representation emphasizes that representation is a symbol that generates emotional responses among constituents (i.e., feelings and beliefs about politics or government).

Pitkin's classification of the four types of representation has become a mainstay of research on gender and legislative politics. Numerous studies have built upon it in an effort to understand why women get elected to office (descriptive representation), what women do once they are in office (substantive representation), and what the symbolic consequences of women's election to office are for the electorate (symbolic representation). Yet, gender and politics scholars often ignore one important point that Pitkin makes about the concept of representation—that it cannot be disaggregated into its component parts, with each dimension studied in isolation from the others. Instead, Pitkin (1967, 10–11) argues that the only way to fully understand representation is by examining all four dimensions and the relationships among them. In other words, representation must be conceived of as an integrated whole (Schwindt-Bayer and Mishler 2005).

Specifically, the dimensions of representation relate to one another in three key ways. First, formal representation influences descriptive representation. Electoral rules that determine how elections take place, for example, can have a strong effect on how well a representative body reflects social or ideological diversity in society. Second, formal and descriptive representation can influence substantive representation. Electoral rules provide incentives for representatives to "act for" their constituents in different ways. Further, legislatures that more fully mirror diversity in society provide greater opportunities for representation of society's diverse political interests. Finally, formal, descriptive, and substantive representation influence the way the electorate views government. An underrepresented group, for example, is likely to have greater trust in government if it feels that the institutions electing the legislature emphasize representativeness, if there are members of that underrepresented group in power, and if the legislature passes legislation that addresses their unique concerns and policy priorities. Figure 1.1 illustrates this integrated conceptualization of representation.

In this book, I use this theoretical framework for conceptualizing representation to study women's representation. In the next three sections of this chapter, I define and operationalize the four dimensions of representation, articulate the theoretical links between the dimensions and explain how they apply to women's representation, and develop a set of hypotheses about women's representation to test empirically in Latin America. Each section focuses on a different set of relationships (shown in boxes in figure 1.1)—formal and descriptive representation; formal, descriptive, and substantive representation; and the full model. I conclude with a concise summary of the model and a justification for why an integrated theory of women's representation offers the best theoretical framework for studying women's political representation in Latin America.

Formal and Descriptive Representation

The integrated model of representation suggests that formal representation is a key explanation for descriptive representation. But what exactly are formal and

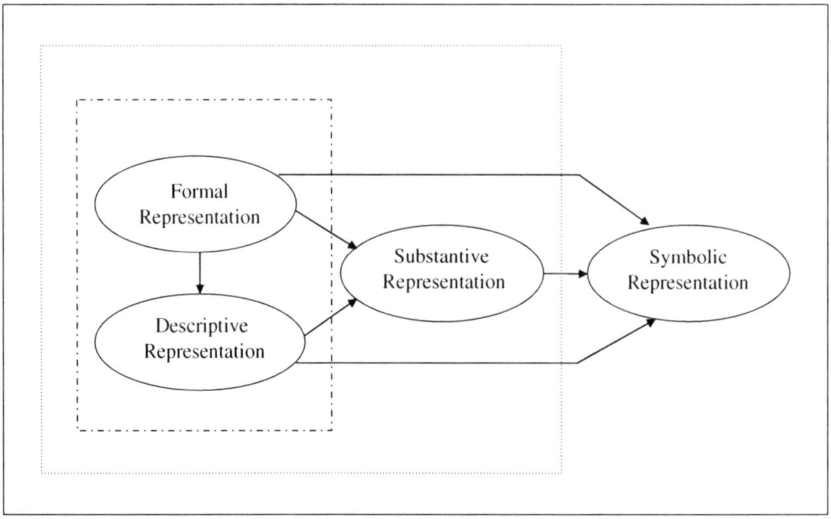

FIGURE 1.1. An Integrated Model of Representation

descriptive representation, and how does formal representation affect descriptive representation of women? Formal representation refers to the institutional arrangements that define the process by which representation occurs. Pitkin argues that formalistic views of representation are about "how it is initiated or how it is terminated," rather than who the representatives are or the act of representing (Pitkin 1969, 9). Formal representation brings together two distinct views of representation. It captures Hobbes' view of representation as giving the elected the *authority* to act in the name of the represented alongside the *accountability* view of representation in which representatives must be held responsible for their actions (Pitkin 1967; Przeworski et al. 1999). Formal representation can be operationalized as the rules and procedures regulating the selection and removal of representatives—in other words, electoral rules.

Descriptive representation refers to the extent to which those elected "stand for" their constituents. It focuses on the degree to which the composition of a legislative body provides "an accurate resemblance" of the citizenry (Pitkin 1969, 11). In other words, it refers to the *representativeness* of the system. Legislatures can be descriptively representative based on occupational correspondence between representatives and the represented or on geographic or territorial correspondence (Marsh and Wessels 1997). They can also be representative in terms of social characteristics, such as race, ethnicity, class, and gender (Norris and Franklin 1997). Descriptive representation is arguably the most studied of Pitkin's four dimensions partly because the composition of the legislature is highly visible and easily measured.

I argue that formal representation affects the descriptive representation of women in legislatures through two types of electoral institutions. First are proportional electoral rules, referring to the proportionality of electoral formula, district magnitude, party magnitude, and the structure of ballots, which all contribute to explaining how representatives get into office and can make it easier or more difficult for women to win office. Second are women-specific electoral institutions, in other words, gender quotas, which require political parties to include a minimum percentage of women on party ballots (or a maximum percentage for any one gender). Quotas are designed specifically to increase the presence of women in politics.

Proportional Electoral Rules

The most prominent explanation for variation in women's representativeness has been electoral institutions. Proportional electoral rules increase the number of women elected to legislatures by creating incentives for women to run for office, encouraging political parties to nominate women to party ballots, and translating votes into seats in a proportional way. Existing literature has found that proportional representation (PR) electoral rules, large district magnitudes, and large party magnitudes are key factors for increasing the number of women elected to legislatures (Duverger 1955; Castles 1981; Norris 1985; Engstrom 1987; Rule 1987; Matland 1993; Oakes and Almquist 1993; Darcy et al. 1994; Matland and Taylor 1997; Kenworthy and Malami 1999; Yoon 2004; Schwindt-Bayer 2005; Paxton and Hughes 2007; Tremblay 2008b). They influence the election of women by making it easier for parties to nominate women without eliminating men from the ballot. This occurs because parties can win multiple seats in any district and because seats get allocated in proportion to the votes that parties receive. Consequently, political parties may be more likely to "risk" the nomination of nontraditional candidates (i.e., women) for the nth seat in multimember districts with proportional representation rather than for the only seat in single member district plurality systems.

In addition, research suggests that the type of party ballot may affect the likelihood that women get elected. For example, proportional representation can be applied in the form of closed lists, in which voters cannot disturb the political party's predetermined ordering of candidates on the ballot, or open lists, in which voters select individual candidates rather than just mark a political party preference. Similarly, majoritarian systems can allow voters to mark multiple candidate preferences, as in the alternative vote (AV) system used in the Australian House of Representatives, or restrict their vote to a single vote for a party or candidate, as in the U.S. House. Allowing voters to mark candidate preferences could help or hurt women regardless of whether it occurs in a proportional or majoritarian system. In societies that are supportive of gender balance, for example, preference voting could lead to more women in office than would party voting (Kittilson 2005; Schmidt 2008b; Tremblay 2008a).

Gender Quotas

Gender quotas are a relatively recent phenomenon in legislatures around the world (Krook 2004, 2009). In the 1930s, India and Pakistan were the first countries to experiment with what have become known as reserved seat quotas by setting aside seats for women in the national parliament (Krook 2009). In the 1970s, Western European socialist parties started the trend for voluntary party quotas in an effort to increase representation of women in the party's parliamentary delegation (Caul 2001). In the 1990s, countries in Latin America began to adopt legal candidate quotas, which are gender quotas adopted by governments, either as constitutional amendments or legislative changes to electoral or political party codes, that require all parties running candidates for election to the national legislature to ensure that a certain percentage of candidates are women (Krook 2004; Dahlerup 2006b).[2] Argentina became the first country in the world in 1991 to pass a legal candidate quota requiring all political parties running candidates for the national congress to ensure that at least 30% of the ballot in every district was female (Jones 1996).[3] In 1996, Costa Rica and Paraguay adopted similar legislation, and in 1997, another seven Latin American countries adopted quotas—Bolivia, Brazil, Dominican Republic, Ecuador, Panama, Peru, and Venezuela.[4] The last two countries in the region to adopt quotas were Honduras and Mexico, in 2000.[5] As of 2008, twelve Latin American countries have tried legal candidate gender quotas and fifteen other countries from around the world have followed suit. In total, over 100 countries have experimented with some type of gender quota, most in recent years (International IDEA and Stockholm University 2009).[6]

Quotas are a "fast-track" mechanism for gender equality in politics aimed at increasing women's representation quickly (Dahlerup and Freidenvall 2005; Dahlerup 2006b; Kittilson 2006; Archenti and Tula 2008b; Ríos Tobar 2008b; Tremblay 2008b; Tripp and Kang 2008; Krook 2009). Gender quotas increase women's representation by providing incentives for parties to put women on the ballot, and they are expected to translate into more women winning legislative seats. However, the effectiveness of quotas depends on the type of quota, how the quota is designed, and where it is implemented (Htun and Jones 2002; Jones 2005; Araújo and García 2006; Dahlerup 2006b; Krook 2007; Marx et al. 2007; Archenti and Tula 2008b; Ríos Tobar 2008b; Tremblay 2008b; Jones 2009; Krook 2009). For voluntary party quotas, the rules provide incentives to nominate women only for the party that adopted the quota. This may lead to some increase in the number of women in office, but the size of that increase will depend on how many seats the party with quotas wins. For reserved seat quotas, the quota limits the ballot to women only and guarantees that women will be elected from those ballots. However, if only 5% of the seats in the legislature are reserved for women, then the gender representativeness of the legislature may still be quite limited. For legal candidate quotas, the quota requires all parties running candidates for election to put women on ballots. The number of seats that women win, however, depends on whether government enforces the quota, whether parties abide by the quota, where parties place women on the ballot, and the way in which electoral rules distribute seats across parties (Htun and Jones 2002; Jones 2009; Schwindt-Bayer 2009). The adoption of quotas may increase the number of women in national legislatures, but the way that quotas are designed will determine just how much of an increase will occur in different representative bodies.

In chapter 2, I test the effect of formal representation on descriptive representation of women empirically in Latin America. I hypothesize that more proportional electoral formulas, larger district magnitudes, larger party magnitudes, and gender quotas lead to the election of more women to Latin American legislatures. In addition, I expect that the strength of the gender quotas that countries use and the electoral context in which they operate, specifically whether ballots are open or closed lists, influence the number of women elected to office. I test these hypotheses with a statistical analysis of data from multiple elections in all 18 Latin American democracies.

Formal, Descriptive, and Substantive Representation

The integrated model of representation also suggests that formal and descriptive representation can affect substantive representation. Substantive representation is a complex concept with a range of meanings. How representatives do substantive representation and what they are representing can vary widely. In addition, the way in which formal and descriptive representation affects substantive representation is not always straightforward, particularly as it relates to women's representation. The following sections describe how I define and measure substantive representation (and substantive representation of women, more specifically) and how formal and descriptive representation affects substantive representation of women.

Defining and Measuring Substantive Representation

Substantive representation refers to "acting in the interests of the represented in a manner responsive to them" (Pitkin 1967, 209). Most commonly, this implies *policy responsiveness*, or the extent to which representatives enact laws and implement policies that are responsive to the needs or demands of citizens (Miller and Stokes 1963; Achen 1978). Although Pitkin considers policy responsiveness to be central to this dimension of representation, she points out that "there is still room for a whole range of positions concerning the representative's role and his relationship to his constituents" (Pitkin 1969, 20). Eulau and Karps (1977), for example, identify three other ways in which representatives can respond to constituents: *service responsiveness*, which refers to the provision of particularized benefits to individuals or groups; *allocation responsiveness*, which refers to the generation of pork barrel benefits for the constituency; and *symbolic responsiveness*, which refers to intangible gestures made in response to constituent concerns. Other scholars focus on *home style*, which refers to how representatives act in their districts rather than in the capital (Fenno 1978), and the *personal vote*, which focuses on how legislators act to secure constituent rather than party support (Cain et al. 1987), as forms of substantive representation.

In this book, I conceptualize substantive representation broadly. Although much of the research on women's substantive representation focuses on just one or two ways in which substantive representation takes place (such as the policy priorities of legislators, sponsoring bills, sitting on committees, holding leadership positions, roll-call voting, debating, or constituency service), substantive representation actually includes all of these activities (Eulau and Karps 1977; Schwindt-Bayer 2003; Celis 2008; Franceschet and Piscopo 2008). I examine four distinct ways that representatives *act for* and *respond to* constituents—political preferences, policymaking, committees and leadership, and home style. Political preferences refer to legislators' opinions and beliefs about the process of representation and their role in it. It includes the way they view constituents, their policy or issue preferences, and their preferred areas of legislative work.[7] The policymaking process involves the bills that legislators sponsor and cosponsor and their participation in legislative and committee debates on policy. Committees and leadership refers to the positions that legislators hold in chambers and on legislative committees. Finally, home style refers to the nonpolicy work that representatives do aimed primarily at generating votes and frequently taking place in the representative's electoral district rather than in the capital (Fenno 1978). It includes activities such as casework and constituency service, spending time in the district, attending public forums, participating in activities sponsored by special interests in the district, giving public speeches, and talking to the press.

In addition, I distinguish these four components of substantive representation by whether the activities reflect legislators' attitudes or behavior. The first measure of substantive representation, preferences about representation, is a measure of legislators' political attitudes. Policymaking, committees and leadership, and home style reflect legislative behavior. Although often related, attitudes and behavior are distinct concepts that should be studied separately from one another (Wangnerud 2000b; Dodson 2001; Childs 2004; Lovenduski 2005; Schwindt-Bayer 2006). Political attitudes can translate into legislative behavior and help to determine what kinds of bills representatives sponsor, what issues they promote in legislative debates, on which committees they sit, and with whom they interact in the district (Thomas and Welch 1991; Wangnerud 2000b; Dodson 2001; Lovenduski and Norris 2003; Lovenduski 2005; Schwindt-Bayer 2006). However, behavior does not always reflect attitudes due to an array of constraints produced by the legislative environment, such as political party membership, legislative seniority, constituency pressures, or existing legislative norms (Rosenthal 1997; Lovenduski and Norris 2003; Childs 2004; Lovenduski 2005; Schwindt-Bayer 2006; Franceschet and Piscopo 2008). For example, a legislator may feel that foreign affairs is an important political issue but not sit on the foreign affairs committee because he or she does not have enough seniority to get onto this committee. Similarly, representatives from the governing party may place high priority on certain issues but not sponsor any bills on these issues because the president is responsible for sponsoring legislation in that area. Because preferences do not always translate into legislative action, it is critical to examine both the political preferences that representatives bring to the legislative arena and how they act on those preferences to capture the extent to which substantive representation takes place.

Studying substantive representation *of women* also requires clarification about who and what is to be represented. In this book, I argue that creating a complete picture of substantive representation requires examining how legislators represent women and women's issues in comparison with how they represent issues of concern to other groups in the electorate, more broadly. To do this, it is necessary to determine just what women's issues are and how to distinguish them from other types of political issues.

Scholars have long-debated the notion of *women's interests* or *women's issues*. Some scholars voice a normative critique that classifying women as a group with identifiable interests that are waiting to be represented is essentialist (Mansbridge 1999; Young 2000; Weldon 2002b; Mansbridge 2005). Assuming that women have a common interest means that "members of certain groups have an essential identity that all members of that group share and of which no others can partake" (Mansbridge 1999, 637). This is problematic because it reinforces the idea that women are inherently different from men, that women are a homogeneous group who can be classified together as an interest group, and that their issues are less important than men's. Critics point out that women's differences from men are not innate but socially constructed, that women's issues are as important as men's, and that women have an array of identities, such as those emerging from race, ethnicity, class, religion, or ideology, that may intersect with their gender identity (Weldon 2006). These critics worry that creating a dichotomy of *women's issues* and *men's issues* reinforces subordination of women and women's issues (Peterson and Runyan 1999). To avoid falling into the trap of essentialism, scholars have recently suggested defining women's issues as issues that emerge from women's long-standing status as subordinate to men and the problems that this subordination has produced rather than as emerging from sex differences between women and men (Mansbridge 2005). Women's issues, then, are issues that derive from the long history of gender inequality in society.

Another concern with the notion of women's issues is more empirical. Some scholars argue that it is inappropriate to classify issues as women's issues or men's issues *a priori*. Instead, it is better to let interview subjects define women's issues or for the researcher to determine them inductively from the political context under study (Celis et al. 2008; Mackay 2008; Zetterberg 2008). These scholars emphasize that women's issues in one country, at one point in time, and as defined by one woman may not be the same as in another country, at another point in time, or as defined by another woman. Consequently, women's issues may be identified more reliably by exploring public opinion toward women's issues, by determining what issues women's groups and social movements are promoting, and by interviewing feminists to determine their view of these issues.

In this study, I take these concerns into account and create a three-part categorization of political issues. Specifically, I distinguish between women's equality issues, social or compassion issues, and men's issues.[8] Women's equality issues are issues related to gender inequality that deal specifically with feminist concerns, such as women's rights, discrimination, sexual harassment, women's access to education and income, and women's health.[9] Borrowing from Bratton (2005, 107), they are issues "that directly address and seek to improve women's economic, political, and social status." Beckwith and Cowell-Meyers (2007, 556) provide a comprehensive list of the types of policy issues that fall into this category: "policies liberalizing divorce and reproductive rights; equalizing the civil rights of men and women in terms of education, employment, pay, training, property ownership and inheritance, marriage, mobility, and political representation; providing family and medical leave, subsidizing childcare, addressing domestic abuse, sexual assault, violence against women; and providing for women's health care; among others." The second set of issues is compassion or social issues.[10] These refer to issues that traditionally have been considered part of the "women's domain"—the home or private sphere—and emerge from women's traditionally defined private sphere gender roles as caregivers and homemakers. This category includes issues such as children and family, education, health, public/social welfare, and the environment. Specific examples of policy in these areas are building new schools, modifying education curricula, improving hospital care, providing low-income housing, instituting programs and discounts for seniors, or protecting the environment. Finally, I distinguish women's issues and social issues from men's issues. Men's issues are issues that traditionally have been considered to be in the "men's domain"—the public sphere—and emerge from men's traditional gender role as head of the household. These include issues such as the economy, agriculture, employment, fiscal affairs, and foreign affairs.

This classification scheme takes existing concerns about classifying women's issues into account in several ways. First, it defines women's issues in a nonessentialist way that does not imply that women have unique interests with which all women identify or that all women are defined by one, and only one, identity. Instead, it derives from theories of women's historical subordination and women's socially defined gender roles (Phillips 1995; Mansbridge 1999; Young 2000; Mansbridge 2005), emphasizing issues on which women's experiences of subordination are likely to make them more similar to one another than to men. Further, it does not mean that *all* women recognize these interests and promote them, but in general, women are *more likely than men* to recognize the nature of women's subordination and the unique issues that have emerged from that subordination.

Second, it addresses some of the empirical concerns with classifying women's issues, such as taking political context into account while still maximizing generalizability across studies and allowing public opinion or women's groups to determine which issues are women's issues. Specifically, this classification is comparable with those used by other scholars working on women's substantive representation in the developed world (Dodson and Carroll 1991; Reingold 2000; Swers 2002), while at the same time providing a classification of issues that is valid in Latin America (Chaney 1979; Molyneux 1985; Zambrano 1998; Craske 1999, 2003; Htun 2003).[11] It also builds on public opinion research that finds gender gaps in the way citizens view various political issues (Jaquette and Wolchik 1998; Norrander 1999; Wangnerud 2000a; Inglehart and Norris 2003; Lindgren et al. 2009) and emphasizes women's rights issues that women's groups in many Latin American countries have brought to the political forefront in recent years, such as divorce laws, domestic violence, and women's reproductive rights. Recent studies of women's representation in Latin America have used similar classification schemes (Jones 1997; Taylor-Robinson and Heath 2003; Schwindt-Bayer 2006). Finally, it distinguishes *feminist* women's issues (women's equality issues) from more *feminine* issues (social and compassion issues) and distinguishes both types of issues from men's issues, allowing broader and more accurate conclusions than a focus on just one type of issue would permit (Dodson and Carroll 1991; Thomas 1994; Schwindt-Bayer 2006). Overall, it creates a theoretically driven set of issues from which I can generate hypotheses about how formal and descriptive representation affect women's substantive representation.

Descriptive and Substantive Representation

One of the best-researched areas of the women's representation literature examines how descriptive representation affects substantive representation of women. The majority of this research focuses on how women represent women and women's issues. A smaller but equally important segment of the literature, however, focuses on how women represent other concerns, such as social issues or men's issues. Both of these approaches are part of the integrated model of representation and are necessary to understand the nature of women's representation fully.

WOMEN REPRESENTING WOMEN

A common argument for electing women to legislative office is that women will represent differently than male legislators. They will bring new issues, such as women's equality concerns, to the legislative arena by sponsoring legislation on these issues, negotiating women's equality bills through to policy passage, sitting on women's issue committees, bringing a women's perspective to legislative debates, and even feminizing the legislature to make it a more cooperative, collegial, and respectable political space. Yet, scholars do not always agree that descriptive representation of an underrepresented group automatically means or even should mean substantive representation of that group's interests (Dolan and Ford 1995; Mansbridge 1999; Tremblay and Pelletier 2000; Dovi 2002; Vincent 2004; Childs and Krook 2006; Celis et al. 2008; Mackay 2008). Even Pitkin had reservations about linking descriptive representation to substantive representation: "We tend to assume that people's characteristics are a guide to the actions they will take, and we are concerned with the characteristics of our legislators for just this reason. But it is no simple correlation; the best descriptive representative is not necessarily the best representative for activity or government . . . a lunatic may be the best descriptive representative of lunatics, but one would not suggest that they be allowed to send some of their numbers to the legislature" (Pitkin 1967, 89).

In regard to why women may not represent women, some scholars note that not just any woman will do because some women have a gender consciousness and feminist attitudes whereas others do not (Dolan and Ford 1995; Tremblay and Pelletier 2000; Dodson 2001; Dovi 2002; Waylen 2008). In other words, substantive representation of women does not simply require women but a set of "critical actors" (Childs and Krook 2006; Celis et al. 2008). Although this is indeed a valid concern, numerous empirical studies point out that women are more likely to be feminist and have a gender consciousness than men (Dolan and Ford 1995; Tremblay and Pelletier 2000; Dodson 2001; Childs 2004). Perhaps partly because of this, women, in general, may be more likely than men to represent women.

Others criticize the argument that women will act for women because it reinforces male assumptions of women's inferiority and reinforces traditional gender stereotypes (Mansbridge 2005). In legislatures that prioritize the masculine over the feminine, women's issues are widely considered by male legislators and party leaders to be less important political issues than men's issues such as economics, finance, agriculture, and foreign affairs. If female legislators are the predominant political actors working on women's issues, this reinforces long-standing stereotypes that these are issues for women only rather than gender issues or human rights issues that should be priorities for both men and women. It reduces women to an inferior status in the legislature (Vincent 2004; Franceschet 2005; Macaulay 2006).

A final counterargument suggests that women may be less likely to represent women unless a *critical mass* of women has been elected to office. However, empirical research on critical mass theory has not found consistent support for this line of thinking. Some scholars have found that women's and men's political preferences and behavior are more similar to one another than different when only a few women are present in office (Saint-Germain 1989; Thomas 1991, 1994; Towns 2003; Grey 2006). Other critical mass scholars have found the opposite effect—that "token" women do represent women—and that larger numbers of women in office leads to greater similarity in how men and women represent because women's issues become mainstream and enmeshed with traditional legislative concerns (Diamond and Hartsock 1981; Thomas 1994; Crowley 2004; Bratton 2005). These inconsistent findings have led scholars to seriously question the utility of critical mass theory in recent years (Childs and Krook 2006; Dahlerup 2006a; Grey 2006; Tremblay 2006).

In contrast to these critiques of the link between descriptive and substantive representation, there are many reasons to think that descriptive representation of women will lead to greater substantive representation of women in representative democracies (Young 1990; Phillips 1995; Williams 1998; Mansbridge 1999; Lovenduski 2005). According to Mansbridge (1999, 639), descriptive representation of an underrepresented group will allow individuals in that group to represent it under three conditions: (1) when the electoral process intentionally and systematically underrepresents specific groups in the population, (2) when the underrepresented group believes that they can adequately represent themselves, and (3) when there has been a long-standing historical prejudice against the group. She argues that African Americans in the United States and women meet these criteria. Women may be better representatives of women than men because they have faced a common historical discrimination against their participation in politics and in society, more broadly.[12] This does not mean that men cannot represent women and women cannot represent men, but that "particularly on issues that are uncrystalized or that many legislators have not fully thought through, the personal quality of being oneself a member of an affected group gives a legislator a certain moral force in making an argument or asking for a favorable vote on an issue important to the group" (Mansbridge 1999, 648). Weldon (2002b) corroborates this, arguing that women may have a greater interest in representing women not because they have shared interests but because they may be more likely to understand and empathize with women or have a desire to learn about women's concerns.

Drawing on these arguments, female legislators may be more likely than male legislators to focus on women's issues in the legislative arena for three key reasons. First, female representatives may promote women's issues more than men because of the common experiences of subordination that women face (Williams 1998; Mansbridge 2005). Experiences of discrimination could produce a strong gender consciousness in female legislators giving them incentives to work to eliminate gender inequality. Mansbridge (2005) argues that the long history of structural discrimination against women makes it likely that female representatives will represent women's issues more than men because they have greater concern for women and because female representatives are able to communicate with women better than men. Their shared gender may increase women's empathy for women's concerns and interest in learning about and representing them (Mansbridge 2005). Second, female legislators may see themselves as "surrogate" representatives and feel a special responsibility to represent women, regardless of electoral district, or think that women in society expect them to focus on women's issues (Mansbridge 1999; Reingold 2000; Carroll 2002; Mansbridge 2003; Tremblay 2003; Childs 2004). The belief that women *should* represent women may lead to a self-fulfilling prophesy. Franceschet and Piscopo (2008) point out that this may be exacerbated in countries with gender quotas because campaigns to adopt quotas often emphasize women's differences and the special contributions they could make to politics, generating a *mandate effect* in which women feel obligated to represent women. Third, female representatives may view focusing on women's issues as a way to cater to women in their electoral district (Thomas 1994; Lovenduski 2005). From a rational choice perspective, catering to women could be a way to generate votes for oneself and one's political party.[13] Although this is less frequently discussed in the literature, the rationality perspective underlies many assumptions about how women's presence may translate into action. Women may be more likely than men to choose representing women as a strategy for ensuring their political future because of a belief that female constituents will vote for them. Indeed, this strategy has been attributed to male presidents and political leaders pushing for the adoption of gender quotas (Krook 2004; Araújo and García 2006; Krook 2009).

A significant amount of research already supports the hypothesis that women represent women's issues more than men do. Female representatives in the U.S Congress and U.S. state legislatures have been found consistently to place greater priority on women's rights issues than men (Leader 1977; Welch 1985; Saint-Germain 1989; Thomas and Welch 1991; Reingold 1992; Thomas 1994; Jones 1997; Swers 1998; Arnold 2000; Reingold 2000; Carroll 2001; Poggione 2004). Similarly, female parliamentarians in the United Kingdom and Scandinavian countries have been found to prioritize issues related to gender equality and more specific women's issues, such as child care legislation, equal opportunity policies, maternity leave policies, and equal employment (Skard and Haavio-Mannila 1985; Norris 1996; O'Regan 2000; Wangnerud 2000a; Bratton and Ray 2002; Lovenduski and Norris 2003; Childs 2004; Childs and Withey 2004; Childs 2008; Kittilson 2008). Even in Latin America and some countries in Africa, studies of women's policy priorities have found support for the idea that women represent women's equality concerns (Jones 1997; Taylor-Robinson 2002; Goetz and Hassim 2003; Bauer and Britton 2006; Schwindt-Bayer 2006; Franceschet and Piscopo 2008).[14] Differences in legislators' preferences for women's equality issues also have been found to translate into differences in legislator behavior once in office, specifically the bills they sponsor, the committees on which they work, and the issues on which they speak during floor debates (Thomas and Welch 1991; Wangnerud 2000a; Dodson 2001; Swers 2002; Walsh 2002; Wolbrecht 2002; Childs 2004; Bratton 2005; Chaney 2006; Schwindt-Bayer 2006; Childs 2008; Franceschet and Piscopo 2008).

Based on the theoretical reasons that women are likely to represent women and existing empirical evidence, I generate two hypotheses for how descriptive representation affects substantive representation of women and gender inequality issues in Latin America. First, I expect that female legislators will place higher priority on representing women and women's equality issues than male legislators. More specifically, I expect gender differences in legislators' *attitudes* toward female constituents and women's issues. Due to their shared historical experiences of discrimination in the region, possibly feeling a special responsibility to prioritize women and women's issues, or a strategic calculation that promoting gender issues will boost their political career, female representatives may be more likely than male representatives to prioritize female constituents and women's issues in their political preferences.

Second, in representative democracies, such as those in Latin America, where mainstream political parties at least pay lip service to issues of gender equality and have electoral incentives to promote women's rights, I expect that female legislators will spend more time than men crafting and sponsoring gender inequality bills, debating these bills, working on women's issue committees, doing casework on behalf of female constituents, and interacting with women's groups in society that are pushing a feminist political agenda. In other words, I expect gender differences in legislative *behavior* on behalf of women and women's issues. If women have distinct preferences from men on representation of women and women's issues, then these differences should translate into the legislative work that representatives do. The job of political representatives is to "act for" their constituents representing their policy concerns and their non-policy needs and demands.

WOMEN REPRESENTING ALL CONSTITUENTS

Much of the research on women's representation is driven by concerns with whether women represent women and, thus, do politics differently than men. Other research, however, emphasizes the equality view of women's representation, which "stresses women's entitlements to be in politics on the same terms and in the same numbers as men" (Lovenduski 2005, 2). Although critics of the equality view fear that it "implies that women representatives will become political men" (Lovenduski 2005, 2), the equality view does not require assimilation (Lovenduski 2005; Squires 2007). Women achieving equality inside the legislature does not have to occur by women giving up their goals of changing the masculine norms on which most legislatures are based. In fact, allowing women equal access to power may generate greater transformation of the legislative arena into a less masculinized and less male-dominated environment (Lovenduski 2005).[15] Here, I draw on the equality view of women's representation to argue that in addition to bringing legislative attention to women's issues, female representatives have a responsibility to represent other groups of constituents and other, nonwomen-specific political issues (Dahlerup 1988; Thomas 1994; Carroll 2002; Lovenduski 2005; Grey 2006). Just like men, women are elected first and foremost to represent their constituents—both women and men. Just like men, female representatives are rational actors whose primary goal is to get reelected or seek higher office in order to continue representing the interests of the citizenry. Female representatives must walk a fine line between representing women and representing other nongender-based interests to be fully representative of their constituents.[16] One way that female representatives can do this is by placing priority on issues other than women's equality issues and participating in many different parts of the legislative process. Women can be different (represent women) *and* strive for greater equality in the legislative arena (represent a wide array of issues and participate in the full spectrum of legislative activities).

Evidence from Latin America and other countries around the world finds some evidence of equality concerns motivating women in politics. For example, research shows that women in many legislatures do prioritize male constituents just as they do female constituents and place high priority on issues other than women's equality issues (Rodríguez 2003; Childs 2004; Schwindt-Bayer 2006).[17] In Mexico, Rodriguez (2003, 189) found that "gender concerns come in second in the policy agendas of most female officeholders, trailing behind whatever their principal policy priorities may be (labor, human rights, transportation, education, social welfare, health, etc.)." She goes on to point out that "most of the women who are politically active seek to support and promote women's causes when they can fit them in alongside their main goals" (189). Similarly, Childs (2004) reported that MPs to the British Parliament saw themselves as representatives of all constituents first and talked about representing women only when prodded.

This leads to the third set of hypotheses for this study. Because women have a responsibility to be representative of all constituents, not just women, they are likely to recognize all constituents as important to their political work. As a result of this, they should prioritize issues from across the policy spectrum and view a wide range of legislative activities as important. Specifically, I expect that male and female representatives will place similarly high priority on issues that traditionally have been considered "women's domain" (social issues) and those traditionally considered to be in the "men's domain" (economics, foreign affairs, agriculture, fiscal affairs). I also expect that the gender of the representative will not affect the priority that legislators place on the wide array of legislative activities—policymaking, sitting on committees, holding leadership posts, and working in the district. Both of these hypotheses focus on the *attitudes* of legislators toward representation.

If female and male representatives place similar priority on representing a wide array of political issues and legislative activities, are they equally able to translate those preferences into legislative behavior? I argue that turning preferences into legislative action is likely to prove much more difficult for female legislators than male legislators due to one important constraint—the gendered legislative environment.[18] Scholars have recently drawn attention to the institutional constraints that legislatures pose for female legislators, emphasizing that electoral rules, political parties, and informal legislative norms create a gendered institution that prioritizes "the masculine" and marginalizes "the feminine" (Marx 1992; Duerst-Lahti and Verstegen 1995; Rosenthal 1997, 1998; Hawkesworth 2003; Vincent 2004; Htun and Power 2006; Franceschet and Piscopo 2008; Mackay 2008; Zetterberg 2009). Legislatures are comprised of rules, norms, and values that were created by men, have been dominated by men, and continue to privilege men over women (Phillips 1995; Hawkesworth 2003; Beckwith 2005; Duerst-Lahti 2005; Lovenduski 2005; Chappell 2006; Mackay 2008). Men control a majority of seats in almost all legislatures.[19] They control most positions of leadership in the legislature including committee leaderships, legislative party leaderships, and congressional leadership posts. Men have formal and informal networks that they constructed in the male-dominated legislative atmosphere and in which most of their political allies reside. They also continue to be leaders of most political parties.[20] This creates an "atmosphere of discrimination" that leads to marginalization of women in representation (Duerst-Lahti 2005). In other words, women in the legislature may face a "backlash" against their presence (Lovenduski 2005; Mansbridge and Shames 2008; Sanbonmatsu 2008; Thomas 2008). Duerst-Lahti (2005, 234) describes women in legislatures as facing a catch-22: "the gendering of the electoral environment produces atmospheric discrimination against women and structures that entrench male privilege. Under such conditions, even when women win a place in the institutions, they are faced with a catch-22 dilemma: they can perform the masculine better than males and in the process reinforce the masculinist preferences that make it hard for them to succeed, or they can remain outsiders and face enormous challenges to being effective."

In this book, I argue that marginalization of women by the male-dominated legislative environment is a primary obstacle that female legislators face when trying to turn their political preferences into legislative action. Women are likely to recognize electoral demands to promote all constituents, not just women, and a full range of political issues and to participate in a variety of legislative activities to represent their constituents. Thus, their political preferences are likely to be similar to men's. However, the influx of women into the legislative arena may make male representatives feel that their long-standing and unchallenged political power is threatened and lead them to seek ways to minimize women's political influence. They can do this by pressuring or encouraging women to focus on issues that the male majority considers less important and less prestigious, such as compassion issues, while preserving work on what they consider to be higher value issues, such as economics, finance, agriculture, or foreign affairs, for themselves. They may pressure or encourage women to focus on certain kinds of legislative activities that are less likely to generate political influence, such as constituency service, while preserving prestigious leadership positions and committee assignments for themselves.

Specifically, this yields a fourth set of hypotheses that drive this research. Marginalization of women may result in two behavioral outcomes. First, female representatives are likely to spend more time on home-style activities and less time sponsoring legislation, sitting on committees, and holding leadership posts than men, despite placing similar attitudinal importance on these activities. Second, female and male legislators will have similar political preferences for issues, but female legislators will be more likely than their male counterparts to sponsor and cosponsor bills, participate in debates, sit on committees, and do home style on social issues (education and health) and less likely than men to participate in these activities on traditional men's issues (economics, fiscal affairs, agriculture, and foreign affairs).[21]

Gender differences in legislative activities already have been found in many areas of legislative work and in many different legislatures. For example, female representatives have been found to sponsor bills on compassion issues more often than male representatives, sponsor bills on economics and business issues less often than men, and be more likely to cosponsor bills rather than individually sponsor legislation (Thomas 1991, 1994; Jones 1997; Swers 1998; Wangnerud 2000a; Schwindt-Bayer 2006). Women are more likely to sit on committees such as education, health, and welfare, whereas men are present across the board (Diamond 1977; Johnson and Carroll 1978; Skard and Haavio-Mannila 1985; Thomas and Welch 1991; Norton 1995; Towns 2003; Heath et al. 2005). Women have been found to do more constituency service than their male counterparts and have different home styles (Diamond 1977; Thomas 1992; Richardson Jr. and Freeman 1995; Norris 1996; Friedman 2000), and female legislators are often less vocal on committees and in hearings dominated by male colleagues (Blair and Stanley 1991; Kathlene 1994, 1995; Broughton and Palmieri 1999; Taylor-Robinson and Heath 2003; Catalano 2008). Lastly, they have been much less likely to hold positions of leadership in legislative chambers and on committees (Skard and Haavio-Mannila 1985; Rosenthal 2005; Saint-Germain and Metoyer 2008), although female state legislators in the United States became more likely to hold these positions in the 1990s than in the early 1970s (Dolan and Ford 1997; Rosenthal 1998).

Some scholars view these behavioral differences as evidence of *difference theory*—the argument that men and women have distinct issue preferences emerging from their different genders and traditional gender roles (Chaney 1979; Sapiro

1981). They often put a positive spin on gender differences, viewing them as an indication that women are transforming the way that politics is done and perhaps doing it better than men (Dodson and Carroll 1991; Thomas 1994; Wangnerud 2000a; Marx et al. 2007; Catalano 2008). Women may make politics less competitive and confrontational and more cooperative instead, in effect "feminizing" the legislature (Thomas 1994; Childs 2004; Lovenduski 2005). This line of thinking has been touted as a possible explanation for gender differences in legislator behavior, particularly in Latin America where women's difference from men has traditionally been promoted as justification for feminism (e.g., maternal feminism) and women's movements (Chaney 1979; Jaquette and Wolchik 1998; Craske 1999; Franceschet 2005).[22]

Other scholars, however, view gender differences in legislative behavior as an indication that women and women's voices are discriminated against and sidelined in the legislative arena (Marx 1992; Kathlene 1994; Rodríguez 2003; Childs 2004; Franceschet 2005; Heath et al. 2005; Schwindt-Bayer 2006; Zetterberg 2008). In other words, women are being marginalized in the political arena. Lyn Kathlene (1994), for example, found that women were much less likely than men to participate in committee hearings in U.S. state legislatures. She concluded that "as the proportion of women increases in a legislative body, men become more verbally aggressive and controlling of the hearing. Women legislators may be seriously disadvantaged and unable to participate equally in legislative policymaking in committee hearings" (560). Similarly, Heath et al. (2005) showed that when male party leaders or male chamber presidents control committee assignments in Latin American legislatures, women end up on social issue committees and are kept off of power committees. They argue that committees are scarce political resources that the male majority has an incentive to protect, and when male leaders control the distribution of those resources, they can and do marginalize women. Zetterberg (2008) examines whether Mexican female legislators' committee preferences translate into the desired assignment as a measure of marginalization. He finds little evidence of marginalization in his analysis, but he does view the translation of preferences into behavior as an important indicator of it.

One of the difficulties with these two theories is that they offer very different explanations for one phenomenon—gender differences in legislative behavior. In this book, I suggest that one way to distinguish between them is by comparing representatives' political preferences to their behavior. In order for difference theory to be supported, gender differences in behavior should reflect gender differences in representatives' political preferences. Women's distinct gender roles should drive them to both think *and* act differently than men. For example, women would place higher priority on social issues and spend more time working on those issues in office. In contrast, the marginalization thesis suggests a different pattern of attitudes and behaviors. It suggests that the gendered legislature is intervening in the process of women translating their preferences into behavior such that they are not able to act on behalf of the issues they prioritize. I argue that this may appear as hypothesized above—women and men placing similar priority on traditional women's domain and men's domain issues but women being more likely to act on behalf of traditional women's domain issues and not able to work on issues traditionally in the men's domain. Marginalization of women may also occur in other ways in legislative politics, but in this book, this is the pattern of marginalization for which I empirically test.

Formal, Descriptive, and Substantive Representation: Explaining Variation across Political Settings

Thus far, this theory of substantive representation suggests that the relationship between descriptive representation and substantive representation will be the same in all legislatures. Yet, women's representation may vary across legislative settings. Indeed, scholars often point out that substantive representation is different in different political contexts (Rosenthal 1997; Carroll 2001; Weldon 2002b; Tremblay 2003; Vincent 2004; Tremblay 2006; Beckwith and Cowell-Meyers 2007; Dovi 2007; Celis 2008; Celis et al. 2008; Franceschet and Piscopo 2008; Mackay 2008; Waylen 2008; Zetterberg 2008). Some scholars argue that the explanation for these differences lies in the nature of political parties and the party system (Htun and Power 2006; Macaulay 2006; Tripp 2006). Others have suggested that women's ability to represent women depends on the strength and quality of democracy in the political system (Goetz and Hassim 2003; Creevey 2006; Longman 2006). Still others emphasize the role of societal forces, such as women's movements or international pressures (Goetz and Hassim 2003; Bauer and Britton 2006).

In terms of the conceptual framework of representation that underlies this study, I focus on how formal representation mediates the way descriptive representation translates into substantive representation. Specifically, I argue that electoral institutions may affect the extent to which male legislators marginalize women. Under certain configurations of electoral rules, male legislators may have more power and incentive to prevent women from acting on behalf of their political preferences. I focus on two possible mechanisms by which formal representation may mediate substantive representation—electoral rules that strengthen the power of the male majority and gender quotas.[23]

ELECTORAL RULES

Building upon literature that argues that strong parties facilitate powers of marginalization, I argue that marginalization of women will be greater where political institutions give political parties and party leaders significant influence over the behavior of legislators (Goetz and Hassim 2003; Vincent 2004; Tripp 2006; Franceschet and Piscopo 2008; Mackay 2008; Zetterberg 2008). Specifically, where electoral rules encourage party-centered rather than personalistic legislative behavior, political parties and party leaders (who are most often male) have greater incentive and power to marginalize women. In party-centered systems, party leaders have substantial influence over the distribution of legislative resources and over the actions of legislators. They often decide who sits on which committees, who will hold which leadership posts in the legislature, who will get nominated to party ballots in future elections, and who will receive appointment to higher political office if the party maintains political power. Indeed, Kittilson (2006) and Caul (1999; 2001) emphasized the importance of parties for women's representation in Western Europe. In these studies, Miki Caul Kittilson showed that the inclusion of women on the national executive committees of political parties leads to more women getting elected to parliaments and increases the likelihood that a party will adopt women-friendly policies, such as gender quotas. Just as the presence of women in party leadership can bring about changes in women's representation, the absence of women from party decision making is likely to further women's marginalization in politics.

If electoral institutions encourage personal vote seeking, however, legislators have more incentive to focus on the needs and demands of constituents in their district, and party leaders have far less influence over legislators (Cain et al. 1987; Carey and Shugart 1995). These rules encourage legislators to act independently from their parties and cultivate their own reputations. Their political future is tightly tied to their support in the electorate, rather than in the political party, making them more independently minded representatives. In personalistic systems, women may still face marginalization from the male majority in the legislature and other gendered legislative institutions, but marginalization may be more limited because party leaders have less control over legislative resources and little influence on the way legislators represent. In personalistic systems, female and male legislators' substantive representation should be more similar to one another (Macaulay 2006).[24]

Specifically, I hypothesize women's marginalization in the legislature will be greater under party-centered electoral rules than personalistic electoral rules. Male party leaders, like the male majority in most gendered legislatures, are likely to see female newcomers as an incursion into their political space. In party-centered systems, they have sufficient power and influence over elected representatives to sideline women into working on traditional women's domain issues, such as social issues, rather than branching into men's domain issue areas, or appoint women to social issue committees, rather than the more powerful and prestigious men's domain committees. Female representatives have little ability to oppose party leaders if they want to ensure their future political career. Thus, party-centered electoral rules add an additional set of obstacles to women's substantive representation because women face discrimination from the male majority in the legislature and the male-dominated party leadership that controls most legislative resources.[25]

GENDER QUOTAS

Another possible influence on the extent to which women may be marginalized in legislatures is gender quotas. Only recently has empirical research examined how quotas affect women in office (Vincent 2004; Xydias 2007; Franceschet and Piscopo 2008; Zetterberg 2008), but many of the arguments presented in debates over the adoption of quotas express concern that quotas create "token women" who play little role in the legislative process and are easily marginalized (Bauer and Britton 2006). Gender quotas, as a mechanism of formal representation, could generate backlash from male representatives who feel their political future threatened by requirements to put women on ballots and compensate for that by marginalizing women in the legislature and preserving power for themselves (Zetterberg 2008). In legislatures with quotas, women may have a particularly difficult time translating their preferences into behavior.

Although the theoretical reasons for quotas to have a negative effect on women's substantive representation are logical, empirical research finds mixed support for this argument. One study that does support this thinking is by Vincent (2004). She claims that party quotas in South Africa have solidified that "women gain power only through access to men" and have led to women avoiding women's issues in their political behavior, citing changes from the prequota period to the postquota period. In contrast, voluntary quotas have been in place in Western European parties since the 1970s, yet little evidence suggests that they have led to marginalization of women in legislative politics. In fact, the parties that adopted quotas were most often leftist and socialist parties that had progressive political agendas that complemented the quotas they adopted. In Germany, Xydias (2007) examined transcripts of legislative debates, finding that gender quotas there have led to women participating more frequently in debates, speaking "more meaningfully than men," and being interrupted less often. This is the opposite of what one would expect were men marginalizing women in the chamber. Franceschet and Piscopo (2008) argued that quotas in Argentina have reinforced male dominance in the Congress and led to more marginalization of women, but the congresses from which they draw these conclusions already had quotas. This makes it difficult to know if quotas produce this phenomenon or if some other aspect of the legislative environment is responsible, such as Argentina's party-centered electoral rules. Zetterberg (2008) also argued that quotas may lead to greater marginalization of women but found few differences among women elected under quotas and those elected without quotas in his study of Mexico. Instead, he suggested that candidate selection rules and the predominance of strong parties in some countries increase the risk of marginalization of women. Devlin and Elgie (2008) also found that quota women and nonquota women are treated similarly in Rwanda. Although empirical evidence finds little support thus far for quotas increasing marginalization of women, the hypothesis still needs further testing.

Summarizing the Theory of Substantive Representation

In sum, this theory of women's substantive representation argues that the election of women brings new issues to the political agenda, specifically women's equality issues, but also results in marginalization of women inside the legislative arena. This marginalization is most likely to appear in the policymaking process, in legislators' committee assignments and leadership positions, and their home-style activities. The extent to which women represent diverse issues and gain access to all parts of the legislative process, however, may depend on the institutional context. Electoral institutions that empower party leaders and the adoption of gender quotas may produce more significant gender differences in legislative activities, even when women and men may be increasingly similar to one another in political preferences. In contrast, fewer gender differences are likely to emerge in personalistic systems and in legislatures without quotas.

I test this theory empirically in Latin America in chapters 3–6. Chapter 3 examines how gender affects legislators' attitudes toward representation, focusing on key political issue areas and the types of activities representatives engage in. Chapters 4 through 6 examine legislator behavior by examining policymaking (chapter 4), committee membership and chamber leadership (chapter 5), and home style (chapter 6). In the conclusion to the book (chapter 8), I compare the findings on attitudes and behavior in these chapters to determine what role formal representation plays in marginalizing women in Latin American legislatures.

Formal, Descriptive, Substantive, and Symbolic Representation

Symbolic representation is similar to descriptive representation in that it refers to representatives "standing for" their constituents (Pitkin 1969). But symbolic representation interprets "standing for" in a different manner. Representatives stand as symbols that can evoke feelings and attitudes about representation among the population. Pitkin makes clear that it is not the symbol itself that is of interest, but the reaction to that symbol that is of particular interest in symbolic representation: "it requires working on the minds of the audience rather than on the symbol itself, and in politics this usually means working on the minds of the represented" (1969, 13). She draws a comparison to the example of a flag as a symbol representing a nation. What matters is not the flag or symbol itself, but "the symbol's power to evoke feelings or attitudes" (Pitkin 1967, 97). Interest in the symbolic or emotive aspects of politics, even beyond representation, has grown into a notable research area of political science (Edelman 1964; Ragsdale 1984).

A common way to measure symbolic representation is public attitudes toward representatives, representative institutions, and government, more broadly. Symbolic representation occurs when the public feels that its elected officials are trustworthy or has confidence in the system of government and how it operates.

A sizeable literature exists that studies public support for government (see, for example, Hibbing and Patterson 1994; Mishler and Rose 1997), and much of this research argues that variation in public support results from the public's perceptions of how well their representatives are performing (Jackman and Miller 1996; Powell 2000). Symbolic representation can also be specific to underrepresented groups and focus on whether these social groups feel represented by their elected officials. Numerous measures of public feelings or support for government are available offering a wide range of ways to assess this fourth and final dimension of the "concept of representation."

Symbolic representation of underrepresented groups, such as women, is critical for representative democracy. Governments that are run by an elite and homogenous group of male representatives who are unresponsive to constituents' problems and concerns are likely to be viewed as unrepresentative and untrustworthy, yielding an electorate with little confidence or engagement in democracy. In contrast, those that are more diverse, that pass policies that deal with citizens' concerns, and provide mechanisms for citizens to participate more in democracy may be perceived as more credible, more trustworthy, more democratic, and in touch with the people. Having an electorate that feels represented, satisfied with, and trusting of democratic institutions is crucial for the quality and stability of democracy. What makes the electorate feel this way, however, is the subject of much debate.

The integrated model of representation suggests that formal, descriptive, and substantive representation shapes symbolic representation. Specific to women's representation, I argue that a country's use of more proportional electoral formula and gender quotas (formal), the presence of women in office (descriptive), and the adoption of female-friendly policies (substantive) will make constituents feel more represented by their government. On one hand, symbolic representation may affect female citizens only, but on the other hand, it may indicate to men that their democracy is more representative and inclusive and improve their perceptions of government as well. Indeed, recent research suggests that variation in political factors, social dynamics, and historical contexts can have important conditioning effects on citizen attitudes toward politics and women's involvement in politics, more specifically (Sapiro and Conover 1997; Morgan et al. 2008).

Formal and Symbolic Representation: Gender-Inclusive Institutions

The idea that formal institutions can directly affect citizens' views of government is not new. Duverger (1954) argued half a century ago that electoral rules have both mechanical *and* psychological effects on political outcomes. Specifically, he suggested that plurality electoral rules yield two-party systems whereas proportional rules yield multiparty systems in part because voters in plurality systems realize that their votes for small parties are "wasted" and so they vote for one of the two largest parties in the system. In proportional representation systems, voters realize that they can vote for smaller parties and help those parties win some representation. Since Duverger's Law, the idea of electoral institutions having psychological or symbolic effects on citizens has expanded beyond voting to the way citizens feel about their government, in other words, symbolic representation. A small but growing body of literature looks at how electoral rules, such as proportional representation electoral systems, consensus democracies, multiparty and parliamentary systems, and preferential voting rules, affect the electorate's attitudes and beliefs toward the political system (Anderson and Guillory 1997; Banducci et al. 1999; Lijphart 1999; Norris 1999; Anderson et al. 2005; Farrell and McAllister 2006; Aarts and Thomassen 2008).

For women's representation, electoral institutions may help to explain the fact that men and women in many countries have very different views of government. In the United States, studies have found that American women express greater trust in Congress than do men (Hibbing and Theiss-Morse 1995; Sanbonmatsu 2003). Comparatively, wide variation exists in the gender gap, with men being more supportive than women in some countries whereas women are more satisfied than men in other countries (Karp and Banducci 2008). Electoral institutions, such as proportional representation electoral rules, large district magnitudes, or preference voting, are designed to maximize representativeness and give the electorate a say in the individuals who represent them. The use of these institutions could send signals to the electorate of representativeness and inclusiveness, psychologically triggering positive feelings toward government among the citizenry, especially women (Kittilson and Schwindt-Bayer 2008; Kittilson 2010).

Relatedly, the use of gender quotas could affect symbolic representation. Gender quotas are designed to increase women's numbers in office, but quotas can also act as symbols that generate feelings of support for the political system (Kittilson 2005; Zetterberg 2009). Kittilson (2005, 644) argued that gender quotas have two important, but sometimes overlooked, effects: they "reshape attitudes, values, and ideas toward women's roles in politics" and "can be a powerful symbol for democracy and justice beyond national borders." Zetterberg (2009) suggested that quotas could have signal effects on women's political attitudes and activities whereby quotas send signals to women in society that they are accepted as citizens and that the political environment is open to women. Others emphasize the symbolic role that quotas play as part of debates about adopting quotas. A commonly cited motivation for the adoption of quotas is to gain domestic and/or international legitimacy (Htun and Jones 2002; Araújo and García 2006; Krook 2006; Squires 2007). By adopting quotas, governments hope to send signals to their citizens that gender equality is important. This may result in increased citizen trust in and support for government, particularly among women, and may lead to greater political engagement by female citizens. Thus, formal representation, via gender quotas and other political institutions, may provide important symbols that psychologically improve citizens' attitudes toward politics.

Descriptive and Symbolic Representation: The Presence of Women

One of the most powerful justifications for the election of more women to political offices has been the symbolic effects that women's presence may have (Phillips 1995; Young 2000). Even where female legislators do not advocate a distinctly "female agenda" or respond to women's policy concerns, a visible presence of women in the legislature may directly enhance public confidence in representative bodies and government through a role model effect (Zetterberg 2009). Role model effects occur because the presence of women in office provides intangible, symbolic benefits to women in society that the presence of men does not (Phillips 1995; Young 2000; Childs 2004). Thus, increased descriptive representation of women may improve the attitudes that female citizens have toward government and their participation, more generally. Indeed, an array of existing research suggests that constituents are more likely to identify with the legislature and to defer to its decisions to the extent that they perceive a significant percentage of "people like themselves" in the legislature (Phillips 1995; Mansbridge 1999; Gay 2001; Banducci et al. 2004). Aarts and Thomassen (2008), for example, find that perceptions of representativeness are directly related to satisfaction with democracy such that those who perceive the system to be more representative have higher democratic satisfaction. Research also provides some evidence that the presence of women in politics has symbolic effects on women in society, making them more politically engaged in and satisfied with democracy (Norris and Franklin 1997; Sapiro and Conover 1997; High-Pippert and Comer 1998; Atkeson 2003; Sanbonmatsu 2003; Atkeson and Carrillo 2007; Wolbrecht and Campbell 2007; Karp and Banducci 2008; Reingold and Harrell forthcoming).

Increased descriptive representation of women also may lead to more positive feelings about democracy among both women and men. The election of women is a direct symbol for women who have previously been excluded from politics and may view increased election of women as evidence that they too can be more involved. At the same time, however, the election of women can serve as a more general symbol of increased representativeness and inclusiveness of the political system, which may spur more positive feelings toward government by men too. Indeed, several studies on how women's increased presence in government affects women in society have found that women's presence improves men's engagement and attitudes toward politics as well (Lawless 2004; Schwindt-Bayer and Mishler 2005; Atkeson and Carrillo 2007; Karp and Banducci 2008; Kittilson and Schwindt-Bayer 2008).

Substantive and Symbolic Representation: Women's Rights Policies

Finally, substantive representation of women may affect the way citizens feel about their government, particularly female citizens. Policy performance, specifically economic and political performance, has long been seen as a key explanation for citizens' evaluations of government (Jackman and Miller 1996; Powell 2000; Mishler and Rose 2001). When the economy is performing poorly, for example, citizens blame government, expressing less satisfaction with democracy and trust in democratic institutions (Mishler and Rose 2001). The passage of other types of policies also could improve citizen affect toward government. I argue that governments that tackle women's issues and produce more policies aimed at gender equality or overcoming gender discrimination should produce greater support among citizens, particularly women who see their concerns being addressed by government. This logic has been used as one reason that getting more women into office is important—it could produce more women-friendly policies and generate greater support for the political system (Phillips 1995; Mansbridge 1999; Atkeson 2003; Karp and Banducci 2008).

Interestingly, however, only one study has tested the intervening role for substantive representation empirically. A co-authored study that I performed (Schwindt-Bayer and Mishler 2005) found no direct effect for the link between substantive and symbolic representation, and instead found that it is the electoral system and the percentage of the legislature that is female that influence women's confidence in government. Yet, we focused on the state of existing women's policies in countries rather than recent passage of women's issue policies.[26] I suggest here that it is the act of passing women's issue policies that generates press coverage and public discussion of these policies, thereby making the electorate feel more represented by government. The focus on recent policy passage may generate a different outcome.

In chapter 7, I provide a statistical analysis of symbolic representation in Latin America that tests the theory that formal, descriptive, and substantive representation of women affects men's and women's perceptions of their democratic government. Specifically, I focus on the effect of gender quotas and the proportionality of electoral rules, the presence of women in the legislature, and the passage of women's policies on four measures of symbolic representation—citizens' satisfaction with democracy, perceptions of corruption, trust in the legislature, and trust in government. Based on the theory just outlined, each of these should affect symbolic representation by making the Latin American electorate feel better about their democratic government. Women's representation should make women, particularly, but perhaps men as well, feel more included in and engaged in their democracy.

Summarizing the Theory of Women's Representation

In short, the overarching theoretical model of women's representation articulated here argues that women's representation is comprised of four distinct dimensions that are related to one another in three important ways. First, formal representation should influence descriptive representation in that electoral institutions, such as gender quotas and proportional electoral systems, will facilitate the election of women to legislative office. Second, descriptive representation is related to substantive representation such that the election of women should bring new political issues, specifically women's equality concerns, to the political agenda. At the same time, however, women face a political environment long dominated by men in which it is difficult for women to break into the informal networks that underlie the power structure. This results in women not gaining access to important political resources, such as prestigious committee assignments, leadership posts, or sponsorship of diverse types of legislation, and being marginalized in legislative politics into less important legislative activities and work on traditionally "feminine" policy issues. Marginalization is not universal, however. The degree of marginalization that women face depends on electoral institutions (formal representation). Specifically, it depends on whether electoral rules encourage personalistic or party-centered legislator behavior and whether gender quotas are used to elect legislators to office. Third, the theory suggests that formal, descriptive, and substantive representation will affect symbolic representation. The use of gender-inclusive political institutions, the passage of women-friendly public policies, and a large presence of women in the legislature should generate feelings of being represented among the electorate and result in higher levels of satisfaction with representative democracy and greater trust in representative institutions.

Women's representation is not just about explaining how women get elected or what kinds of policies they produce once there. Instead, it is a multifaceted and integrated concept comprised of the gendered nature of electoral institutions (formal representation), the presence of women in legislatures (descriptive representation), the way in which women represent (substantive representation), and citizen perceptions of that representation (symbolic representation). To fully understand women's representation, it is necessary to examine all of these dimensions of representation and the ways in which they influence one another. Doing so has several benefits.

First, it generates more accurate conclusions about the nature of women's representation. For example, if scholars examine only women's descriptive representation, they would conclude that women's representation is improving in many countries around the world because the number of women in office has increased in recent years. Yet, focusing on substantive representation may reveal extensive marginalization of women in these very legislatures that prevents them from playing a powerful legislative role. From this, a very different conclusion would be drawn. Similarly, if scholars study only how quotas affect descriptive representation of women, they may conclude that quotas have a positive effect on women's representation because many countries with quotas have seen dramatic increases in the number of women elected to the national legislature. Yet, examining how quotas influence substantive representation may reveal that quotas facilitate marginalization of women, having a negative effect on women's representation. Second, an integrated theory of women's representation makes room for the possibility that although women get elected to office in growing numbers and effect positive evaluations by the electorate, their presence may not translate into equal representation inside the legislative arena. In other words, it allows the election of women to have different effects on the way representatives "act for" constituents in different political settings, and it explains why female legislators' issue preferences are not always reflected in their legislative behavior. Finally, this theory offers answers to the questions that are at the heart of this book—what causes women's growing presence in politics, and what are its consequences?

An Empirical Study of Women's Representation in Latin America

This theory of women's representation answers questions about why women have been elected in increasing numbers in some legislatures but not others, what this means for the legislative process and policy outputs, and how it affects citizens more broadly. In this book, I apply this theory to Latin American legislatures, where we still know relatively little about women's representation (see, however, Chaney 1979; Marx 1992; Franceschet 2005; Macaulay 2006; Marx et al. 2007; Archenti and Tula 2008b; Saint-Germain and Metoyer 2008).

A study in Latin America offers a useful test of this theory for several reasons. First, the region offers wide variation in women's formal, descriptive, substantive, and symbolic representation. In terms of formal representation, most countries use some variant of proportional representation electoral rules for their lower chambers, but some upper chambers have majoritarian electoral rules. The size of the electoral districts within countries also vary widely, from those as small as 1 or 2 in Panama to those as large as 100 in the Colombian Senate. Twelve Latin American countries have experimented with gender quotas, but the remaining six have not. Further, the adoption of quotas in most countries occurred in the late 1990s, making it possible to compare politics before and after the implementation of quotas in many countries. In terms of descriptive representation, women's election to Latin American democracies has increased over the past 30 years but to varying degrees across Latin American democracies (table 1.1). This makes it possible to examine both why women's representation has increased and why it remains low in some countries but is higher in others. The countries also vary in substantive representation. Some countries, such as Costa Rica, have passed several significant policies protecting women's rights. Others are still struggling to fight the influence of the powerful Catholic Church in the region and promote basic protections of women's reproductive or marital rights (Htun 2003; Franceschet 2005; Squires 2007). Finally, in terms of symbolic representation, citizen perceptions of Latin American governments vary significantly across countries. In some countries, citizens are fairly supportive of their representative democracies, but in others, they are incredibly frustrated with democracy. In Uruguay, for example, 80% of citizens were satisfied with the way democracy was working in the country in 2006 (Americas Barometer). In Paraguay, however, only 20% of citizens felt positively about democracy (Americas Barometer). This type of variation in women's representation creates an excellent setting for a test of hypotheses about women's representation.

Second, Latin America is representative of many democracies around the world. It is a region where gender equality is increasingly, though not entirely, seen as status quo. Despite a lingering culture of machismo, society increasingly values women's work outside the home and views women as capable political leaders (Gallup Organization 2001; Latinobarómetro 2004). The characterization of traditional gender roles is also changing as women are moving out of the private sphere and into the public sphere and entering the workforce and institutions of higher education in large numbers (Craske 1999). Women's groups and the women's movement also have become respected entities in civil society and play critical roles pressuring governments to respond to their demands and tackle lingering women's rights problems (Jaquette 1994; Franceschet 2005; Macaulay 2006; Waylen 2007). In addition, religion and state are largely separate in the region. Although the Catholic Church still has a strong influence over politics in some countries (Franceschet 2005), its power has been significantly diminished in many. This has freed governments in these countries to address women's demands for equality. Finally, Latin America today is a region of democracies. In the mid-1970s, only 3 countries in Latin America were democratic (Colombia, Costa Rica, and Venezuela). Today, all but one (Cuba) of the remaining 19 Latin American countries have transitioned from authoritarian states to electoral (and in some cases liberal) democracies. This yields a set of countries whose governments are representative democracies and whose elected leaders are accountable to the electorate (Samuels and Shugart 2003; Samuels 2004). This increases the generalizability of the findings from Latin American legislatures.

A third reason that Latin America is a good locus for study is that it is a region where politics is still a "man's game" (Marx 1992; Franceschet 2005; Macaulay 2006). Despite the influx of women into legislatures and the fact that citizens view politics as being more open to women, Latin American legislatures and political parties are gendered institutions that prioritize men and the masculine over women and the feminine. The vast majority of leaders in Latin American political parties are men, and in no legislature have women become the majority. Legislative rules and norms were designed by men and continue to privilege men over women. It is in this type of setting that the theory above suggests that marginalization of women in legislatures is likely. Latin America also offers variation on the formal institutions, electoral rules that encourage party-centered over personalistic behavior and gender quotas, which may exacerbate women's legislative marginalization.

Finally, a study of Latin America is useful because this theory suggests a different view of women's representation in the region than has traditionally existed. Latin America is a region where scholars have traditionally emphasized *difference* arguments over *equality* arguments for explaining women's political representation (Chaney 1979; Jaquette and Wolchik 1998; Craske 1999). Elsa Chaney (1979) first articulated this view in a study she conducted in the 1960s and 1970s that found that women in politics in Latin America were *supermadres*—super mothers who translate their traditional private sphere roles of caregiver and homemaker into the public sphere. This way of thinking about women in Latin American politics became dominant in the region and complemented similar arguments that emphasized women's identities as mothers and caregivers as justifications for their political mobilization against authoritarian regimes during the 1970s and 1980s (Molyneux 1985; Schirmer 1993; Bayard de Volo 2001). Yet, the cultural, socioeconomic, and political changes of the past 30 years provide reasons to suspect that *difference* is not the only (or even primary) motivation for women in politics in Latin America today. Women entering politics today may still base some of their claim to power on difference theory by using their gender to justify promoting women's rights issues in politics, but they also may see a need for equality in politics and try to attain legislative clout that affords them the political power they need to effectively represent not just women but all constituents. As Lovenduski (2005) suggests, difference versus equality is not an either/or. Indeed, recent research on the applicability of the supermadre model to women in Latin American politics suggests that it does not hold over time or across all Latin American countries (Furlong and Riggs 1996; Macaulay 2006; Schwindt-Bayer 2006).

The Cases

In this book, the empirical test of formal representation's effect on descriptive representation (chapter 2) and the analysis of explanations for symbolic representation (chapter 7) focus on women's representation across almost the entire region of Latin America. The chapters on substantive representation (chapters 3–6), however, narrow the focus of the study to four legislatures in three countries—the Argentine Chamber of Deputies, the Colombian Senate and Chamber of Representatives, and the unicameral Legislative Assembly in Costa Rica.[27] The intensive data collection needed for a study of the political attitudes that representatives bring to the political arena, their policymaking behavior, their committee and leadership assignments, and their home-style activities necessitates a narrow study of just three countries. The choice of Argentina, Colombia, and Costa Rica is not arbitrary. They are representative of many other Latin American countries on these dimensions, increasing the generalizability of findings from these three countries to other countries in the region. Perhaps most important, these three countries minimize variation on culture and socioeconomic factors that could affect how women legislate and maximize variation on legislative electoral rules and gender quotas. This allows a test of how formal representation mediates substantive representation as outlined previously.

Compared to countries in other regions of the world, Argentina, Colombia, and Costa Rica are very similar to one another in terms of their cultural and socioeconomic environments and have been over time. Argentina, Colombia, and Costa Rica are all Catholic-dominant cultures and are countries where society has become increasingly tolerant in recent years of women moving out of the private sphere and into the public sphere (Gallup Organization 2001; Latinobarómetro 2004). The three countries have similar scores on the Gender-related Development Index (GDI) and Gender Empowerment Measure (GEM), indicating that they are similar socioeconomically as well.[28]

Argentina, Costa Rica, and Colombia are dramatically different from one another, however, in their electoral rules. In terms of gender quotas, Argentina has had quotas since 1991 and Costa Rica has employed them in elections since 1998. Colombia does not have a gender quota for legislative elections. In terms of the incentives that electoral rules provide for personalistic or party-centered behavior, Argentina and Costa Rica have electoral systems that inhibit personal vote seeking, whereas Colombia's rules encourage it (Carey and Shugart 1995). Argentina and Costa Rica have closed-list proportional representation electoral systems in which parties have near complete control over their electoral lists. Political party leaders nominate candidates to ballots and rank candidates in the order in which they want them to win seats. Voters must vote for the party as a whole and cannot change the order of candidates on the party list. Colombia, on the other hand, has a variant of open-list proportional representation, in which parties have almost no control over their ballots. Parties can run multiple lists in any district, and because of this, most candidates who want to run on a party's ballot simply create a new ballot on which they are the first candidate.[29] When voters go to the polls, they are essentially selecting the individual candidates (rather than parties) that they prefer. This creates strong incentives for personal vote seeking and personalistic behavior among representatives (Ingall and Crisp 2001). Thus, Argentina's and Costa Rica's electoral rules provide strong incentives for legislators to be responsive first and foremost to the demands of party leaders, whereas Colombia's rules provide incentives for legislators to be responsive directly to the constituents in their district.

Because Argentina has quotas and a party-centered system whereas Colombia lacks quotas and has a personalistic electoral system, focusing just on these two countries makes it impossible to distinguish which type of electoral rule explains differences in substantive representation. Including Costa Rica eliminates this problem. Costa Rica is party centered and has quotas, but it has used quotas only since the 1998 election. Because some of the analyses in this book are time serial, it is possible to examine pre- and postquota periods in Costa Rica and isolate the effect of quotas from the effect of party-centered electoral rules. Similarly, the use of time-serial data in Argentina allows a comparison of prequota congresses with postquota congresses.

Studying these three countries makes it possible to test whether female legislators represent differently than male legislators, whether these differences vary across countries, and whether electoral institutions are part of the explanation for different patterns of women's substantive representation, as the theory argues. With only three cases, it is impossible to control statistically for country-level characteristics, such as culture, socioeconomics, or electoral institutions. Instead, it is necessary to use case controls. In other words, the use of these three cases approximates Mill's *method of difference* or a most similar systems design (Przeworski and Teune 1970). Culture and socioeconomic factors are near constants across the cases, whereas electoral rules vary.

Conclusion

Latin America is a region that has often been overlooked in research on women's representation. The relatively recent emergence of representative democracy in the region and the attention that women's movements in those transitions to democracy have drawn is part of the reason for this. Yet, it is a region in which we need a better understanding of the causes and consequences of women's growing presence in office. In this chapter, I articulated a theory of women's representation and developed a series of hypotheses that help to answer these questions. The remainder of the book examines this theory in Latin America. In doing so, this book makes several important contributions to our understanding of women's representation generally and women's representation in Latin America more specifically. First, previous research studies women's representation by focusing on only one or two dimensions of representation rather than recognizing the integrated nature of women's representation and the extent to which formal, descriptive, substantive, and symbolic representation are inherently linked to one another. Previous studies provide only disparate pieces of the puzzle of women's representation. By drawing on an integrated model of women's representation, this study suggests a more complete theory of women's representation.

Second, this study broadens the definition of substantive representation beyond its common focus on policy responsiveness to include other aspects of legislative work such as committee assignments, constituency service, interactions with interest groups and media, and presentation of public personas, and it distinguishes between legislators' attitudes and behavior in these areas. It develops a theory of women's substantive representation that explains why gender differences in legislators' work in these areas may vary within any given legislature (male marginalization of women in certain legislative tasks) and explains why women's substantive representation may vary across legislative settings (formal representation). In testing this theory, it draws on original data collected in Latin America—a survey of legislators in Argentina, Colombia, and Costa Rica, data on 7,000 bills sponsored in these legislatures, and interviews with female legislators conducted in 1999 in Costa Rica, 2002 in Colombia, and 2006 in Argentina.

This book also responds to recent calls for greater attention to how political context and political institutions affect women's representation (e.g., Celis et al. 2008). It does this by bringing institutions to the forefront of women's representation and emphasizing its centrality as a determinant of descriptive, substantive, and symbolic representation. Electoral institutions help to explain variation in the gender representativeness of legislatures, citizen perceptions of their representative democracies, and the way in which women are substantively represented. Institutions also are behind the argument that the gendered nature of legislatures mediates women's representation by providing incentives for marginalization of women in office and are a likely explanation for different patterns of substantive representation across political settings. This book brings institutions front and center to the study of women's representation.

Finally, and perhaps most important, this book advances our understanding of representation and democracy in Latin America. The rise of women's participation in government has important implications for the quality and functioning of democracy. This is particularly important in new democracies with still-fragile and malleable institutions. This study offers some answers to questions about representation and democracy, such as, what does it mean for democratic governance that culture, the socioeconomic environment, and institutions can help or hinder the election of women? What does it mean for democracy that women and men do not differ in the types of legislative activities they perform but that they do differ when it comes to women's issues? How does the presence of women in office affect perceptions of representative democracy, if at all? Similarly, this study answers questions about the reality of women and representative democracy in Latin America. It offers important contributions to our understanding of the growing participation of women in democratic politics in the region and its consequences.

2

Descriptive Representation

Electing Women in Latin America

Over the past 30 years, the number of women elected to Latin American legislatures has increased dramatically. Argentina's first election of the current democratic period in 1983 resulted in only 4% of the Chamber of Deputies being female. By 2008, women comprised 40% of the chamber. Costa Rica, one of Latin America's longest standing democracies, had only 3 female deputies (5%) in the 1974–1978 Legislative Assembly, but after the 2006 election, 37% of the assembly was female. The percentage of the legislature that is female today in Colombia is much smaller than Argentina and Costa Rica, but it too has grown from about 5% in the House of Representatives in 1974 to 13% in 2002 and 1% in the 1974–1978 Senate to 12% after the 2006 election. What explains the fact that some Latin American countries are nearing parity in the election of men and women yet other countries lag far behind?

Explanations for Gender Representativeness

The model of representation articulated in chapter 1 emphasizes formal representation as the determining factor in the extent to which legislatures reflect diversity in the electorate. However, representation does not occur in a vacuum. The broader cultural, societal, economic, and political context in which representation takes place also shapes descriptive representation (Norris 1985; Rule 1987; Oakes and Almquist 1993; Kenworthy and Malami 1999; Reynolds 1999; Inglehart and Norris 2003; Paxton and Hughes 2007; Schmidt 2008a).

Culture

One argument for why women are significantly underrepresented is culture. Cultural dynamics can hinder the ascension of women to national political office because in some countries traditional cultures continue to view women's place as "in the home" and either legally prevent women from running for office or more subtly discourage women from participating in the public sphere. Until the early 1900s, women in most countries did not have the right to run for political office. Although most countries today allow women to participate in politics, many societies continue to envision distinct gender roles (or *separate spheres*) for women and men—women being responsible for the home and family (the *private sphere*), and men being responsible for generating income and participating in politics (the *public sphere*). The separate spheres logic is an obstacle to the election of women for two reasons. One, it discourages many women from even considering a run for political office. Women are socialized to believe that they do not belong in politics, and consequently, do not pursue political careers. Lawless and Fox (2004), for example, find that a lack of political ambition among women in the United States is the key reason that Congress is only 13% female. Two, it suggests that women who do run may face discrimination from voters who believe that women should not be in politics.

Most research on the way in which culture hinders the election of women finds some support for these ideas. Norris (1985) found that societies with favorable attitudes toward women in politics have more women in office. This was corroborated in Inglehart and Norris (2003), Paxton and Hughes (2007), and Tremblay (2007), although Tremblay finds it matters only in older democracies. Similarly, Yoon (2004) finds that patriarchal cultures in sub-Saharan Africa significantly encumber women's accession to legislatures. A country's dominant religion is another cultural barrier. Rule (1987), Reynolds (1999), Tripp and Kang (2008), and Kenworthy and Malami (1999) find that religion is correlated with the election of women: certain religious denominations with more restrictive views of women's equality, such as Catholicism, have fewer women in office than those with more accepting views of gender equity, such as Protestantism. Rule (1987), Reynolds (1999), and Kenworthy and Malami (1999) also find that the number of years that women have had the right to vote or stand for office in a country influences the proportion of women in office.

Yet, not all of the existing explanations for women's representation matter in all political contexts (Tremblay 2007; Stockemer 2008). In Latin America, religion and political attitudes may not be as important for explaining women's election to national legislatures because Latin American countries are more similar than different on some major cultural dimensions. As described in chapter 1, the Catholic Church is a strong influence in society and politics in all Latin American countries, with only minimal variation across countries. Further, the more traditional view of gender roles whereby women and men occupy separate spheres has changed throughout the region. As of 2004, only one-third of Latin Americans think that men make better political leaders than women (Latinobarómetro 2004). This ranges from as few as 14% of respondents (Mexico) believing that, to as many as 50% (Dominican Republic). However, these attitudes have not been found to affect the number of women elected to national legislatures in Latin America (Jones 2009).

What may matter are differences in the *democratic* culture of Latin American countries. The length of time that countries have had to develop a cultural norm of women participating in politics varies across Latin America as does the number of years that countries have been democratic. Women in all Latin American countries have legally had the right to participate in politics for almost 50 years, but women received this right at different points in time in different countries (table 2.1). Ecuador was the first country to grant women the right to vote in 1929, and Paraguay was the last to do so, in 1961.[1] Mexico's 1917 constitution technically gave the right to vote to "all Mexicans," but the government denied this right to women until 1953, when the Mexican states finally ratified a constitutional amendment clarifying women's suffrage (Miller 1994; IPU 2008). El Salvador gave women the right to vote in 1939, but it was only in 1961 that they could run for office.

The newness of democracy in Latin America may also affect women's representation. The struggle for political rights in Latin America was long, challenging, and frequently interrupted by periods of nondemocratic rule during which all citizens' political participation was restricted. Despite achieving the legal right to participate in politics by the mid-twentieth century, women's access to power since then has been hindered by the absence of real democracy in most countries. It was only in the last few decades of the twentieth century, as part of the "third wave" of democratization (Huntington 1991), that most Latin American countries became democratic (table 2.1). The two longest standing democracies in the region are Costa Rica (since 1948) and Venezuela (since 1959), but even these countries had limited participation by women until after the so-called second-wave of feminism in the 1970s. Most other Latin American countries had been authoritarian since the early twentieth century or underwent only intermittent experiments with democracy. Limited democracy in the region made it difficult for women to make inroads into elected office in many countries until the 1980s and 1990s. Consequently, the weaker democratic culture in Latin America's newer democracies may hinder women's descriptive representation.

TABLE 2.1. Cultural and Socioeconomic Characteristics of Latin American Countries

	Right to Vote/ Stand for Office	Transition to Democracy	Percentage of Women in Paid Labor Force[a]		
Country	Year	Year	1980	2005	Change
Ecuador	1929	1979	24	64	40
Brazil	1932	1985	41	61	21
Uruguay	1932	1985	37	66	29
El Salvador	1939/1961[b]	1984	42	50	8
Dominican Republic	1942	1978	31	49	18
Guatemala	1946	1985	30	35	5
Panama	1946	1989	37	55	18
Venezuela	1946	1959	32	62	30
Argentina	1947	1983	31	61	30
Chile	1949	1989	31	41	10
Costa Rica	1949	1948	27	49	21
Bolivia	1952	1982	40	64	24
Mexico	1953	1994	31	43	11
Colombia	1954	1974	26	66	39
Honduras	1955	1982	34	56	22
Nicaragua	1955	1990	39	37	−2
Peru	1955	1980/2001[c]	30	61	31
Paraguay	1961	1989	40	69	28
Region Average			34	55	21

Sources: IPU (1995); Payne et al. (2002); World Bank (2007).

[a] 1980 is the first year in which data were collected. These figures include working-age women only (ages 15–64).

[b] El Salvador is the only country that granted women the right to vote and the right to stand for election at two different points in time.

[c] Peru's main transition to democracy occurred in 1979. In 1993, President Fujimori instigated a self-coup, rewrote the constitution, and called new elections. Many observers consider the remainder of his regime, until 2001, a period of authoritarianism in Peru.

Socioeconomic Environment

Along with culture, the socioeconomic environment of a country helps to determine the representativeness of legislatures (Rule 1981; Norris 1985; Randall and Smyth 1987; Rule; Oakes and Almquist 1993; Kenworthy and Malami 1999; Reynolds 1999). This occurs by increasing or decreasing the likelihood that women will be part of the *candidate pool* and able to run for and win national office. Most candidates for public office have similar educational and occupational backgrounds, such as university educations and advanced degrees, relevant private or public sector jobs (e.g., lawyer, business leader, or professional), or previous political experience. These qualities are important because voters and political parties see them as unwritten qualifications for public office. As women attain these qualifications, parties may be more likely to nominate women as candidates and voters may be more likely to vote for women, making them viable contenders for election.

One of the most common measures of gender equality in the socioeconomic environment is the extent to which women participate in the paid labor force (Rule 1981; Norris 1985; Randall and Smyth 1987; Rule 1987; Studlar and McAllister 1991; Oakes and Almquist 1993; Kenworthy and Malami 1999). As traditional views of gender roles break down, women enter the labor force in large numbers. This in turn places them in the candidate pool because they attain skills and experiences that are valued by political parties and society when selecting legislative candidates. Factors such as literacy rates, women's participation in education, unemployment rates, and fertility rates also affect women's representation, but their impact has been smaller and less consistent across studies.

An additional socioeconomic factor of interest is the level of economic development in a country (Rule 1981; Matland 1998; Paxton and Hughes 2007; Tremblay 2007; Schmidt 2008a). Although level of development is not a direct measure of women gaining qualifications for public office, it provides a broader indication of a country's socioeconomic status. Economically developed countries tend to have less social inequality, contributing to greater gender equality. Further, economically developed countries have more money to spend on education and public welfare, creating a better educated electorate and larger middle class. Related to economic development is gendered development. Recent research shows that the GDI (the U.N.'s Gender-related Development Index) also captures the relationship between socioeconomic conditions and the elections of women (Reynolds 1999). Socioeconomic environments that put more women in the candidate pool also elect more women to national legislatures.

Similar to culture, socioeconomic factors may not be as important to explaining descriptive representation of women across countries in Latin America. Socioeconomic variation within Latin America is rather limited, particularly when compared to differences between Latin America and other regions of the world. Where socioeconomic factors may matter is explaining variation over time within countries. Vastly changing socioeconomic conditions have accompanied the transitions to democracy in Latin America. As late as the 1970s, women's participation in the workforce was far below men's—only one-third of women participated in the paid labor force compared to nearly 85% of men (World Bank 2007). By 2005, over half of Latin American women participated in the paid labor force (table 2.1). In some countries, such as Ecuador and Colombia, the change in women's participation rates from 1980 to 2005 is as large as 40 percentage points. In contrast, the poverty-stricken countries of Central America—El Salvador, Guatemala, and Nicaragua—have witnessed much smaller changes in women's workforce participation, and Nicaragua has actually seen a slight drop in women working outside the home since the socialist Sandinista regime was in power from 1980 to 1989. Although women and men have not yet reached parity in formal workforce participation rates, women's involvement in the paid labor force has increased. This could explain some of the increase in women's political representation in Latin America over time.[2]

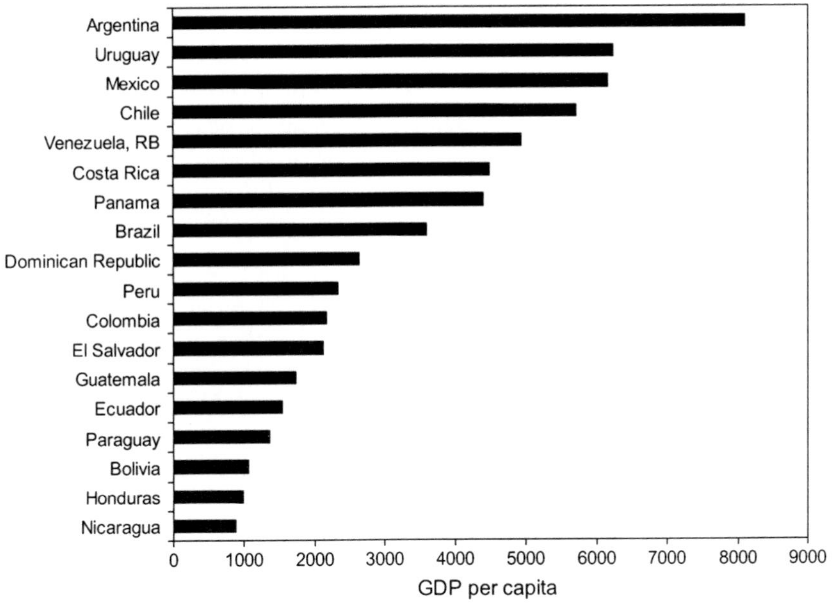

FIGURE 2.1. GDP per Capita in Latin American Countries, 2005 (World Bank 2007)

Latin American countries also vary in their levels of economic development, but not as widely as other regions of the world (figure 2.1). The region as a whole had an average GDP per capita in 2005 of $3362 (World Bank 2007). GDP per capita was highest in Argentina, where it reached $8094, but Nicaragua and Honduras had a GDP per capita of less than $1000. Economic development may explain some of the variation in women's representation in Latin America because it reflects the economic obstacles that women must overcome to balance private sphere and public sphere activities. Lower levels of economic development make it more difficult for women to gain the experience necessary to enter the candidate pool, get on party ballots, and ultimately win seats in national legislatures.[3]

Formal Representation

Culture and socioeconomic conditions are important influences on women's representation, but the election of women is significantly challenged without political institutions that encourage representativeness. Women-friendly electoral rules provide incentives for parties to put women on ballots, and through the formulas that translate votes into seats, increase the numbers of women elected to legislatures. The effect of institutions, specifically the type of electoral system, district magnitude, and party magnitude, on the election of women has long been documented (Duverger 1955; Castles 1981; Norris 1985; Engstrom 1987; Rule 1987; Matland 1993; Oakes and Almquist 1993; Darcy et al. 1994; Matland and Taylor 1997; Kenworthy and Malami 1999; Yoon 2004; Schwindt-Bayer 2005; Paxton and Hughes 2007; Tremblay 2008b). Recent research, however, stresses the importance of gender quotas for women's representation (see, for example, Dahlerup 2006b; Archenti and Tula 2008b; Ríos Tobar 2008b; Tremblay 2008b; Tripp and Kang 2008; Krook 2009). Given that quotas have been very popular in Latin America in recent years, it is crucial to understand just how they affect the election of women in the region.

Electoral Rules

Electoral institutions are the rules that define how the election process works, and these rules can help or hurt the election of women. The most prominent argument is that proportional representation (PR) electoral systems are more favorable to women than majoritarian systems (or plurality rules). PR electoral rules allocate seats in proportion to the percentage of votes the candidate or party receives. Majoritarian electoral rules allocate seats to the candidates or parties that win the most votes. Because PR stresses proportionality, it facilitates representativeness in terms of gender and other descriptive characteristics, whereas majoritarian or plurality rules favor the majority, who are almost always men. Indeed, numerous studies have shown a strong relationship between proportional representation and the election of women (Duverger 1955; Rule 1981; Norris 1985; Rule 1987; Darcy et al. 1994; Rule 1994; Matland and Studlar 1996; Caul 1999; Yoon 2004).

Some scholars argue that the distinction between PR and majoritarian systems is too simplistic and misses the diversity that exists within each type of system (Taagepera and Shugart 1989; Cox 1997). A more nuanced characteristic of electoral systems is the size of the electoral district (i.e., district magnitude). In a single member district system, winning a legislative seat is a zero-sum game in which a candidate from only one sex can win the election. Because women have long been excluded from the political process, parties have little incentive to fill the one position they could win with female newcomers. As district magnitude increases, however, winning a seat in a PR system is no longer a zero-sum game because multiple candidates can be elected from each district. Larger districts are more favorable to the election of women because they make room for female newcomers without displacing male candidates. Parties have incentives to nominate both men *and* women to their ballots, and indeed, larger district magnitudes have been linked to the election of more women (Engstrom 1987; Rule 1987; Matland and Brown 1992; Schwindt-Bayer 2005; Tremblay 2008b).

Some studies, however, have found no relationship between district magnitude and the election of women (Welch and Studlar 1990; Studlar and Welch 1991; Matland 1993; Matland and Taylor 1997; Kittilson 2006; Schmidt 2008b, 2008a). Matland (1993) and Matland and Taylor (1997) suggest that, instead of district magnitude, party magnitude determines the proportion of seats won by women because it measures the number of seats that *each party is likely to win* in a district rather than the overall number of seats available. Because it is rare for one party to win every seat in a district, parties make calculations about whether to include women and where to put them on the ballot based on the number of seats in the district that they expect to win. Thus, party magnitude provides a more accurate estimate of how district size affects the election of women. District magnitude could be large, but if many parties are running and party magnitude is small, then party leaders may be less likely to allocate the one or two seats that the party might win to women (Jones 2009).

Gender Quotas

Theoretically, the goal of gender quotas is to increase representation of women on party ballots, and ultimately, in the legislature. Yet, it is still unclear just how effective quotas have been at increasing women's representation, particularly in Latin America (Jones 1998; Jones and Navia 1999; Htun and Jones 2002; Baldez 2004a; Jones 2004b; Schmidt and Saunders 2004; Jones 2005; Baldez 2007; Archenti and Tula 2008b; Ríos Tobar 2008b; Jones 2009). The theory for why quotas should increase the election of women lies in their mechanical and psychological mechanisms. Mechanically, quotas require parties to nominate female candidates to positions that increase their chances of winning legislative seats. Psychologically, quotas increase women's representation by encouraging women to consider running for public office and encouraging parties to seek out qualified female candidates for their ballots. The presence of quotas signals to women in society that the government views women's political participation as important and desirable. This could lead to more women aspiring to office, which increases the pool of interested and qualified women from which parties select candidates. As Luz Sapag, an MPN senator in Argentina notes, "I believe that the system of quotas has contributed to women finding fewer obstacles to occupying spaces, and maybe it opens the possibility to many women who before did not see politics as an environment for them" (Sapag 2006).

Most cross-national statistical research on the effect of gender quotas on the election of women has operationalized quotas as simply being in place or not, and results have been mixed. Some studies find that adopting a quota puts more women into office (Caul 1999; Kittilson 2006; Stockemer 2008; Tripp and Kang 2008), but other studies have uncovered only weak, if any, effects for gender quotas (Reynolds 1999; Htun and Jones 2002; Kunovich and Paxton 2005; Tremblay 2007; Schmidt 2008a). Htun and Jones (2002, 51), in one of the first comparative studies on the effectiveness of quotas, found that the adoption of quotas in Latin America had little effect: "With the exception of Argentina, quotas have been a relatively painless way to pay lip service to women's rights without suffering the consequences." One reason for this may be that quotas in some countries have not been in place long enough for the psychological effects of quotas to work. Another may be that simply having a gender quota is not sufficient for increasing the election of women. Instead, the design of quotas and the context in which they are implemented may condition the impact of quotas (Htun and Jones 2002; Jones 2005; Araújo and García 2006; Dahlerup 2006b; Krook 2007; Marx et al. 2007; Archenti and Tula 2008b; Ríos Tobar 2008b; Schmidt 2008a; Tremblay 2008b; Jones 2009; Krook 2009). "Stronger" gender quotas should lead to the election of more women than weaker quotas or the absence of quotas. Indeed, some recent statistical studies provide empirical support for this. Yoon (2004), for example, finds that "substantial quotas" have a statistically larger effect on the number of women in sub-Saharan African parliaments than "minor quotas" or "no quotas," and "minor quotas" have a statistically larger effect than the absence of quotas. Jones (2009) offers an analysis of quota effectiveness in recent Latin American elections using data on party ballots and finds that "well-designed" quotas elect more women than "lax" quotas or no quotas. Further, "well-designed" quotas implemented in a closed-list proportional representation electoral system have a larger impact on the election of women than those in open-list PR systems.

Quotas in Latin America are very diverse. Argentina's quota law stipulates that women comprise 30% of candidate lists and that women must be in "electable" positions on the party ballot. The electoral authority can reject party lists that do not comply with the quota. In contrast, Honduras's gender quota law mandates that parties allocate 30% of the ballot to women, but the law does not require parties to place women in winnable positions, nor did the law stipulate any enforcement mechanism by which the electoral commission can ensure that parties abide by the law. After the 2001 election in Argentina, 33% of the Argentine Senate and 31% of the House of Deputies was female. The gender quota is widely considered to be a success (Jones 1996, 2009). In the Honduran Congress, women won only 5.5% of legislative seats in the first postquota election (2001). Honduras's quota law was unsuccessful at increasing the election of women.[4]

In Costa Rica, the gender quota passed in 1996, specifying that 40% of candidates be female. Although 40% is a large percentage, the quota did not mandate that parties place women in winnable positions. Deputy Virginia Aguilar articulated the problem with this (Aguilar 1999):

> There is a required minimum percentage of 40% of the lists being women. The problem is that lists have a quantity of eligible positions and a quantity of ineligible positions. Say that there are ten positions on the list, the law requires four women and six men, at least. So they put in the first six positions, the men, and in the four that follow, women. The law does not require women to be in positions where they can actually be elected.

Indeed, representation of women in the 1998–2002 Legislative Assembly was only 4 percentage points higher than it was before Costa Rica adopted its quota law.

It was not until a 1999 ruling by the Supreme Electoral Tribunal that parties were required to place women in positions on the party ballot where they had a real chance of winning (Jones 2004b). Also in this ruling, the tribunal stated for the first time that it would reject party lists that did not adhere to the quota. In the first election after this change (2002), women won 35% of the assembly's seats, and Costa Rica became another example of successful quota law implementation (Jones 2009).

As these examples make clear, legal candidate quotas in Latin America vary significantly, and this diversity may be important for explaining differences in descriptive representation of women across countries. The simple presence of a gender quota may lead to some increase in the election of women over time by signaling government support for representation of women, but the design of the quota and its implementation in a compatible electoral system may be even more important for increasing descriptive representation of women in Latin America.

THE DESIGN OF CANDIDATE QUOTA LAWS

Legal candidate quotas vary widely across countries, but the major differences occur along three key dimensions that make quotas "stronger" or "weaker" than one another (Htun and Jones 2002; Jones 2005; Krook 2007; Tremblay 2008b). Table 2.2 describes these for Latin American countries. The first dimension on which laws differ is the size of the quota—the percentage of women that the quota requires political parties to nominate. In theory, this could range from 1% to 50% (gender parity), but in Latin American countries, it ranges from 20% in Paraguay and Ecuador (when it was first adopted in 1997) to 45% in Ecuador's 2006 election. As the target increases, the percentage of women elected to the legislature should increase as well (Jones and Navia 1999; Schmidt and Saunders 2004). However, it may not be a one-to-one relationship because of the nature of legal candidate quotas—they simply give women access to a certain percentage of a party's ballot rather than guarantee a specific percentage of legislative seats. The percentage of seats that women win ultimately depends on other factors such as the proportionality of electoral rules, the size of the electoral district, the electoral formula, and electoral thresholds.

The second dimension is whether the quota includes a placement mandate. A placement mandate stipulates that parties must place female candidates in winnable positions on party ballots. About half of the Latin American countries with quotas include placement mandates. A number of studies have stressed the importance of placement mandates for gender quotas (Jones 1996; Htun and Jones 2002; Gray 2003; Baldez 2004b; Jones 2004b; Matland 2006; Archenti and Tula 2008a; Schmidt 2008a; Jones 2009). They argue that without a placement mandate, fewer women will be elected because parties will be unlikely to put women in positions where they can actually win office. This does not mean that quotas without

TABLE 2.2. Gender Quota Laws in Latin America

Country	Year Adopted	Legislative Chamber to Which Quota Applies	Target Percentage	Placement Mandate	Enforcement Mechanism
Argentina[a]	1991	Lower and upper	30	Yes	Strong
Bolivia[b]	1997	Lower and upper	33/25	Yes	Strong
Brazil[c]	1997	Lower	25/30	No	Weak
Costa Rica[d]	1996	Unicameral	40	No/yes	None/strong
Dominican Republic[e]	1997	Lower	25/33	No/yes	Strong
Ecuador[f]	1997	Unicameral	20/30/45	Yes	Strong
Honduras	2000	Unicameral	30	No	None
Mexico[g]	2000	Lower and upper	30	Yes/no	Strong
Panama	1997	Unicameral	30	No	Weak
Paraguay	1996	Lower and upper	20	Yes	Strong
Peru[h]	1997	Unicameral	25/30	No	Strong
Venezuela[i]	1997	Lower and upper	30	No	Weak

Sources: Electoral codes, International IDEA and Stockholm University (2009) and existing literature on quotas in Latin America. See also Schwindt-Bayer (2009).

[a] The quota applied to the Argentine Senate beginning in 2001 when the Senate was directly elected for the first time. It has applied in the Chamber of Representatives since the 1993 election. The initial quota law passed in 1991 did not include a placement mandate. This was added with Executive Decree 379/93, which was passed March 8, 1993 (Marx, Borner, and Caminotti 2007). The placement mandate was passed prior to the first election under the quota law in 1993, which is why I do not note the addition of the placement mandate in the table. A few parties had already nominated candidates for the 1993 election when the decree was passed, and they received an exemption, but the full law was in place for this election (personal communication with Argentine quota expert Mark Jones, March 6, 2008). In 2000, the law was again qualified with Executive Decree 1246/00 to require, among other things, that parties nominating only two candidates include a woman in one of those two positions, but the size of the quota remained 30%, which applied to most parties (Marx, Borner, and Caminotti 2007; Jones 2009).

[b] I code the Bolivian lower house quota as 33% because Law 3153, rather than setting a specific percentage, specifies that at least 1 of every 3 candidates must be female. Other studies have classified the quota as 30%, however, rather than 33% (Costa Benavides 2003; Krook 2005; Jones 2009). The placement mandate for the Senate requires parties to nominate at least 1 woman for every 4 positions for the upper house, which is 25%.

[c] Brazil's quota law (Law 9540) set the quota to 25% for the 1998 election and 30% for all elections afterward.

[d] Costa Rica implemented a placement mandate and enforcement mechanisms in 1999, such that they applied from the 2002 election onward (García Quesada 2003; Jones 2004b).

[e] In 1997, a reform to the electoral law (Law 275/97) added a 25% quota and specified that lists would be rejected by the Central Electoral Agency if they violated the law. An additional modification in 2000 increased the target to 33% and added a placement mandate (Law 12/00). Some scholars code the Dominican Republic as not having a placement mandate because they argue that the adoption of an essentially open-list PR system in 2000 minimizes the effect of the placement mandate (Jones 2009). Because this study is trying to determine just what effect quota design has, however, I do not make that assumption. In theory, the 1997 law extends to the Dominican Senate; however, it was impossible to implement practically due to the Senate's electoral rules ((Jiménez Polanco 2008).

[f] Ecuador's quota law passed in 1997 with a target of 20%. In 2000, a revision to the quota increased the target to 30% and specified that it should increase by 5% with every succeeding election—including municipal elections. Consequently, in the most recent national election (2006), the quota was 45% (del Campo and Luengo 2008).

[g] Mexico's quota has a placement mandate for seats allocated in proportional representation elections but not for the single member district plurality seats (Baldez 2004a; Jones 2009). The placement mandate is for the lower chamber only, not the Senate. Mexico first implemented a quota *recommendation* in 1993, but it was only in 2000 that a law requiring all parties to comply with a clearly articulated national quota was passed (Reynoso 2008).

[h] In 2000, Peru increased the quota to 30% with Law 27387 (Schmidt 2003).

[i] Venezuela's quota lasted only until 1999 (Htun and Jones 2002). The quota adopted in 2004 in the new Bolivarian Republic of Venezuela is only a recommendation (International IDEA and Stockholm University 2009).

placement mandates have no effect; they can still have a symbolic effect by encouraging more women to run for office or encouraging parties supportive of the quota to put women in winnable ballot positions, as Jones (2004b) found in municipal elections in Costa Rica. But in general, placement mandates should make quotas more effective and should increase women's representation more than when mandates are absent.

The third dimension is the strength of the quota law's enforcement mechanisms. Enforcement mechanisms are stipulations in the constitution or electoral law that prescribe consequences for political parties that do not abide by the quota. They make it easier for electoral authorities to punish parties that overlook or choose not to employ the quota and, consequently, should lead to more parties abiding by the quota and more women getting elected to office (Jones 1996; Htun and Jones 2002; Baldez 2004b; Matland 2006). In Latin America, some countries specify no means by which the quota can be enforced (e.g., Honduras), whereas others include hefty consequences for parties that submit lists of candidates that do not comply with the quota (e.g., Argentina).

Enforcement mechanisms are more diverse than simply having them or not. There are varying degrees of strength of enforcement. Some quota laws have weak penalties for parties that violate the quota law. Brazil, for example, has a stipulation whereby parties that do not meet the required percentage of women must eliminate men from candidate lists (Araújo 2008). Although this balances out the number of men and women on the ballot and encourages parties to comply, it does not require parties to seek out more women for the quota. In an open-list PR system, this does very little to increase the likelihood that women will get elected. Panama's enforcement mechanisms are also weak. The law allows parties that are unable to meet the quota to nominate any candidate wishing to run (male or female). This essentially makes the quota a mere recommendation—if a party makes a good faith effort but claims to find few qualified women, they can resort to additional male candidates. These relatively weak enforcement mechanisms contrast with stronger ones employed in Argentina, Bolivia, Costa Rica, Mexico, Paraguay, and Peru. In these countries, enforcement consists of independent electoral authorities reviewing lists and rejecting those of political parties that do not comply with the quota. Parties must meet the quota or they cannot run any candidates in the districts that violate the quota. I classify these differences in the strength of enforcement mechanisms as *no enforcement*, *weak enforcement*, and *strong enforcement*. Stronger enforcement mechanisms should lead to the election of more women.[5]

QUOTA-COMPATIBLE ELECTORAL CONTEXTS

Much of the research on gender quotas suggests that the electoral context in which quotas are implemented has an important mediating effect on the impact of quotas (Jones and Navia 1999; Htun and Jones 2002; Gray 2003; Schmidt and Saunders 2004; Jones 2005; Mansbridge 2005; Araújo and García 2006; Krook 2007; Frechette et al. 2008; Ríos Tobar 2008b; Jones 2009; Krook 2009). Electoral contexts vary in many ways, but one important characteristic of the electoral context that may mediate the effectiveness of quotas is whether ballots are closed or open (Jones and Navia 1999; Htun and Jones 2002; Baldez 2004a; Archenti and Tula 2008a; Miguel 2008; Schmidt 2008a; Jones 2009).[6] Closed-list ballots are those in which parties determine the order of candidates on the party ballot and prohibit voters from voting for individual candidates. Open-list ballots allow voters to determine which candidates get elected by expressing preferences for individuals.[7]

In open-list systems, gender quotas may be less effective for a couple of reasons. One, preference voting allows voter biases against women to play a role in the election process. Although some studies have found that voter discrimination (for or against female candidates) is rare (Norris et al. 1992; Darcy et al. 1994; Matland 1994), others find that candidate gender does affect the number of votes that candidates receive in some contexts (Sawer and Simms 1984; Cook 1994; Schwindt-Bayer et al. forthcoming). Two, it makes little sense to use placement mandates when voters have a say in the candidates who get elected (Schmidt 2008a; Jones 2009). Open-list systems make it less likely that rules about how many women are on the ballot and where they are placed will translate into a large number of women elected (but see Schmidt 2008b). Jones and Navia (1999) examine open-list municipal elections in Chile and provide statistical evidence that gender quotas would be less effective in open-list elections. Similarly, Miguel (2008) argues that the open-list PR system in Brazil is the primary reason that quotas have not led to the election of more women to Congress. Jones (2009) finds that effective quotas in open-list systems do not work as well as they do in closed-list systems but that the difference is smaller than expected.

Closed ballots, in contrast, facilitate the implementation of gender quotas because parties tightly control the number and placement of women on the ballot, and electoral authorities can ensure that parties abide by the quota. At election time, voters vote for the entire party list as it was constructed by the parties, making it much more likely that the number of women on party ballots will translate into a comparable number of women elected. In Latin America, closed-list systems are more common than open-list systems, but some countries do allow preference voting. These include Brazil, the Dominican Republic (since 2002), Ecuador, Honduras (since 2005), Panama, and Peru. It is in these countries that the strength of gender quotas is less likely to matter for the election of women to national legislatures.

As this discussion suggests, simply having a gender quota may be insufficient for increasing the election of women in Latin America, but strong quotas that are implemented in the right electoral context should produce more gender-representative legislatures. The gender quotas that are most effective at increasing women's representation should be those that combine high quota targets, placement mandates, and enforcement mechanisms, and that are implemented in closed-list proportional representation electoral systems. As the theory of women's representation suggests, these aspects of formal representation should be important explanations for variation in women's descriptive representation in Latin America.

An Empirical Test

To test the relationship between formal and descriptive representation, I used data from elections to the lower and upper chambers of all 18 Latin American democracies' national legislatures from 1974 (or the first democratic election) through April 2008.[8] This was as few as 4 elections in Panama and Nicaragua, where the first democratic elections did not occur until 1990, and as many as 12 elections in Argentina, which became democratic in 1983 and holds legislative elections every 2 years in the lower chamber.[9]

The dependent variable is the percentage of women in the legislative chamber after each election between 1974 and 2008. I test the effect of formal representation on the election of women using the three measures described above. The first variable is the type of electoral system, which is divided into three categories: plurality or "semi-PR", mixed plurality/proportional representation, and pure proportional representation (PR). Almost all lower chambers in Latin American democracies have mixed systems or pure PR systems, but several upper chambers use plurality rules or semi-PR, which approximates plurality elections more closely than it does proportional representation elections.[10] Due to the proportionality of the electoral formulas, pure PR systems should have significantly more women in the legislature than plurality/semi-PR systems. Mixed systems should have more women than plurality/semi-PR systems but fewer than pure PR systems due to the combination of plurality and PR rules (Kostadinova 2007; Hinojosa 2008; but see Moser 2001; Curtin 2008).

The second set of formal representation measures are two variables that measure the average number of seats in each electoral district (i.e., district magnitude) and the average number of seats that political parties expect to win in each district (i.e., party magnitude). These provide a more nuanced measure of how proportionality affects the number of women in office. Importantly, the size of the district varies across both plurality and proportional representation systems. For example, Chile has a modified majoritarian electoral system with two-member districts. A party has to win twice as many votes as the other party to win both seats. Similarly, the Argentine and Bolivian senates use modified plurality rules to elect senators to three-member districts. The first two seats in the district go to the party that wins the most votes, whereas the third seat is awarded to the party that comes in second. Proportional representation systems can have district magnitudes as small as 2 and as large as the entire legislature. The Colombian Senate, for example, elects the entire legislature from one district with a magnitude of 100. In the models that follow, I logged both district magnitude and party magnitude because they are skewed, with a few country chambers having unusually large district and party magnitudes. In addition, it is theoretically more likely that district magnitude and party magnitude will have a *diminishing returns* effect, with a larger impact at lower magnitudes than at higher magnitudes (Schwindt-Bayer 2005; Jones 2009).

The third measure of formal representation is gender quotas. I measured quotas in two ways. First, I coded a dichotomous gender quota variable, indicating whether a quota applies to the legislative election (coded "1") or not (coded "0"). Then, I created an index of the strength of legal candidate quotas. This is a multiplicative index combining the size of the gender quota, which is an indicator of whether or not there is a placement mandate (coded "2" or "1," respectively) and the strength of the enforcement mechanisms (coded "1" for no enforcement, "2" for weak enforcement, and "3" for strong enforcement).[11] Figure 2.2 compares the quotas that Latin American countries use according to the index of quota strength. Theoretically, the index could range from 1 to 300,[12] but among Latin American countries, it ranges from 30 in Honduras, which has the weakest quota design, to 270 in Ecuador's 2006 election, which has the strongest quota design—a 45%

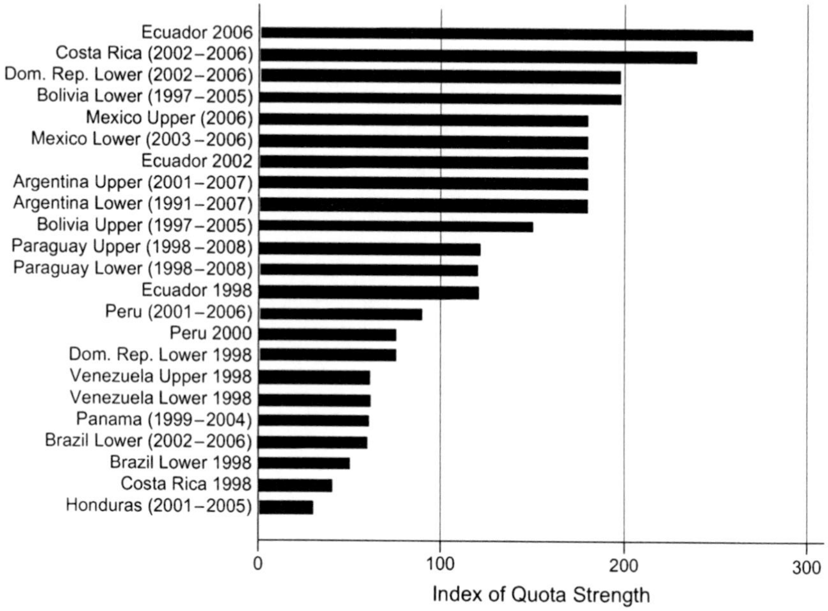

FIGURE 2.2. Strength of Gender Quotas in Latin American Countries

target with placement mandates and strong enforcement.[13] As hypothesized above, quotas should be more effective when party ballots are closed rather than open. I included a variable for whether the quota is adopted in a closed-list PR system (closed = 1, open = 0) and interacted it with the strength of the quota index to measure the conditioning effect of electoral context.

To isolate the effect of formal representation from other factors, the empirical tests that follow included measures of democratic culture and the socioeconomic environment, as described at the beginning of this chapter.[14] Specifically, the models control for the number of years that a country has been democratic (Payne et al. 2002), the number of years that women have had the right to run for political office (IPU 1995), the percentage of women who work in the paid labor force (World Bank 2007), and GDP per capita logged (World Bank 2007). Table 2.1 and figure 2.1 illustrated some of the variation in these measures. The statistical models also include a lagged dependent variable—the percentage of the legislative chamber that was female after the previous election—because women who were elected in one election have an incumbency advantage for getting reelected in the next election. This makes it likely that the percentage of women elected in any given year is in part determined by the percentage of women who won in the previous year.[15]

Explaining the Election of Women in Latin America

Table 2.3 presents the results of four statistical models that explain variation in the percentage of women elected to national legislatures in Latin America.[16] The table reveals that formal representation is indeed linked to descriptive representation of women in Latin America through the use of higher district and party magnitudes and gender quotas. In none of the models, however, is the broad measure of the type of electoral system, PR or mixed,[17] a significant influence on the election of women. At first glance, it appears that this supports some recent literature that finds that proportional representation electoral systems have no effect on women's representation in developing countries (Matland 1998; Moser 2001; Tremblay 2007; Stockemer 2008; but see Yoon 2004). However, when I exclude district magnitude or party magnitude from the models, PR systems do elect more women than plurality systems. The average increase in the percentage of women elected from one election to the next is 1.5% higher in proportional representation system than plurality systems—a statistically significant, but not substantively large, change. Thus, it is likely that PR is not significant because district or party magnitude overwhelms the effect of PR systems.

District magnitude and party magnitude both influence descriptive representation of women in Latin America (models 1 and 2, respectively). As the average number of seats in electoral districts increases logarithmically, the percentage of seats won by

TABLE 2.3. Explaining the Election of Women in Latin American Legislatures (percentage of the legislative chamber that is female)

	Model 1: District Magnitude	Model 2: Party Magnitude	Model 3: Quota Index	Model 4: Preference Voting Interaction
PR system	1.10	.98	2.86	2.15
	(.71)	(.64)	(2.13)	(2.26)
Mixed system	.24	.01	1.34	.41
	(1.02)	(.90)	(1.89)	(2.16)
District magnitude (log)	.27*	—	−.17	−.16
	(.15)		(.55)	(.46)
Party magnitude (log)	—	.36**	—	—
		(.16)		
Gender quota	3.34***	3.33***	—	—
	(.95)	(.93)		
Quota strength index	—	—	.01	.00
			(.01)	(.02)
Closed-list PR	—	—	—	−7.21**
				(3.40)
Quota strength index*Closed-list PR	—	—	—	.04
				(.03)
Years democratic	.06**	.06**	.13***	.14***
	(.03)	(.03)	(.04)	(.04)
Right to run for office	.02	.03	−.06	−.13*
	(.03)	(.03)	(.07)	(.07)
Women in workforce	−.01	−.01	−.06	−.07
	(.03)	(.03)	(.06)	(.07)
GDP per capita (log)	.73	.66	.75	.73
	(.55)	(.53)	(1.14)	(1.18)
Lagged % women	.84***	.84***	.82***	.80***
	(.06)	(.06)	(.09)	(.09)
Constant	−6.34	−5.74	1.16	8.25
	(4.31)	(4.16)	(12.43)	(14.10)
R^2	.87	.88	.90	.90
N	164	164	47	47
Rho	−.25	−.27	−.35	−.31

Prais-Winsten regression coefficients with panel corrected standard errors in parentheses.
$^*p < .10$, $^{**}p < .05$, $^{***}p < .01$

women increases as well. Indeed, a diminishing returns effect exists whereby the increase is larger at small district magnitudes and smaller at large magnitudes. The graph at the top of figure 2.3 illustrates this.[18] The figure also shows that district magnitude has a rather small effect on the election of women because the predicted percentage of the legislature that is female varies only between 11% and 12.2% as district magnitude moves from its minimum value (1 seat per district in the Dominican Republic upper chamber and in every other election to the Brazilian upper chamber) to its maximum (200 seats per district in the Mexican mixed system). The effect is very similar for party

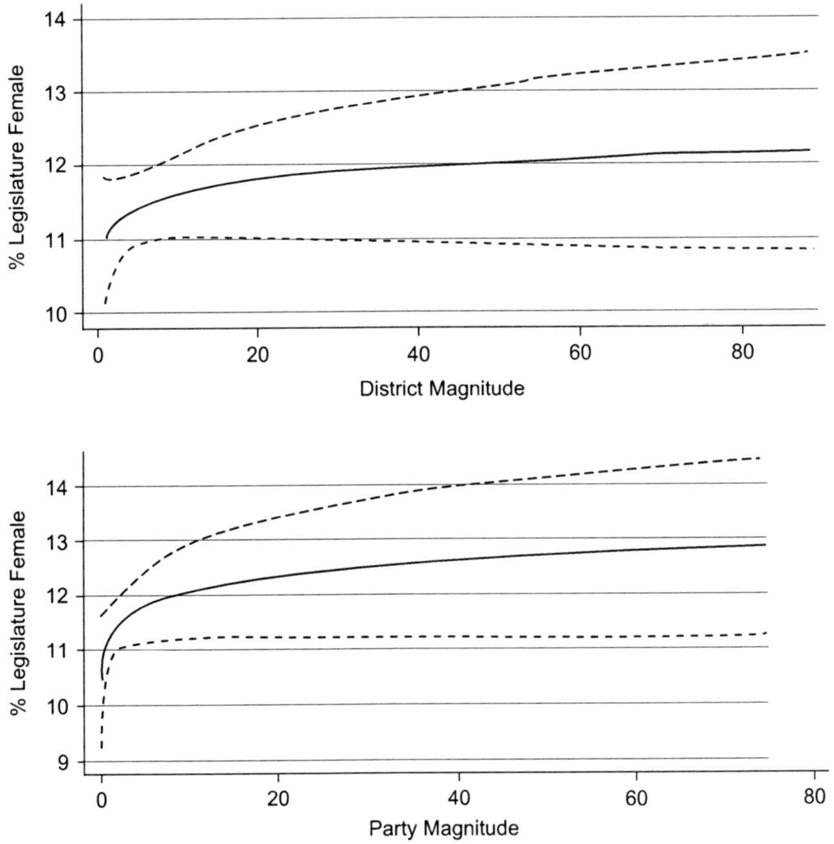

FIGURE 2.3. Predicted Effect of Logged District Magnitude and Logged Party Magnitude on the Percentage of the Legislature that Is Female (dashed lines are confidence intervals)

magnitude (graph at the bottom of figure 2.3). As the average number of seats that a party wins increases, the percentage of seats won by women increases more rapidly at small party magnitudes and more slowly at large party magnitudes. The predicted percentage of women in the chamber ranges from 10.5% to near 13%, indicating a larger effect for party magnitude than district magnitude.

As expected, gender quotas play an important role in the election of women in Latin America. Models 1 and 2 of table 2.3 illustrate the effect of simply having a gender quota or not. On average, legislative chambers with gender quotas elect 3.3% more women from one election to the next than chambers that do not use quotas. The mere presence of quotas does generate greater representation of women, offering support for the theory that quotas have psychological effects that encourage more women to participate in formal politics. However, the effect of quotas is relatively small, most likely because it does not take into account the wide variation in quota laws illustrated in table 2.2. It combines countries such as Peru, whose quota has a target of only 25% and no placement mandate, with countries such as Costa Rica, which has a 40% target, placement mandates, and strong enforcement mechanisms. Doing so provides a rough estimate of the effect of a quota but reveals no information about how varying types of quotas influence the proportion of women in office.

Models 3 and 4 of table 2.3 take into account the strength of the quotas and the electoral context in which the quota operates. These models show that the strength of the quota design does affect the election of women but only in closed-list systems. Model 3 includes the strength of quota index without interacting it with electoral context and finds no significant effect. Simply having a stronger quota does not guarantee more women in office. Model 4 presents the results of a model in which the strength of the gender quota is interacted with whether the electoral system is closed-list PR or open-list PR. Although the interaction term does not reach statistical significance in the model, calculating the conditional effects and standard errors reveals that the strength of gender quotas has a statistically significant and substantively strong effect on the percentage of women in office in closed-list systems. Figure 2.4 presents this relationship graphically. When electoral laws prohibit preference voting, as in most Latin American countries, the strongest quotas led to a predicted 24% of seats won by women compared to only 14% under the weakest quotas, all else being equal. In systems that permit preference voting, however, strong quotas do not increase the percentage of women in the legislature.

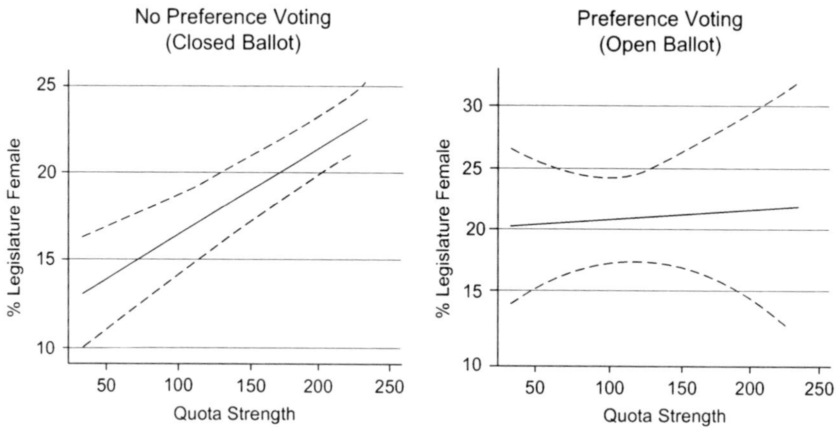

FIGURE 2.4. The Effect of Gender Quota Strength on the Percentage of the Legislature that Is Female in Closed-Ballot and Open-Ballot Systems (dashed lines are confidence intervals)

Clearly, the design of gender quotas and their compatibility with electoral contexts helps to explain the widely varying percentages of women in Latin American legislatures with quotas. A couple of examples help to illustrate this. Costa Rica elected women to almost 40% of the seats in the Legislative Assembly in 2006, yet Ecuador's National Congress had only 25% of its legislative seats held by women after the 2006 election. Both countries have strong quotas, but Costa Rica applies that quota in a closed-list electoral system whereas Ecuador applies it in an open-list system. Because of the open-list system, Ecuador's quota has very little effect on the election of women. In the 1997 and 1998 elections, Argentina and the Dominican Republic both used closed-list PR electoral rules and gender quotas. However, Argentina had a strong quota, requiring 30% of party ballots to be female, placement mandates, and strong enforcement, which resulted in 27% of the Chamber of Deputies being female. The Dominican Republic had a weaker quota—a target of 25%, no placement mandate, but strong enforcement—and elected women to only 15% of the seats in the Chamber of Deputies. Because the Dominican Republic's quota was weak, it generated a much smaller percentage of women in office than Argentina, with a stronger quota. Quota design matters but so too does electoral context.

In contrast to the strong effect of formal representation, the broader cultural and socioeconomic environment of Latin American countries has little influence on the election of women. Only the number of years that the country has been democratic and the lagged percentage of women in the legislature increase the percentage of women in office. Countries that have been democratic longer have larger increases in women's representation than those with shorter democratic histories.[19] Similarly, the percentage of women in the previous legislature strongly correlates with the percentage of women elected in the next election. This suggests some incumbency effect whereby women are likely to stay in office once elected. In contrast, the length of time since suffrage, level of development, and women's workforce participation have little effect on the representation of women in Latin American legislatures.

The null findings for the number of years that women have had the right to run for office are not too surprising given that women in all Latin American countries have had this right for quite some time—since 1961—and got the right to run for office within a narrow window of 32 years (see table 2.1). This may have mattered in the first years after suffrage, but it no longer affects women's descriptive representation in the region.

Although some cross-regional studies have found evidence that cultural and socioeconomic factors help explain the percentage of legislative chambers comprised of women (Norris 1985; Rule 1987; Oakes and Almquist 1993; Kenworthy and Malami 1999; Reynolds 1999; Schwindt-Bayer 2005; Schmidt 2008a), others have found that institutional and other factors overwhelm the role that socioeconomic and cultural contexts play (Paxton 1997; Britton 2008;

Stockemer 2008; Tremblay 2008a). This appears to be the case in Latin America. Economic development, women's workforce participation, and the years since suffrage have had little effect on the election of women. Instead, institutional factors are the most important explanations for descriptive representation of women in Latin America.

Conclusion

The theoretical model of women's representation purports that formal representation is tightly linked to descriptive representation. Specifically, it suggests that formal institutions that emphasize proportionality and representativeness produce legislatures that are more representative of diversity in society. Drawing on data from multiple elections in 18 Latin American democracies, this chapter showed that formal representation is a key explanation for women's descriptive representation in Latin American legislatures. More proportional electoral rules, specifically higher district magnitudes and higher party magnitudes, and gender quotas lead to the election of more women to national legislatures in the region. Further, differences in the design of gender quotas and the electoral contexts in which they are implemented affect representation of women in countries with quotas. Stronger gender quota designs (those requiring larger representation of women on the ballot, those with placement mandates, and those with strong enforcement mechanisms) lead to more women in office than those with weaker quota designs. This only occurs, however, when they are implemented in quota-compatible electoral contexts. Gender quotas and proportional electoral rules are key explanations for women's descriptive representation in Latin America.

The central place for formal representation in explaining descriptive representation of women in Latin America confirms what much of the existing literature has argued. Duverger (1955) was the first to assert that single-member district electoral systems create significant obstacles for the election of women, and empirical evidence from numerous studies of the developed world and some countries of the developing world supports this. In addition, recent research emphasizes the importance of quotas, even if not all studies have found empirical support for quotas increasing women's representation (Reynolds 1999; Htun and Jones 2002; Kunovich and Paxton 2005; Tremblay 2007). In Latin America, research on how electoral institutions affect women's descriptive representation has tended to be country specific or built upon bivariate statistics, yet it too has found that electoral rules and gender quotas are important explanations for women's descriptive representation in Latin America (Jones 1998; Baldez 2004a; Jones 2004b; Schmidt and Saunders 2004; Araújo and García 2006; Archenti and Tula 2008b; Ríos Tobar 2008b; Stockemer 2008). Franceschet (2005), for example, argues that women's underrepresentation in the Chilean Congress is in part due to the highly disproportional binomial electoral system that disadvantages women and the fact that parties have strongly resisted gender quotas. As all of this literature shows, formal representation is crucial to understanding descriptive representation of women.

These findings also validate the thinking of female legislators in Latin America who see quotas as a positive mechanism for improving women's representation. Argentine Deputy Josefina Abdala was against the adoption of quotas in Argentina but credits the law with ensuring her election and the election of many other women:

> I was one of those who did not want the *Ley de Cupos* [quota law] because to me it seems that women have the same possibilities as men. I always say that we have to go out and fight for our place. But also, I have to recognize that, thanks to the *Ley de Cupos*, there are many more women in politics. It is as simple as that. If it weren't for the *Ley de Cupos*, I would be third on the ballot. But the *Ley de Cupos* put me second. (Abdala 2006)

In Costa Rica, Deputy Sonia Villalobos highlights the need for quotas in a region long dominated by a sexist culture:

> In a country like ours, it is necessary. I do not believe that all countries should have quotas, but in a society of *machismo* where people believe that politics is a right of men, it is necessary to have quotas. I believe that it is going to help us, over a short period of time, to increase the numbers of women not only in the Legislative Assembly, but in the provinces, ministries, executives, and other arenas of decision-making. We need a quota to overcome the societal belief of *machismo* that prioritizes men and views politics as a right of men. (Villalobos 1999)

In sum, this chapter offers a cross-national, time-serial statistical analysis that shows that electoral rules and quotas are important explanations for women's descriptive representation in Latin America. At the same time, it generates additional questions about the consequences of the election of women to legislatures. What effect has the presence of women in politics had for representation of women and women's issues? What effect has it had on gender equality among legislators inside the legislature? Do formal institutions that clearly influence women's descriptive representation also have an effect on women's substantive representation? In the next three chapters, I explore the relationship between formal representation, descriptive representation, and substantive representation of women in Latin America.

3

Preferences and Priorities

Gender and the Political Attitudes of Legislators

The political preferences that legislators bring to the political arena are the starting place for substantive representation. They provide information about the priorities that legislators place on constituents, legislative activities, and political issues, which in turn can affect the way that representatives behave in office. Although attitudes and behavior are often similar, they are not identical. A legislator may think that women's equality is an important political issue but not expend any policymaking effort toward women's equality issues. Thus, it is necessary to examine both the attitudes and behavior of elected representatives to determine whether female legislators represent women—and if not, why.

In this chapter, I analyze the political attitudes of representatives in Argentina, Colombia, and Costa Rica to determine whether female representatives have different preferences and priorities than men. Specifically, this chapter answers three of the overarching questions posed in chapter 1: do female representatives represent women through their political preferences, do they represent *all* constituents to the same extent that male representatives do, and to what extent do gender differences in political preferences vary across countries? I answer these questions using data from an original survey of legislators in the three countries. Findings from analyses of these data provide a baseline from which to compare the behavior of female representatives analyzed in the following chapters.

Gender and Political Preferences in Latin American Legislatures

In Latin America, Elsa Chaney's (1979, 21) seminal research suggested that women in office are *supermadres*—"tending to the needs of her big family in the larger casa of the municipality or even the nation." She found evidence of this by interviewing women in government in Chile and Peru in the 1960s and early 1970s. Chaney's conclusions about women in office being supermadres dominated thinking about women's representation in the region for many years (Chaney 1998; Jaquette and Wolchik 1998; Craske 1999). What her conclusions suggest is that female and male representatives will differ from one another in their attitudes toward social issues and traditional men's issues, with women tending to social issues and men focusing on men's issues. Yet, Chaney's research took place when few women worked outside the home, entered institutions of higher education, or participated in politics. Over the past 30 years, women's status has changed significantly (Craske 1999).[1] Societal views of women in the region are more supportive of women entering the labor force and being in politics (Gallup Organization 2001; Latinobarómetro 2004). Women are working in the paid labor force and entering institutions of higher education in growing numbers (World Bank 2007). And they have entered legislative and executive branches of government with increasing regularity (Escobar-Lemmon and Taylor-Robinson 2005; IPU 2008). As a result of these changes, the political attitudes of female representatives may differ today, such that the supermadre label no longer fits.

Indeed, recent research questions the applicability of the supermadre model in Latin America and lends support to the hypothesis articulated in chapter 1 that women will place higher priority on women's issues than men and may be similar in the importance that they place on social issues and men's issues (Furlong and Riggs 1996; Htun and Power 2006; Schwindt-Bayer 2006). Furlong and Riggs (1996) found little evidence to confirm Chaney's classification of women in government as supermadres in Costa Rica. They showed that women in government still accept traditional gender roles in the private sphere but not in the public sphere. In office, women see themselves as being highly capable officeholders who could hold a wide range of political positions, not just traditionally feminine ones. Similarly, Saint-Germain and Chavez Metoyer (2008) found that female representatives in Central America have strong predispositions to representing women but see this as being above and beyond their responsibilities to constituents or their political party. Statistical research also has shown that women represent women's issues but are not very different from men in the importance they place on more feminine issues or men's issues (Htun and Power 2006; Schwindt-Bayer 2006). Htun and Power (2006) found that female legislators in Brazil are more supportive of gender quotas and labor rights but that party matters more than gender in explaining attitudes toward abortion rights and gay rights. In an earlier study, I reported that female legislators in Latin America view women's equality and children and family issues as more important issues than men do but that no differences exist on issues of education, health care, or the economy (Schwindt-Bayer 2006). Thus, initial evidence supports the theory that although female representatives are likely to prioritize women's issues more than men do, fewer differences may emerge in the areas of traditionally defined gender issues—social issues and men's issues.

Building on the theoretical framework posed in chapter 1, I test five specific hypotheses in this chapter. The first two address the question of whether women are representing women through their political preferences—specifically, preferences toward women as a constituency and women's issues. I argue that female representatives should place higher priority on female constituents and women's groups than male representatives due to their shared history of societal subordination and feeling a special responsibility as women to represent women (Phillips 1995; Mansbridge 1999; Young 2000; Weldon 2002a; Mansbridge 2003). This should also lead female legislators to place higher priority on women's issues. The second three hypotheses address whether women are representing *all* constituents through their political attitudes. Female elected officials are likely to recognize that they cannot ensure their political future or fully do their job as representatives by focusing only on women (Dahlerup 1988; Thomas 1994; Carroll 2002; Grey 2006). As a result, they should seek out a range of other important constituencies to represent. Female and male representatives are likely to place similar priority on constituencies, such as the poor, ethnic minorities, farmers and fishermen, and blue-collar workers. In addition, female constituents should view all legislative activities—policymaking, sitting on committees, constituency service, giving public speeches—as important vehicles for representation. Finally, I expect that female representatives will give social issues and men's issues the same priority that male representatives give them. Men's and women's similar preferences should reflect the fact that they are first and foremost representatives of their parties and constituents, not just of women.

In 2001–2002, I conducted a survey of legislators in Argentina, Colombia, and Costa Rica asking about their political preferences, backgrounds, previous political experiences, and political ambition (see appendices A and B). In this chapter, I use the legislators' responses to examine the priority that representatives in Argentina, Colombia, and Costa Rica place on different types of constituents, various legislative activities, and a range of political issues. Representatives were asked to respond to all of the questions about their preferences on a 5-point scale from "very low" priority to "very high" priority. I analyze these responses using ordered probit statistical models that estimate the probability that a legislator will give each of the five possible responses. Rather than presenting numerous tables of statistical results, however, I present figures and tables of the substantive effect that a legislator's gender has on political priorities that emerge from the models (i.e., the predicted probabilities).[2] These illustrate where men and women have statistically significant differences in their preferences and show the substantive size of these differences.

The variable of most importance here is the gender of the legislator. But other factors also affect the political preferences of representatives, and sometimes outweigh the effect of gender (Tremblay and Pelletier 2000; Wangnerud 2000b; Poggione 2004; Htun and Power 2006). In this chapter, all of the statistical models control for four sets of additional influences on legislators' political preferences—legislators' personal characteristics and backgrounds, their prior political experience, their political ambition, and the nature of their electoral district. Specifically, the control variables are a representative's ideology, age, marital status, education level, occupation, legislative experience, prior political experience, political ambition, and urbanness of the electoral district.[3] Appendix C details the coding of these variables. By controlling for these additional influences on legislators' political preferences, it is possible to isolate the effect of a legislator's gender from other factors that may affect their attitudes.

Perceptions of Constituents

Most research on representation assumes that a legislator's constituents are the citizens living in the district from which the representative was elected. In other words, representation takes place *dyadically* between a representative and the constituents in his or her electoral district (Miller and Stokes 1963, Bartels 1991). Building on the idea that constituents are located within an electoral district, Fenno (1977) argued that representatives have four concentric circles of constituents within their district. A representative begins with a geographic constituency of all voters in his or her district, then maintains a reelection constituency separating supporters from nonsupporters, then focuses on a primary constituency by dividing strong from weak supporters, and finally distinguishes the closest circle of personal supporters. The representative has different relationships with the different constituencies and represents them in different ways.

However, *constituency* does not refer *only* to citizens in a geographic district. The concept of a constituency can be perceived in a myriad of ways. Some representation scholars argue that representatives should view all citizens in the country as their constituents and representatives from one district can represent those in another district—in other words, collective representation or surrogate representation (Weissberg 1978; Hurley 1982; Mansbridge 1999, 2003). Mansbridge (1999, 642) wrote that "in the United States, voters have many of their most vital interests represented through the 'surrogate' representation of legislators elected from other districts. Advocates of particular political views who lose in one district, for example, can hope to be represented by advocates of those views elected in another district." This view suggests that women elected from one district can be surrogate representatives for women in other districts who may not have a female member of congress. Similarly, Eulau and Karps (1977, 248) argued that constituents could be viewed as solidary or functional groupings of organized and unorganized interests. In other words, constituents could be the individuals residing in a representative's electoral district, but they could also be organized groups, such as women's groups, unions, religious organizations, or unorganized groups of individuals with common characteristics, such as women, minorities, or the poor. Both of these views of *constituency* underscore that representatives may view women as a constituency whose interests and concerns deserve representation. Whether legislators actually view women this way, however, is an empirical question.

Existing literature finds strong empirical evidence that although female representatives first and foremost view their job as representing all constituents in their district, they also view women as an important constituency (Thomas 1994; Reingold 2000; Wangnerud 2000a; Childs 2001; Carroll 2002; Childs 2004; Saint-Germain and Chavez Metoyer 2008). In interviews she conducted with female British MPs, Sarah Childs (2004) found that women identify their district as the primary locus of representation but many also recognize a need to represent women. Similarly, in her earlier research, Childs (2001) found that female MPs in Britain see representation as a way to generate closer ties between female constituents and representatives. Wangnerud (2000a) found that in Sweden women were significantly more likely to view promoting "the interests/views of women" as very important—55% of women felt this way compared to 10% of men. They also were more likely to interact with women's groups.

In a study of two U.S. states, Reingold (2000) found that although all legislators reported viewing women as an important group, female legislators were more likely to see female constituents as strong supporters. Her study found few gender differences in representational activities of Arizona and California representatives, but their perceptions of constituencies was one area in which legislators differed. Similarly, Thomas (1994, 69) found that "57 percent of women state legislators considered representing women very important; only 33 percent of men responded similarly." This pattern also emerged in the U.S. Congress. Almost all female representatives and senators felt that "in addition to representing their districts," they have a special obligation to represent the concerns of women (Carroll 2002, 53). In addition, most of the female legislators in Central America interviewed by Saint-Germain and Chavez Metoyer (2008, 188–189) said that they feel a special obligation to represent women; however, few female representatives mentioned women as a special constituency prior to being asked about it.

Interviews that I conducted with female representatives in Argentina, Colombia, and Costa Rica illustrate that women almost always state that their first and foremost responsibility is to the people, their constituents, or their political party. Argentine Deputy Graciela Rosso stressed that it is not her party, her province, or her gender that she represents but ideas: "It is ideas that we defend. The most important thing is to defend that which betters the lives of the people who live in our country" (Rosso 2006). Similarly, another Argentine deputy stressed that her

> political obligation as a deputy is to represent the people . . . I believe that one should represent the interests of the people in general. As a political theme, I always work for the most vulnerable sectors. Poor women in Argentina are a very vulnerable sector . . . Women and poor women are, for me, one of the most important political groups . . . But that doesn't mean that a woman only represents feminine interests. I also have other interests. (di Tullio 2006)

Sonia Villalobos in Costa Rica stressed that nonwomen's groups have been critical to her career as a deputy in the Assembly (Villalobos 1999). In her district, Puntarenas, the fishing industry is very large. She developed a strong relationship with this group, composed almost entirely of men, and the group has helped her immensely in politics. She points out that it is necessary to have strong support not only from women and women's groups but from all camps. One Argentine deputy described her priorities very clearly: "For me, I am fanatic about my district. I represent the people first. After that, I represent my gender and after that my party" (personal interview, June 20, 2006).[4]

Many female legislators, however, also emphasize the importance of representing women. Deputy Alicia Fournier wrote in the Costa Rican Legislative Assembly's parliamentary journal, "Today we are confronted with a new responsibility, to be adequate channels for feminine voices that clamber for justice and respect for human rights" (Fournier Vargas 2001, 38). Deputy Isabel Chamorro of Costa Rica noted that "women [in society] depend on us. The role that we play is important for the future representation of women in the congress" (Chamorro 1999). Costa Rican Deputy Sonia Picado attributed her desire to get elected to the Legislative Assembly in part to wanting to represent women: "I think that just by being here I am sending a message to other women that we can do it" (Picado 1999).

Survey Results

Do empirical analyses support this anecdotal evidence that women in Argentina, Colombia, and Costa Rica view women as an important constituency to represent? Analysis of the survey results in these countries reveals that women view all constituents as important, but also place special priority on women. I analyzed two survey questions to determine this—the first question dealt with views of various social constituencies (unorganized groups), and the second question asked about representatives' views of different organized groups in society.

Male and female legislators in all three countries place relatively high priority on most unorganized social constituencies. Specifically, men and women both view minorities, the poor, environmentalists, business owners, blue-collar workers, professionals, farmers, and fishermen as important constituencies in their districts. Significant gender differences do exist in some countries, however, in whether legislators view women as an important unorganized constituency. In Argentina and Costa Rica, statistical models reveal that female legislators place much higher priority on female constituents than do male legislators. Figure 3.1 shows the predicted probabilities that emerge from the multivariate models in each country. In Argentina, 59% of female legislators see women as a "very high" priority compared to only 15% of men. Almost all female legislators place "high" or "very high" priority on women, whereas only 70% of men do. In Costa Rica, 80% of female deputies place "very high" priority on women, whereas only 67% of male deputies

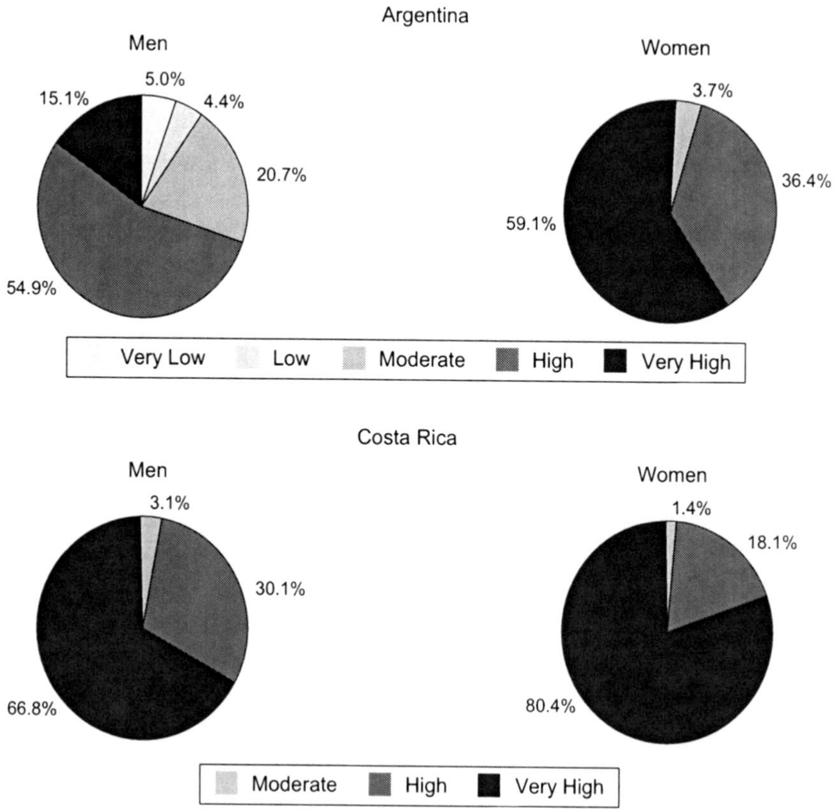

FIGURE 3.1. Predicted Percentages of Legislators with Priorities for Women as a Constituency

place a similar priority on female constituents. In contrast to the significant gender differences that exist in Argentina and Costa Rica, no gender differences emerge in Colombia after accounting for legislators' backgrounds, political experience, ambition, and electoral district. Women and men are equally likely to place priority on women as a constituency needing representation.

Another view of constituents is as organized groups whose interests are promoted by interest groups and NGO's. Quite a few significant gender differences emerge in the importance that legislators place on various organized constituencies, after accounting for legislators' backgrounds, prior experience, political ambition, and electoral districts. Of primary interest here, female representatives place significantly higher priority on women's groups than do male representatives in Argentina, Costa Rica, and the Colombian Chamber of Representatives but not in the Senate (table 3.1). In Argentina, 46% of female legislators are predicted to place "very high" priority on women's groups, and 84% give them either "very high" or "high" priority. In contrast, only 18% of male representatives rank women's groups as a "very high" priority, and a little less than half (42%) think they are only a "moderate" or "low" priority.[5] In the Colombian Chamber of Representatives, female representatives also view women's groups as more important than do men, but the difference is primarily in the extent to which they place "very high" priority on women's groups. As table 3.1 shows, the statistical model predicts that 77% of female legislators view women's groups as a "very high" priority compared to less than half of men. Most male and female representatives, however, think that women's groups are of at least high importance to their legislative work.

This pattern is similar to what the priorities of deputies in Costa Rica reveal (table 3.1). The probability that female deputies will place "very high" priority on women's groups is 0.89 compared to 0.70 for male deputies. The probability is less than 0.05 that male and female deputies will rank them as having less than "high" priority. The gender difference in Costa Rica is partially related to the fact that

TABLE 3.1. Predicted Probabilities of Priority that Legislators Place on Women's Groups

	Argentina		Colombian Chamber		Costa Rica	
	Men	Women	Men	Women	Men	Women
Low	.21	.06	.08	.02	<.05	<.05
Moderate	.21	.10	.09	.03	.03	.01
High	.40	.38	.35	.18	.26	.10
Very high	.18	.46	.48	.77	.70	.89

Note: The statistical models from which these predicted probabilities are calculated also control for the legislator's ideology, age, marital status, highest education level, occupational experience, number of terms in the legislature, prior office-holding experience outside of the legislature, future political ambition, and whether they represent an urban district. The predicted probabilities are estimated in Stata 10.0 with CLARIFY holding continuous variables at their mean and dichotomous variables at their mode.

women are disproportionately more likely to be single rather than married. When marital status is omitted from the statistical model, the gender difference is strongly significant and the substantive difference in priority is larger. Once the fact that women are less likely to be married than men is controlled, however, the size and significance of a legislator's gender shrinks ($p = .09$). Single women appear to be more likely to prioritize women's groups as a constituency than married women.

In addition to differences in views of women's groups, a legislator's gender also influences the way representatives view other organized constituency groups in the three countries, though in varying ways. For example, in Argentina, women place greater priority on unions than do men, but in the Colombian Senate, women place less priority on them than men do. In the Colombian Chamber of Representatives, female legislators think that business groups are a higher priority group than do men, but in the senate, women think they are less important than do men. This lower priority that women place on business groups is also found in Costa Rica. Another organized constituency where gender differences emerge is religious groups. In both the Colombian Senate and Costa Rican Assembly, women prioritize religious groups less than men do.

No gender differences exist in the priority that legislators in Colombia and Costa Rica place on their political party, but statistical models do show that both male and female legislators in Colombia place much less importance on parties than legislators in Costa Rica. In Colombia, only 61% of representatives in the chamber are predicted to place "very high" priority on political parties and only 70% of senators feel that way. Some legislators in both chambers give parties "very low" and "low" priority. In contrast, almost 90% of deputies in the Costa Rican Assembly are predicted to place "very high" priority on political parties, and none of those surveyed accorded them a priority lower than "moderate." This makes sense given that Costa Rica is a more party-centered system than Colombia.

In contrast to the lack of gender differences in Colombia and Costa Rica, male and female deputies in Argentina do have significantly different views of their political parties. Women in Argentina place much higher priority on representing the party and its platform than do men. Figure 3.2 shows the predicted probabilities from a statistical model estimating the effect of gender after accounting for other reasons that legislators may place different priorities on their parties and reveals that almost all women (99.5%) are predicted to view representing political parties as a "very high" priority. In contrast, only 64% of men feel this way about parties. This suggests that a very different dynamic exists between women and parties than men and parties in Argentina. Women appear to be much more dependent upon their parties, which could facilitate their marginalization in office. Whether this occurs or not is the subject of the next several chapters, but this finding suggests that parties in Argentina may have a particularly strong ability to influence their female deputies.

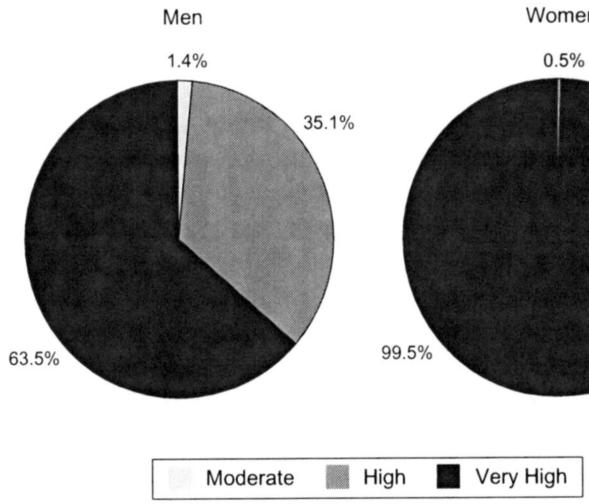

FIGURE 3.2. Importance that Male and Female Legislators in Argentina Place on Political Parties

Overall, these findings show that women and men differ significantly in their views of women as unorganized social constituents in Argentina and Costa Rica and in their views of women's groups in all three countries. Men also place priority on women and women's groups but are significantly less likely than women to view them as a top constituency needing representation. This matches the interview evidence presented earlier from Argentina and Costa Rica, suggesting that women do view women as an important constituency, and corresponds to findings from other countries around the world about how women in office view female constituents and the women's groups that often help get them into office to begin with. These findings also provide an important first piece of the puzzle of women's representation. Representatives represent an array of different constituent groups, and their perceptions of constituents can affect the way they represent them. The importance that a representative places on specific constituency groups, for example, may affect the amount of constituency service that he or she directs toward those groups (Prewitt and Eulau 1969; Zeigler et al. 1974). Representatives who view certain constituents, such as women, as particularly important for their reelection may spend more time working on women's issue policies and speaking on behalf of women in public presentations in an effort to cater to the women's vote. Examining the way that representatives view constituents and the way they view women as a constituency, specifically, is critical for better understanding women's substantive representation.

Perceptions of Legislative Responsibilities

Representatives have numerous responsibilities as part of their job of representing constituents. They sponsor, debate, and amend legislation, sit on legislative committees, hold leadership posts, give public speeches, hold meetings with constituents, do casework on behalf of constituents, and attend political activities in their district. This book groups these responsibilities into three sets of legislative activities that comprise a large part of substantive representation—policymaking, committees and leadership, and home style. Because of the importance of all of these activities to the process of representation, representatives need to participate in all of them to fully represent their constituents. Consequently, female representatives in Latin America should recognize that these are key tools for achieving their representational goals and be as likely as men to place priority on policymaking, committees and leadership, and working with constituents.

Early research on women's representation in countries around the world has found some systematic differences in the types of activities in which men and women participate. Thomas (1994, 38) reported in the United States that "based on the research on women and men legislators of the 1970s, it is clear that women participated in the range of legislative behaviors [participating in committee meetings and floor sessions, meeting with lobbyists and other representatives of various interests, and bargaining with lobbyists and legislative colleagues to achieve desired outcomes] to a lesser degree than men." By the 1980s, female legislators in the United States "participated in all aspects of legislative life" (Thomas 1994, 53). In addition, studies found that women did more constituency service than their male counterparts and had different home styles (Diamond 1977; Thomas 1992; Richardson and Freeman 1995; Friedman 2000). Yet, little empirical work confirmed that women placed greater *priority* on these activities, just that they *participated* in them more often than men. Further, no research in Latin America has analyzed gender differences in representatives' preferences for legislative activities. In this chapter, I examine gender differences with regard to the priority that representatives place on different legislative activities. I use a question from the survey of legislators that asks representatives about the priority they place on six different parts of their job—sponsoring legislation, working in committees, constituency service, distributing pork, giving public speeches, and promoting the political party's platform.

Survey Results

Some gender differences do emerge in legislators' priorities for legislative work, but they vary across countries. In Argentina, gender differences are present in three legislative activities, and in all three, women place higher priority on them than men do (figure 3.3). Specifically, women view distributing pork, sponsoring bills, and promoting the party platform as more important parts of their job than do men, after accounting for how legislators' characteristics, political experiences, ambition, and districts affect their attitudes. Almost 90% of women are predicted to place "very high" or "high" priority on distributing pork and promoting the party platform compared to 70% and 63% of men, respectively. Both men and women think that sponsoring bills is at least a "high" priority, but female deputies are more likely to think that it is a "very high" priority. The higher priority that women place on promoting the party platform echoes the finding from the previous section that women are more likely to view their political party as a very important group. Women in Argentina placed higher priority on the political party than men did.

Fewer differences exist in Colombia and Costa Rica (figure 3.4). In Costa Rica, significant gender differences exist only in the priority that deputies place on sponsoring bills. About 70% of female deputies are predicted to place "very high" or "high" priority on sponsoring legislation, whereas almost all men do. This contrasts with Argentina, where women actually place higher priority on sponsoring legislation than do men. In the Colombian Chamber of Representatives, gender differences emerge only in the area of committee work. Fewer women place "very high" priority on committee work than men, although both are predicted to think that it is at least of "high" priority.

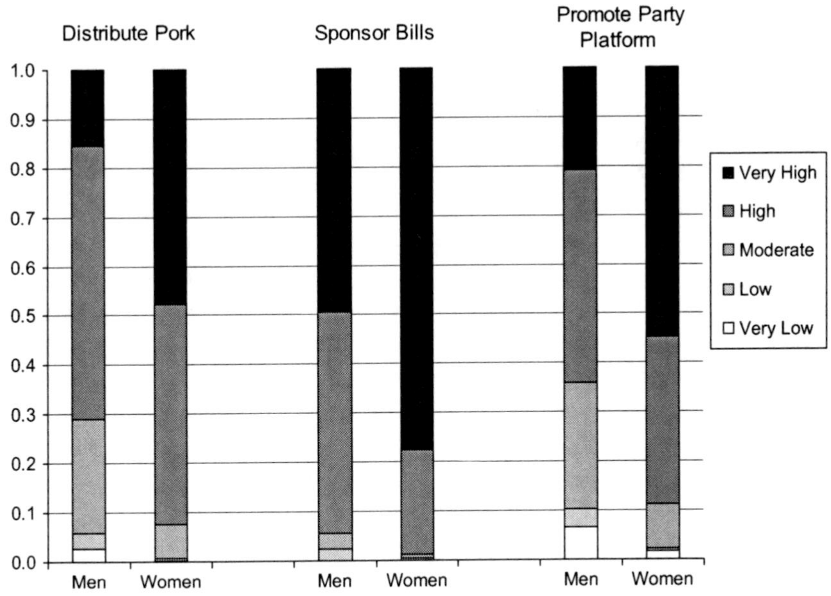

FIGURE 3.3. Predicted Probabilities of the Priority that Legislators Place on Three Legislative Activities in Argentina

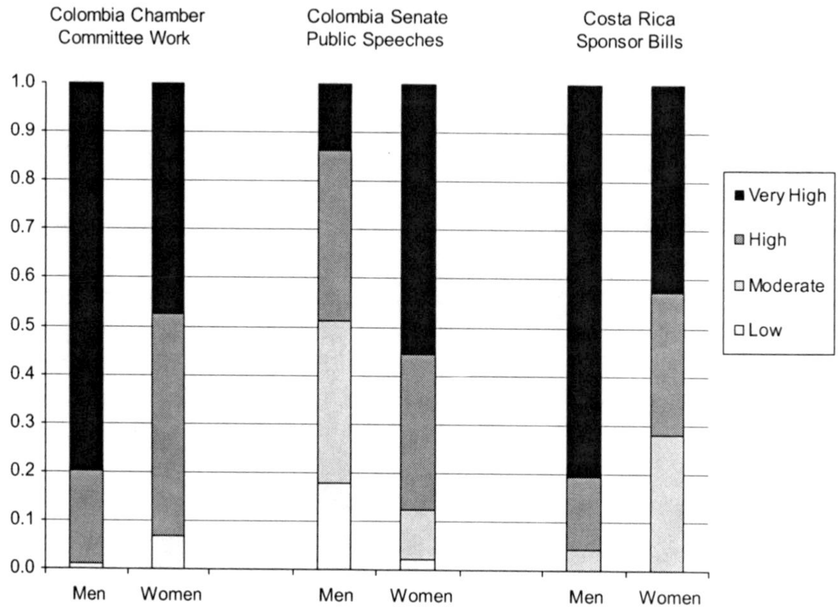

FIGURE 3.4. Predicted Probabilities of the Priority that Legislators in Colombia and Costa Rica Place on Legislative Activities

In the Colombian Senate, women's priorities differ from men's in the activity of giving public speeches and presentations (figure 3.4). Almost 90% of female senators view giving public speeches and presentations as a "high" or "very high" priority. In contrast, just under half of male senators think this is an important priority, and they have a probability of near 0.20 of thinking it is only a "low" priority. This is somewhat surprising given the traditional thinking that women are less comfortable than men with speaking in public and often defer to men in that area. It does, however, suggest that women recognize the symbolic importance of speechmaking to their legislative work. Speeches are often considered a form of symbolic politics that allows politicians to express support or concern for something without having to commit actual time and resources to it (Edelman 1964; Ragsdale 1984). This priority could indicate that women in the Senate are strategic in their behavior. Speechmaking allows them to make themselves seen and heard on a range of issues in a heavily male-dominated environment.

Despite arguments that women prefer certain types of legislative work, these findings suggest that men and women in Latin America are quite similar in the priority they place on different parts of their job. Where women and men differ, it does not match the perception that women prefer less high-profile tasks, such as constituency service. These preferences should translate into legislative behavior as well. Women should be key players in Argentina in promoting the party platform, distributing pork, and sponsoring legislation, given the priority they place on these issues. They may be less active than men in committee work in the Colombian Chamber and less active than men sponsoring bills in Costa Rica because they prioritize these issues less, but they should be equally likely to do other types of legislative work. If they do not, it is not because women and men differ in their preferences for different kinds of activities.

Issue Preferences

The issue preferences that representatives bring to the legislative arena are a key part of substantive representation for several reasons. First, the issues that legislators place priority on give an indication of the issues that are important to the represented. According to the congruence theory of representation, the preferences of the represented should be congruent with the preferences of the legislators that they elect to represent them (Miller and Stokes 1963). Second, legislators' issue preferences can provide information about the personal interests, beliefs, and political issues that motivate them. In addition to bringing the concerns of the represented to the political arena, representatives are also motivated by their own beliefs and experiences. Finally, issue attitudes should be important determinants of the behavior that legislators exhibit with regard to their focus on policymaking, debating, committee work, or constituency service (Thomas and Welch 1991; Wangnerud 2000b; Dodson 2001; Lovenduski and Norris 2003; Schwindt-Bayer 2006).

Comparative politics research has consistently found strong support for the hypothesis that women have more positive attitudes toward women's equality issues than do men. This has particularly been the case in the United States (Diamond 1977; Johnson and Carroll 1978; Thomas 1994). Further, in the 1980s and early 1990s in Sweden, Wangnerud (2000a) found that female MPs had more positive attitudes toward gender equality in society and parliament than male MPs, and she reported similar findings for the Nordic region as a whole (Wangnerud 2000b). In Britain, women have consistently prioritized feminist issues more than men, favoring affirmative action and liberal gender equality issues, in general, and have more liberal positions on issues of abortion, rape in marriage, domestic violence, and equal opportunities for men and women (Norris 1996; Childs 2001; Lovenduski and Norris 2003; Childs 2008). Similarly, research found that female legislators in Rwanda prioritize economic advancement for women, female solidarity within parliament, and international female solidarity issues (Devlin and Elgie 2008).

On other issues, specifically social issues and traditional men's issues, findings have been more mixed. In early studies of women in U.S. state legislatures and

Congress, scholars reported wide differences between men's and women's attitudes toward social welfare issues, economics, and defense, with women being more favorable toward social welfare issues and less interested in economics and defense (Diamond 1977; Leader 1977; Johnson and Carroll 1978; Thomas 1994). These differences persisted into the 1980s, 1990s, and 2000s (Thomas 1994; Poggione 2004) and over time have led to women creating a distinctive set of policy priorities on which they act (Thomas and Welch 1991; Thomas 1994). The issues that have been found to comprise women's distinctive policy priorities in the United States include health, education, social welfare, and the environment. These policy priorities also have been found to carry into women's legislative leadership positions (Little et al. 2001). Gender differences in attitudes toward social issues and men's issues exist in other countries as well. In Sweden, Wangnerud (2000a) found that female MPs were more predisposed toward social welfare issues in the 1980s and early 1990s than male MPs. Other studies, however, have reported more similarities than differences in the gendered attitudes of legislators toward social and men's issues (McAllister and Studlar 1992; Reingold 2000).

Survey Results

Very little research exists on representatives' issue attitudes in Latin America (see, however, Chaney 1979). In this study, I use a question from the survey of legislators asking how important legislators believe various issues to be. Analysis of this question revealed that male and female representatives in Argentina, Colombia, and Costa Rica have very similar issue preferences on a wide array of issues. Specifically, they place similar priority on issues of education, health, the economy, inflation, minority equality, housing, poverty, and political violence. On a couple of issues, significant gender differences emerge among legislators in one country or another. For example, in Costa Rica, women place significantly lower priority on issues of employment than men do, and in Argentina, women place significantly lower priority on crime. In the Colombian Chamber of Representatives, female legislators place slightly higher priority on education than male legislators do. In general, however, male and female legislators bring very similar issue preferences to the legislative arena.

Three exceptions to this are women's equality issues, family and children issues, and agriculture. In all three countries, women place significantly higher priority on women's equality issues than men do after accounting for other factors that affect preferences. As figure 3.5 illustrates, the statistical model predicts that more women will place "very high" priority on women's equality issues than men in all three countries. In Costa Rica and Colombia, more than 60% of women are predicted to place "very high" priority on women's equality compared to approximately 30% of men, and most of the remaining women place "high" priority on this issue. In Argentina, 54% of women are predicted to place "high" priority on

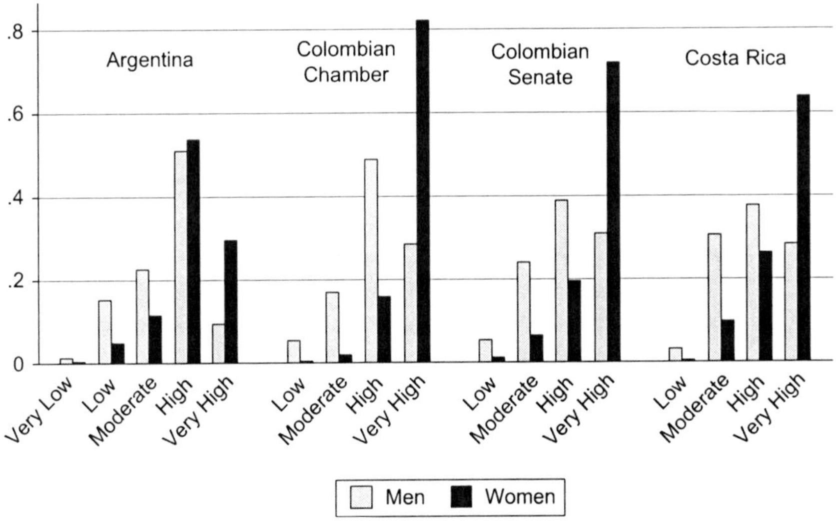

FIGURE 3.5. Predicted Probabilities of the Priority that Legislators Place on Women's Equality

women's equality and about 30% to place "very high" priority on the issue. The disparity between men and women in the "very high" priority category is 20 percentage points. Clearly, women in all three countries view women's equality as a higher priority than do men.

Importantly, however, men do place priority on women's equality issues. The priority that they give it is not as high as women's, but the majority of men see women's equality as being of "moderate" or "high" priority. Whether they truly believe in women's equality as a cause or have learned over time that placing priority on equality is politically correct, they do see women's equality as an important issue. Female legislators, however, see it as even more important.

The different views that male and female legislators have of women's equality issues match the underlying expectation of this study. Women have had different life experiences than men, have suffered decades of discrimination that has only recently abated somewhat, and may have a stronger gender consciousness than men. In addition, women are more likely to view themselves as representatives of women, as the previous section suggested through its findings that women place higher priority on representing female constituents and women's groups than men do. This is clearly observed through the different priority that women place on women's equality as a political issue. These findings also correspond with interview evidence from the three countries. Almost all the women I interviewed for this project stated that they view representing women's issues as very important to their legislative work. At the same time, however, they also stressed the importance of other issues. Argentine Deputy Juliana di Tullio, for example, noted that although the theme of gender is important to her, so too are issues of children, health, social action, and foreign relations (di Tullio 2006).

The importance of nonwomen-specific political issues to female legislators is evident in the survey results. Female and male legislators place very similar priority on most social issues and men's issues. The only two issue areas in which men and women do have different priorities in Argentina, Colombia, and Costa Rica are the family and agriculture. Family and children issues are a higher priority for women than men in the Colombian Chamber of Representatives and Senate, but no gender difference emerges in Argentina or Costa Rica. Figure 3.6 shows that many more women than men in the Colombian Chamber and Senate are predicted to place "very high" priority on family and children issues, after accounting for legislators' backgrounds, political experience, ambition, and electoral district. The disparity in the predicted probabilities is about 0.45 in both chambers. In other words, the difference in the percentage of women and men predicted to place "very high" priority on family and children issues is 45%. Although almost all women place either "high" or "very high" priority on these issues, the majority of men fall into the "moderate" or "high" priority categories. Male legislators in Colombia do see family and children issues as important but not *as* important as women perceive them.

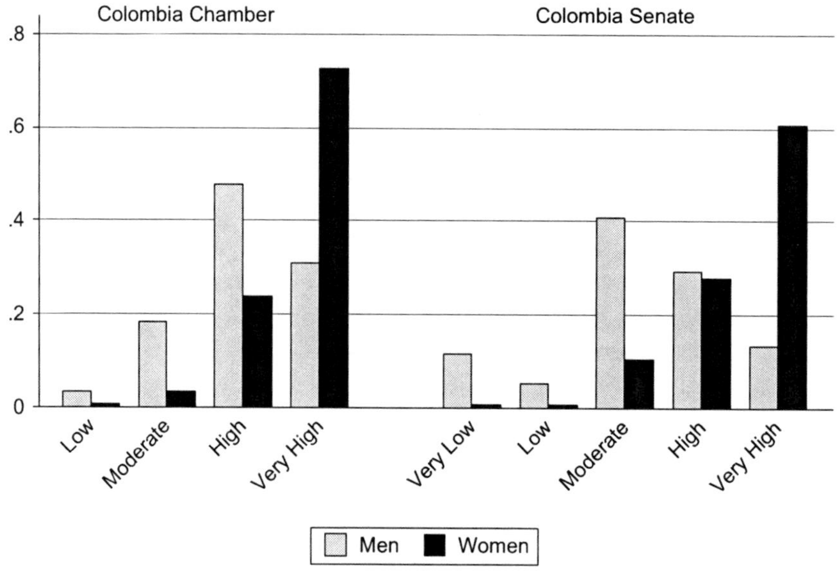

FIGURE 3.6. Predicted Probabilities of the Priority that Legislators Place on Family and Children Issues

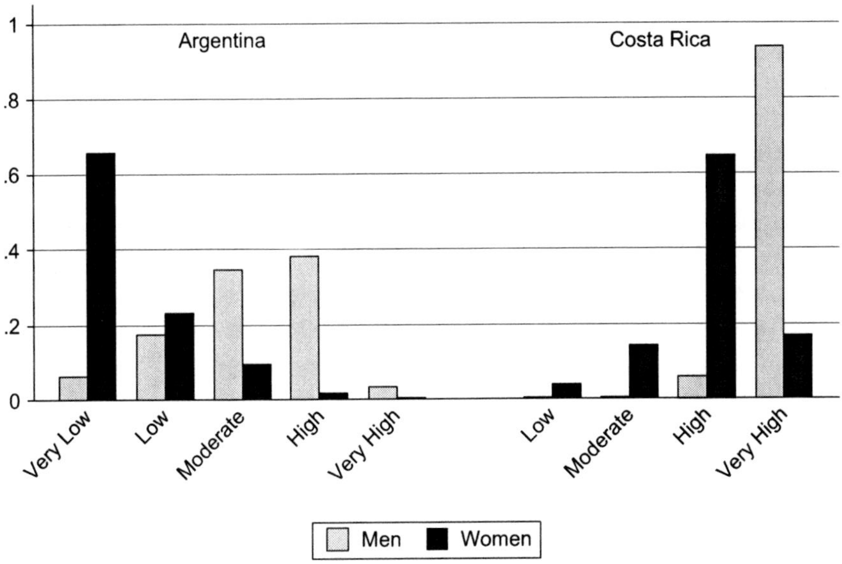

FIGURE 3.7. Predicted Probabilities of the Priority that Legislators Place on Agriculture Issues

The final issue on which male and female legislators differ is agriculture. The differences emerge only in Argentina and Costa Rica (figure 3.7), however, which are the two countries whose economies are still highly dependent upon the agricultural sector. In both countries, women place less priority on agriculture than men. Surprisingly, women in Argentina place almost no priority on this issue. The statistical model predicts that more than 60% of Argentine female legislators place "very low" priority on agriculture issues. This may reflect the fact that agriculture has always been a male-dominated economic activity and one into which women have made few roads in recent years despite the rising numbers of women in the paid labor force. Most women who enter the workforce do so via professional jobs, working class jobs in urban factories or businesses, or the informal sector, which is rarely recorded among national statistics. In 1994, 75% of women worked in jobs classified as being in the service sector, whereas less than 10% of women were involved in agriculture in South and Central America (Women in Development Network 1995). The very low priority that women in Argentina give to agriculture as a political issue clearly reflects this. Male legislators in Argentina also give agriculture less priority than many other issues, but the vast majority of them are predicted to rank it as at least a "low" priority. Although agriculture continues to be a large part of the Argentine economy, legislators give that issue less priority than other issues. In Costa Rica, agriculture is still a top political priority for both male and female legislators but fewer women rank it as a "very high" priority compared to men. The statistical model predicts that only about 18% of female legislators place "very high" priority on agriculture compared to almost all male legislators. Most female legislators rank it as a "high" priority.

Issues that fall into the traditional dichotomy of "women's domain" (e.g., family and children, education, health) and "men's domain" (e.g., economics, inflation, employment, development) yield few gender differences in the priority that legislators place on them. Women in the Colombian Chamber of Representatives do see the family and education as more important than men do, and female deputies in Argentina and Costa Rica place less priority on agriculture. For the most part, however, the traditional distinction between social issues and men's issues does not match the issue preferences that legislators bring to the political arena. This suggests that male and female legislators should represent these issues in similar ways in their legislative activities as well. In contrast, the issue area on which women's behavior should differ from men's is women's equality issues. As this chapter has shown, female legislators in Argentina, Colombia, and Costa Rica think that these issues are more important than do men, and this priority should translate into women placing higher priority on women's issues through the act of legislating. Whether this happens is the subject of the next several chapters.

Conclusion

Three overarching findings emerge from this chapter. First, female representatives do represent women and women's issues more than men do. Female representatives place higher priority on female constituents and women's groups in society (though, not as much in Colombia), and they view women's equality issues as a higher priority than men do. Female representatives in Latin America appear to draw on the shared experiences of discrimination that women have long faced and view themselves as having a special responsibility to be representatives of women and women's equality issues.

Second, female representatives also appear to recognize the need to represent all constituents, not just women. Female legislators do not differ from male legislators in the importance they place on most constituencies, the types of legislative activities that they use to represent their constituents, and various political issues. Like men, they perceive most categories of constituents, activities, and issues as being of at least moderate importance. Women in office have no underlying predisposition to spend more time representing traditionally feminine issues while ignoring traditionally masculine issues, nor do they have a predisposition to focus on female constituents at the expense of other constituents or constituent groups. Instead, women reveal a predisposition to represent constituents, participate in legislative work, and promote political issues to the same extent that men do. Women prioritize women above and beyond other demands of the job.

Third, these findings are more similar than different across countries. Female legislators in all three countries view women's issues as more important than male legislators view them, with the exception of the Colombian Senate. And, similarities in the preferences of men and women dominate in all three countries on most other activities and issues. One exception is that gender differences exist for bill sponsorship in Argentina and Costa Rica but not Colombia. The other exceptions are the gender differences in the priority that legislators place on agriculture issues in Argentina and Costa Rica but not Colombia and the different views that men and women have of children and family issues in Colombia but not Argentina or Costa Rica. For the most part, however, this chapter shows that women are representing women and representing all constituents through their political preferences.

These findings offer important information about the nature of substantive representation of women in Latin America. They show that descriptive representation of women does lead to greater substantive representation of women in terms of the political preferences that representatives bring to the legislative arena. Women in office substantively represent women by seeing them as a special constituency deserving political representation and by holding similar political preferences to them. Just as in the United States and Western Europe, women in office in Latin America are representing women. Of course, this chapter only looks at substantive representation as political attitudes, but it provides one piece of the larger puzzle of women's representation in Latin America.

Finally, the findings in this chapter provide an important baseline for the next three chapters, which examine representatives' behavior in office. Women's political preferences should translate into their political behavior if women have legislative equality with men. Women should turn their higher priority for women, women's issues, and other issues into related legislative action. Yet, as I argued in chapter 1, women in Latin American legislatures are unlikely to be entering a setting in which they have full equality with men. Instead, they enter a gendered institutional environment that has long been male dominated. Male representatives and male party leaders are unlikely to want to cede their dominance or legislative power to female newcomers. As a result, women may be unable to translate their political preferences into legislative behavior. In the next three chapters, I examine the extent to which this holds true.

4

Making Policy

Bill Sponsorship, Cosponsorship, and Debates

One of the primary ways that descriptive representation affects substantive representation of women is through the policymaking process. In this chapter, I examine the role that female legislators in Latin America play in policymaking by analyzing how gender affects the bills that legislators sponsor and cosponsor, their participation in committee debates, and their participation in floor debates on a range of political issues. With this analysis, I answer two important questions about women's substantive representation in Latin America. First, does women's greater priority for female constituents and women's issues in Argentina, Colombia, and Costa Rica translate into policymaking efforts on behalf of women and women's issues? Second, does the near equal priority that male and female legislators place on other political issues—specifically, social issues and men's issues—translate into gender equality in policymaking behavior?

Sponsoring Legislation

One way that representatives "act for" their constituents is sponsoring bills on issues that are important to them and their constituents. Bill sponsorship has been a common indicator of legislators' policy priorities in research on gender and representation, and I use it here as an indicator of whether women's policy preferences are translating into their legislative behavior. In chapter 1, I argued that descriptive representation is likely to translate into substantive representation of women such that female representatives will be more likely to view women's issues as important and to act on those preferences by participating in legislative activities such as sponsoring women's issue bills. Existing research has found evidence in many different countries that female representatives sponsor more legislation on women's issues than men. In the United States, women in Congress and state legislatures have sponsored and cosponsored bills on a range of women's issues and do so more often than men (Thomas and Welch 1991; Thomas 1994; Bratton 2002; Swers 2002; Wolbrecht 2002; Bratton 2005; Swers 2005). Similar findings emerge in Western Europe (Wangnerud 2000a; Childs 2004; Childs and Withey 2004; Kittilson 2006; Childs 2008). In addition, research on women's representation in Latin America provides evidence that female legislators place higher priority than male legislators on sponsoring women's issue bills (Jones 1997; Zambrano 1998; Taylor-Robinson and Heath 2003; Schwindt-Bayer 2006; Franceschet and Piscopo 2008). Studies have also found that the presence of women in legislatures around the world has led to the adoption of more women's issue policies, such as child support laws, domestic violence legislation, and family leave policies (Stevenson 1999; (O'Regan 2000; Bratton and Ray 2002; Weldon 2002a, 2002b; Rodríguez 2003; Kittilson 2008).

At the same time that women are working to make a difference for women, female legislators also have a responsibility to represent other constituents in their district. The last chapter showed that women place high priority on many social issues and men's issues, just as men do. Because legislators' preferences influence their behavior, we might expect women to translate the high priority that they place on these issues into bill sponsorship. Yet, they may be unable to do so because of the gendered legislative environment in which they work. Marginalization of women may occur in bill sponsorship because of traditional gendered views about the types of issues men and women should work on in the political arena. Male representatives and male party leaders may want to preserve sponsorship on the issues that they perceive to be men's issues and that they may perceive to be more important for themselves. In turn, they may encourage female representatives to work more on women's domain issues, such as education, health, children, and family issues. They do this by coordinating who sponsors which bills in their party and directing certain representatives to work in areas that reflect long-standing gendered notions of which issue areas are more appropriate for women and men. Indeed, Senator Piedad Córdoba (2002, 5) wrote about the gendered view that male legislators have of women and women's issues in the Colombian Congress:

> In general, the men in Congress, with very few exceptions, view women's issues with disdain and indifference. Although they do not oppose the discussion openly, when it comes to making a decision they ensure that their majority status prevails, refusing to allow the initiatives to go

> forward. With a few exceptions, the notion continues to weigh in their minds that politics is a matter for men, and they see women members of Congress as immersed in a world that is not their own.

Marginalization also can occur through bill cosponsorship. Male representatives may seek out male cosponsors on economics, agriculture, or foreign affairs legislation, assuming that they are better qualified or would carry more weight in getting the bill sponsored. Female representatives may feel pressure to focus more on social issues and seek out female cosponsors on social issue legislation. Although marginalization of women may occur as outright discrimination (telling a woman not to work on an economics bill because she is a woman), it also may be more subtle (women not being in the networks from which men seek cosponsors). Either way, one means to detect marginalization of women is to examine whether women sponsor or cosponsor more legislation on social issues and less on issues traditionally considered to be men's domain and compare these findings to legislators' preferences for these issues.

Research on the way that gender affects bill sponsorship on social issues and men's issues produces mixed findings. Some studies have found few gender differences in bill sponsorship behavior. For example, Jones (1997) found no evidence in the U.S. Congress or Argentine Chamber of Deputies that women sponsor health-care, education, social welfare, or environmental bills more often than men, and Heath and Taylor (2003) found no gender differences in sponsorship of education and health bills in Honduras. Other scholars, however, have found gender differences in the social and men's issue bills that legislators sponsor (Thomas 1991, 1994; Jones 1997; Swers 1998; Wangnerud 2000a; Swers 2005). Thomas (1991), for example, found that women in U.S. state legislatures sponsor education bills more often than men do and business bills less often. These studies have a hard time determining why women and men differ in their bill sponsorship behavior, however, because they do not take into account representatives' preferences for social and men's issues. It is unclear whether women sponsor bills in these areas because of stronger preferences for social issues or because of marginalization. In this study, I can address this by comparing the bill sponsorship findings to the findings on legislators' preferences in the last chapter.

Women's Issue Bills and Laws in Latin America

Studying bill sponsorship in Latin America is important for many reasons, one of which is that it is a region that traditionally has lagged far behind others in gender equality policies. For example, most countries still have very traditional divorce laws that give women few rights in marriage (Htun 2003). The strong Catholic Church has obstructed efforts to legalize abortion in many countries and has limited other reproductive rights for women (Htun 2003). However, some progress has been made on women's equality issues over the past 30 years. For example, by 1998, twelve countries had passed gender quota laws. All Latin American countries have ratified the U.N.'s Convention on the Elimination of All Forms of Discrimination against Women (CEDAW), and many did so within a few years of signing the convention in 1978. And, some have implemented important protections against domestic violence.

In Argentina, Colombia, and Costa Rica, specifically, recent congresses have passed some notable women's equality laws (table 4.1). Argentina was the first country in the region (and the world) to pass a national quota law for women's election to the national legislature in 1991 (Law 24.012), and in 2001, it passed a

TABLE 4.1. Major Laws on Women, Children, and Families in Argentina, Colombia, and Costa Rica

Country	Laws
Argentina	Quota Law (Law 24.012 of 1991)
	Law on Interfamily Violence (Law 24.417 of 1994)
	Newborn Rights to Identity Law (Law 24540 of 1995)
	Modification to Penal Code regarding crimes against sexual integrity (Law 25.087 of 1999)
	Law for adolescent mothers missing secondary school (Law 25.273 of 2000)
	Sexual and Reproductive Health Law (Law 25.673 of 2002)
	Law reforming previous law to protect pregnant and lactating women in schools (Law 25.808 of 2003)
	Law for Integral Protection of the Rights of Children and Adolescents (Law 26.061 of 2005)
Colombia	Law 82 of 1993—Special protections for female heads of household
	Law 294 of 1996—Prevention, remedy, and sanctions for interfamily violence
	Law 361 of 1997—Mechanisms to integrate citizens with disabilities (especially children)
	Law 548 of 1999—Prohibits military drafting of youth under 18 years of age
	Law 581 of 2000—Quota Law
	Law 679 of 2001—Prevention of Child Pornography and Child Sex Tourism
	Law 721 of 2001—Reforms to the paternity law
	Law 731 of 2001—Sets standards to improve quality of life for rural women
	Law 750 of 2002—Law allowing house arrest or community service for female heads of households convicted of light crimes
	Law 823 of 2003—Equal Opportunity for Women Law
	Reform to Law 294—Increase penalties for crimes of violence against women
Costa Rica	Law of Promotion of Social Equality for Women (Law 7142 of 1990)
	Electoral Code Reform creating gender quotas (Law 7653 of 1996)
	Law against Domestic Violence (Law 7586 of 1996)
	Law against Sexual Harassment in the Workplace and Education (Law 7476 of 1995)
	Law to create the National Institute for Women (Law 7801 of 1998)
	Law to Promote Breastfeeding (Law 7430 of 1994)
	Law against Sexual Exploitation of Youth (Law 7899)
	Law of Responsible Paternity (Law 8108 of 2001)
	Law of General Protection of the Adolescent Mother (Law 7735 of 1997)
	Law to toughen penalties for sex crimes against children (Law 8002 of 2000)

major piece of legislation on women's health—the Sexual and Reproductive Health Law (Law 25.673 of 2002). Costa Rica passed the Law for Real Equality for Women in 1988, which was a landmark piece of legislation promoting women's equality (Saint-Germain and Morgan 1991). Although the law has proven to be more symbolic than substantive, it still represents governmental attention to the plight of women in society and was one of the earliest such laws in Latin America. In July 2008, Colombia passed one of the toughest domestic violence laws in the region, increasing jail time from a maximum of 25 years to 40 years and making sexual harassment a crime punishable with a prison sentence. As Senator Gina Parody pointed out, this was an important accomplishment for Colombia: "Colombia, in contrast to the rest of the countries of Latin America, has a lot of catching up to do and this is the first big step for creating a women's policy agenda in the country" (Colombia: Ley Contra Violencia a Mujeres 2008).

In addition to passing these important laws, legislators in Argentina, Colombia, and Costa Rica have actively been sponsoring women's issue bills in national legislatures. Between 1994 and 2002 in Colombia and Costa Rica and in 1995 and 1999 in Argentina, a total of 187 women's issue bills were sponsored, comprising 2.7% of all of the bills sponsored during those years. Twenty-three of these bills became law (12.3%). The passage rates for women's issue bills in these legislatures have been quite comparable to the rates at which other types of bills have been passed into law. In Argentina, for example, passage rates ranged from 1.5% for fiscal bills to 7.7% for health bills in 1995 and 1999. Women's issue bills fall right in the middle of that range—3.2% of all women's issue bills became law in Argentina during these two years. In Costa Rica and the Colombian Senate, women's issue bills fell closer to the high end of the range. Twenty-two percent of women's issue bills became law in Costa Rica and only education bills had a higher passage rate—of 30%. In the Colombian Senate, 8.8% of women's issue bills became law, the third largest passage rate behind foreign affairs bills and education bills. In the Colombian Chamber of Representatives, women's issue bills were closer to the bottom of the range, but still 15.6% became law. Clearly, legislative activity on women's issue bills has been strong in these three countries in recent years helping to change the overall image of Latin America into one in which women's rights policies are increasingly being promoted and passed into law.

Rules and Motivations for Bill Sponsorship

Legislators sponsor bills for a variety of reasons, and these motivations depend, in part, on rules about bill sponsorship that exist in each legislature. They also depend on whether representatives are *individually* sponsoring or *cosponsoring* legislation. To understand the sponsorship and cosponsorship patterns of legislators in Latin America, particularly the influence that a legislator's gender has on bill sponsorship, it is necessary to clarify the rules within which legislators must operate and the reasons why they sponsor bills in Argentina, Colombia, and Costa Rica.

In Argentina, Colombia, and Costa Rica legislators can sponsor bills on any issue in any chamber, with the exception that budget bills must be introduced in the Colombian Chamber of Representatives whereas international relations bills must start in the Senate. In Colombia and Costa Rica, no limits exist on the number of cosponsors a bill can have, and all signers are considered equal supporters of the bill (i.e., no designated primary sponsor).[1] In Argentina, a maximum of 15 legislators can sign any one bill, and each bill has a designated primary sponsor. Legislators in all three countries compete with the executive when sponsoring bills. The executive branch has the power to introduce bills (and does so), and in Colombia, the president has the power of exclusive bill introduction in several policy areas, most notably the national budget, some fiscal affairs issues, and treaties with foreign nations. Although executives in Argentina and Colombia are more powerful than the Costa Rican president (Shugart and Carey 1992), all three countries have legislatures that exert a check on the executive and are widely considered the primary locus of policymaking (Morgenstern and Nacif 2002).

Legislators initiate bills for many reasons. One is simply to create policy. Some legislators have a personal interest in a policy area and sponsor bills to get that issue on the legislative agenda. Others initiate bills that address policy concerns raised directly by their constituents (and usually match the legislators' priorities as well). Another motivation for sponsoring bills is position taking (Campbell 1982; Koger 2003) or electoral credit claiming (Crisp et al. 2004). Legislators sponsor bills for which they can take credit for bringing benefits to their district and/or votes to their political party to ensure electoral support and a continued political career. All of these things motivate both single-sponsored and cosponsored bills; however, cosponsorship does incorporate additional motivations. Recent research suggests that the key motivation behind cosponsorship is signaling one's policy preferences to other legislators and political parties and showing support for legislation in hopes of increasing the probability that the bill will become law (Krehbiel 1995; Kessler and Krehbiel 1996; Wilson and Young 1997). Legislators may cosponsor a bill with other legislators of similar ideology or party leaders may encourage members to cosponsor bills to show strong and unified support for a bill. Most important for this analysis, women may cross party lines to sponsor legislation with other women to show a unified front behind a women's issue bill. Colombia's recent reform to the violence against women bill was sponsored and pushed through to passage by 27 female legislators representing an array of political parties.

Empirical Study of Bill Sponsorship

In this chapter, I examine bills initiated during two congresses in Costa Rica and Colombia, 1994–1998 and 1998–2002, and 2 years in Argentina, 1995 and 1999, to determine how gender affects bills sponsorship patterns.[2] I classify the bills that were sponsored into eight thematic areas—women's issues, children and family issues, education, health, economics, agriculture, fiscal affairs, and foreign affairs. These categories distinguish between women's equality issues, on which women should be more likely to sponsor bills, and issues traditionally considered to be women's domain issues (children and family, education, and health) and men's domain issues (economics, agriculture, fiscal affairs, and foreign affairs), on which gender differences in bill sponsorship may occur. They also mirror categories of issues in other chapters facilitating comparisons across the different types of substantive representation. Of course, these eight issue areas comprise only about half of all of the bills introduced in a given legislature. The remaining bills fall into other issue areas such as communication, transportation, general social welfare, the environment, and administration, for example. The thematic areas under study here include those that are most relevant to a study of gender and substantive representation.[3]

In all, 6981 bills were initiated by legislators during these congresses—4804 bills were sponsored by only one legislator (i.e., individually sponsored) and 2177 were cosponsored (table 4.2). The overall number of bills sponsored in each country varies but is between 2100 and 2500 bills, yielding a comparable number of bills under study in each country. Some differences do exist, however, in the number of

TABLE 4.2. Number of Bills Sponsored in Argentina, Colombia, and Costa Rica

	Argentina: 1995 and 1999	Colombian Chamber: 1994–1998 1998–2002	Colombian Senate: 1994–1998 1998–2002	Costa Rica: 1994–1998 1998–2002	All Legislatures
Total bills sponsored	2483	1252	1134	2112	6981
Number of bills individually sponsored	1238	1031	956	1579	4804
Number of bills cosponsored	1245	221	178	533	2177
Issues:					
Women's issues	63	32	34	58	187
Children/family	68	20	31	52	171
Education	110	139	71	131	451
Health	78	27	18	49	172
Social and public welfare	228	91	64	233	616
Economics	513	154	178	280	1125
Agriculture	77	41	41	72	231
Fiscal affairs	106	28	34	78	246
Foreign affairs	24	5	5	24	58
Other issue areas	1216	715	658	1135	3724

bills that are cosponsored versus individually sponsored. In Argentina, near-equal numbers of bills were individually sponsored and cosponsored. In Colombia and Costa Rica, cosponsorship of bills was far less common—less than one-fifth of the bills initiated by legislators in the Colombian Chamber of Representatives and Colombian Senate were cosponsored, and only one-quarter of bills sponsored in the Costa Rican Assembly had more than one signature (table 4.2).

The key question that this section asks is what effect a legislator's gender has on the bills that he or she initiates.[4] Here, I use the legislator, rather than the bill, as the unit of analysis. The outcome to be explained in the analyses below is the number of bills that a legislator sponsors or cosponsors overall and in the eight issue areas.[5] Across the four legislatures, 1102 legislators initiated bills during the congresses under study—503 in Argentina, 304 in the Colombian Chamber of Representatives, 181 in the Colombian Senate, and 114 in Costa Rica.[6] The total number of bills initiated by these individuals varied widely.[7] Some legislators sponsored only 1 bill (8% sponsored 1 bill only) whereas three sponsored over 100 bills each during their terms (102, 124, and 148 bills).[8] In Argentina, legislators sponsored anywhere from 1 to 124 bills (median = 22). In Colombia, members of the Chamber of Representatives sponsored between 1 and 50 bills (median = 11) and members of the Senate sponsored between 1 and 57 bills (median = 15).[9] Legislators in Costa Rica make up for the small size of their Assembly (57 deputies) by sponsoring large numbers of bills—between 14 and 148 for each deputy (median = 49), though the second largest number of bills sponsored by any one deputy was only 95. Variation in the number of bills that legislators sponsor carries over into the different subject areas as well. Some legislators initiated no bills in an issue area, whereas others initiated many. For example, the range in the number of women's issue bills sponsored by legislators across all four legislatures is from 0 bills to 8 bills. Nearly 22% of legislators signed at least one women's issue bill. For economic issues, 37% of legislators did not sponsor any economic bills and one sponsored 35 economic bills.

As in the attitudinal analyses from the previous chapter, I include a number of control variables in the statistical models to isolate the effect of gender. Two are similar to those used in the issue preference models—ideology and urban district.[10] Ideology is important because representatives from the left may be more likely to sponsor women's issue or social issue bills than those from the right side of the ideological spectrum. I measure legislators' ideology based on the political party to which they belong and where that party falls on a 5-point ordinal scale from left to right (Coppedge 1997; Rosas 2005; Alcántara 2006). One's electoral district also may affect bill sponsorship behavior. I include a dichotomous measure of whether the legislator's district is urban (higher population density than the country average and coded "1") or rural (lower population density than the country average and coded "0"). This correlates highly with other measures of district demographics such as literacy rates and unemployment rates.

Additionally, I include four variables assessing a legislator's position in the legislative chamber that could influence bill sponsorship patterns. First, I control for whether the legislator is a member of the largest party in the chamber (coded "1").[11] The largest party can set and control the legislative agenda and is better positioned to move legislation through the policy process. Thus, legislators from the largest party might be more likely to sponsor bills, in general, and in specific thematic areas that the party sees as important. Second, senior legislators have greater experience and knowledge of the workings of the chamber and may initiate more bills than junior legislators. I measure legislative experience as the total number of terms a legislator has served including the current term.[12] Third, I account for committee membership to ensure that gender is not picking up the fact that women might be disproportionately situated on women's issue committees, for example, or the fact that legislators may be more likely to sponsor bills on issues dealt with by the committees on which they sit. Committee membership is a dichotomous variable for whether the legislator sits on a committee dealing with bills in the thematic area under analysis (coded "1") or not (coded "0").[13] Finally, I control for whether the legislator served as president of the legislative chamber at any point during the congress (coded "1"). Chamber presidents have numerous responsibilities that detract from the time they can spend sponsoring legislation. Consequently, they should sponsor fewer bills than other legislators.

Finally, I include a variable that controls for the overall number of bills a legislator initiates during the congress and a variable assessing differences in bill sponsorship patterns across congresses. Some legislators initiate many bills, whereas others just a few, in part because legislators vary in their political clout, the size of their staff, and the resources available to them. Otto Guevara Guth, an opposition party leader in the Costa Rican Assembly, sponsored 148 bills in the 1998–2002 congress when the median was only 27. In addition, some congressional terms have more bills sponsored on certain issues due to the issue's relevance to the political agenda. I include a dummy variable for congressional term to ensure that there is no bias from one term or the other within any given country.

Findings on Bill Sponsorship

In the following subsections, I offer three statistical analyses of bill sponsorship.[14] First, I examine whether male legislators individually sponsor or cosponsor more bills than female legislators, regardless of the issues on which the bills focus. The last chapter showed that female legislators in Argentina place a higher priority on sponsoring bills than men whereas women in Costa Rica saw it as less important. Male and female representatives placed similar priority on bill sponsorship in Colombia. This analysis tests whether women are effectively translating the importance they place on bill sponsorship into action. Second, I look specifically at individually sponsored bills to determine gender differences in the percentage of women's issue, social, and men's issue bills that legislators sponsor. Finally, I perform the same analysis on cosponsored bills.

Gender Differences in the Overall Number of Bills Legislators Sponsor

Table 4.3 shows the results of statistical models estimating the effect that gender and other factors have on the overall number of bills that legislators sponsor in the four legislatures. The models predict that women in Argentina and the Colombian Chamber of Representatives sponsor more bills than comparable men do whereas no gender differences emerge in the Colombian Senate or Costa Rica. Women sponsor bills more often than men in Argentina and the Colombian Chamber even after controlling for other factors such as ideology, being in the largest party, legislative experience, being chamber president, and the fact that legislators may sponsor more bills in one congress than another. Calculating predicted values from the statistical models reveals that the average number of bills that men in Argentina sponsor (all else being equal) is 21 compared to 28 for women.[15] In Colombia, the disparity is even wider. The model estimates that men sponsor 8 bills, on average, compared to 17 bills for women.

TABLE 4.3. Explaining Individual Bill Sponsorship (dependent variable = number of bills a legislator sponsors)

	Argentina	Colombian Chamber	Colombian Senate	Costa Rica
Gender	.25*	.54**	−.27	−.12
	(.11)	(.16)	(.21)	(.08)
Ideology	−.97**	−.38	−.79**	−.28**
	(.19)	(.27)	(.27)	(.06)
Legislative experience	.03	.02	−.08*	−.10
	(.03)	(.06)	(.04)	(.10)
Urban district	.06	.21	—	.17*
	(.08)	(.15)		(.08)
Member of plurality party	−.75**	−.22	−.16	−.10
	(.12)	(.14)	(.16)	(.08)
Chamber president	−.99**	−.20	.35	.23*
	(.12)	(.20)	(.23)	(.11)
Congress dummy	.26**	.59**	.34**	.20**
	(.07)	(.10)	(.12)	(.07)
Constant	2.44**	1.49**	2.48**	3.72**
	(.09)	(.22)	(.16)	(.12)
N	503	304	181	114
X^2	83.81**	53.89**	33.98**	63.37**
Alpha	.55	.54	.50	.11

Negative binomial estimates with robust standard errors clustered around the legislator in parentheses.
$*p < .05$, $**p < .01$

In the Colombian Senate and Costa Rican Assembly, significant gender differences do not emerge in overall bill sponsorship patterns, although the estimates are negative and near-significant ($p = .20$ and $p = .14$, respectively). Stronger differences do emerge in Costa Rica, however, if individually sponsored bills are separated from cosponsored bills (models not shown). Women differ significantly from men in the number of bills that they sponsor with other legislators—women cosponsor fewer bills than men do in the Legislative Assembly.[16] The model estimates that women cosponsor an average of 15 bills compared to 20 for men (all other variables held at their means or modes). Examining the other countries, disaggregated by type of sponsorship, also shows that the significant differences in table 4.3 tend to emerge from one type of sponsorship only. In Argentina, women and men individually sponsor similar numbers of bills, but women cosponsor more bills than men do. In the Colombian lower house, female representatives sponsor significantly more bills than men on their own but do not differ from men in the number of bills they cosponsor. No significant differences exist in the Colombian Senate for either individual sponsorship or cosponsorship.[17]

Comparing these findings with the findings from the last chapter on the priority that male and female legislators place on bill sponsorship reveals no evidence that women are being marginalized in the overall number of bills they sponsor. Where women place higher priority than men on bill sponsorship (Argentina), they sponsor more bills. Where they place lower priority on it than men (Costa Rica), they cosponsor fewer bills than men. Where women and men are similar in the priority that they place on bill sponsorship (Colombian Senate), no gender differences emerge in bill sponsorship behavior. Differences in attitudes and behavior do appear in the Colombian lower house, but it is with women sponsoring more bills than the priority they place on bill sponsorship would suggest. This may reflect female representatives having to work harder than men to generate the necessary electoral support to get reelected in a personalistic system with relatively small electoral districts.

Gender Differences in Individually Sponsored Bills on Various Issues

On individually sponsored bills, gender differences do exist in the types of bills that legislators sponsor. Table 4.4 presents the results of models estimating the effect of a legislator's gender on sponsorship of women's issue bills. In Colombia and Costa Rica, women are significantly more likely to sponsor women's issue bills than men. In the Colombian lower house, women sponsor 3.7 times as many women's issue bills as men do, and in Costa Rica, they sponsor 3.3 times as many.[18] Costa Rican deputy Rina Contreras López (1998–2002) was particularly effective at sponsoring women's issue bills and getting them passed into law. During her

TABLE 4.4. Explaining Women's Issue Bill Sponsorship (individually sponsored bills)

	Argentina	Colombian Chamber	Colombian Senate	Costa Rica
Gender	.52	1.30*	2.69**	1.20**
	(.50)	(.64)	(.61)	(.37)
Ideology	.39	−1.23	−1.66	.59
	(1.02)	(.67)	(1.08)	(.35)
Related committee	1.02*	−.79	1.15	.80*
	(.49)	(.71)	(.79)	(.38)
Legislative experience	.27*	−.36	.15	.34
	(.13)	(.26)	(.23)	(.21)
Urban district	−.36	16.15**	—	.64
	(.45)	(.80)		(.56)
Plurality party	1.38*	−.29	−.18	−.57
	(.67)	(.77)	(.52)	(.38)
Chamber president	−15.39**	−18.48**	1.12	−.06
	(1.11)	(.77)	(.94)	(.66)
Total bills sponsored	.03*	.14*	.11**	.03*
	(.02)	(.07)	(.03)	(.01)
Congress dummy	−.66	−1.34*	−1.00*	−.09
	(.47)	(.61)	(.47)	(.38)
Constant	−4.67**	−18.74**	−3.80**	−3.72**
	(.59)	(1.01)	(.80)	(.72)
N	503	304	181	114
X^2	240.53**	2102.82**	34.26**	40.37**
Alpha	2.08	4.10	3.17	.20

Negative binomial estimates with robust standard errors clustered around the legislator in parentheses.
$^{*}p < .05$, $^{**}p < .01$

4-year term in office, she sponsored eight women's rights bill, three of which (38%) became law before the end of the 4-year term—a higher success rate than any other woman achieved for women's issue bills in either the 1994–1998 or 1998–2002 congresses. In the Colombian Senate, the effect of gender is much larger—women sponsor 14.7 times as many women's issue bills. The statistical model estimates that, on average, 32% of female senators in Colombia will sponsor one or more women's issue bills compared to only 5% of men. In Argentina, no significant gender differences emerge, suggesting that both men and women individually sponsor women's issue bills in similar numbers. This is somewhat surprising given the strong findings in other countries, but indeed several men were responsible for sponsoring some notable women's issue bills in 1995 and 1999. These bills included an effort to create a fund to help low-income pregnant mothers, a bill to provide a monthly allowance to women with five or more children, and several bills aimed at better defining and regulating assisted human reproduction (fertility treatments, artificial insemination, etc.).

These results show that women do substantively represent women through individual bill sponsorship. The second question is whether women are as likely as men to individually sponsor social and men's issue bills. Table 4.5 shows the

TABLE 4.5. Explaining Bill Sponsorship on Women's Domain and Men's Domain Issues (individually sponsored bills)

	Argentina		Colombian Senate		
	Economy	Fiscal Affairs	Health	Agriculture	Foreign Affairs
Gender	−.66**	−2.83**	1.74**	−14.60**	−15.51**
	(.26)	(1.05)	(.69)	(.55)	(.87)
Ideology	.94**	1.68	−1.45	.39	−2.09
	(.34)	(1.04)	(1.12)	(1.06)	(1.24)
Related committee	−.01	.89**	.81	1.26*	2.26*
	(.19)	(.35)	(.82)	(.53)	(.99)
Legislative experience	.24**	.19*	.12	−.05	−1.40
	(.05)	(.09)	(.24)	(.21)	(1.31)
Urban district	−.26	−1.18**	—	—	—
	(.19)	(.37)			
Plurality party	.62*	1.08	−.34	−1.10	.94
	(.25)	(.65)	(.54)	(.63)	(.95)
Chamber president	−20.13**	−25.77**	−17.62**	.79	−15.08**
	(1.02)	(1.16)	(.53)	(1.22)	(.92)
Total bills sponsored	.04**	.05**	.08**	.10**	.06*
	(.01)	(.01)	(.02)	(.02)	(.03)
Congress dummy		−.01	−.30	−1.45*	1.92**
	(.17)	(.36)	(.55)	(.61)	(.91)
Constant	−1.81**	−3.53**	−3.64**	−2.32**	−4.93**
	(.25)	(.41)	(.90)	(.85)	(1.55)
N	503	503	181	181	181
X^2	505.43**	927.38**	1335.64**	939.25	714.06**
Alpha	1.04	.01	3.27	4.68	.01

Negative binomial estimates with robust standard errors clustered around the legislator in parentheses.
*$p < .05$, **$p < .01$

results of statistical models for individual bill sponsorship on the issues in which gender is statistically significant. The results show that female legislators in Argentina and the Colombian Senate are more likely to sponsor bills on some social issues and are less likely to sponsor some types of men's domain bills. In the Colombian Chamber of Representatives and Costa Rica, however, women are no more likely to sponsor women's domain issues—children and family issues, education, health—and are no less likely to focus on economic, agriculture, fiscal affairs, or foreign affairs bills.

In Argentina, no significant gender differences emerge for children and family issues, education, or health, but male legislators do sponsor significantly more economic and fiscal affairs bills than women. Female legislators sponsor half as many economic bills as men and one-sixteenth as many fiscal affairs bills. In 1995 and 1999, only 2 of the 39 individually sponsored fiscal affairs bills that were initiated into the Argentine Chamber of Deputies were sponsored by women. In the Colombian Senate, women sponsor 6 times as many bills on health issues as men do, and no women were behind any of the 34 individually sponsored agriculture bills in the 1994–1998 or 1998–2002 terms. Similarly, no women sponsored any of the 5 foreign affairs bills initiated by individual sponsors in these two congresses. The only area for which gender differences emerged in the Colombian lower house and Costa Rican Assembly was children and family issues. In the Colombian Chamber, this was an area on which women placed greater priority to begin with, making it unlikely that women were marginalized into working on these types of bills. In Costa Rica, the absence of gender differences exists both prior to and after the adoption of quotas.

In sum, female legislators in all of the legislatures except Argentina do translate their greater priority for women's issues into legislative behavior by individually sponsoring more bills on women's issues than do men. Thus, female representatives are substantively representing women and women's issues through their legislative behavior. However, women do appear to suffer from some marginalization in the types of bills they sponsor. Despite having similar preferences to men on a range of women's domain and men's domain issues, women in Argentina individually sponsor fewer bills on some men's domain issues, and women in the Colombian Senate individually sponsor more health issues and fewer men's domain issues. As articulated in chapter 1, one reason this may occur is marginalization by the gendered legislative environment.

Gender Differences in Cosponsored Bills on Various Issues

Few studies have disaggregated individually sponsored bills from cosponsored bills in analyses of gender and bill sponsorship (see, however, Swers 2002; Wolbrecht 2002; Swers 2005). Yet, the motivations for cosponsoring the two types of bills can be distinct (as described previously), so gender may have different effects on cosponsored and individually sponsored bills. The analyses presented in table 4.6 show that female legislators in all four chambers are significantly more likely to cosponsor women's issue bills than are men. In Argentina, female representatives cosponsor almost 4 times as many women's issue bills as men do. The statistical model predicts that 40% of women will sign at least one women's issue bill compared to only 15% of men, holding other variables at their means and modes. In Costa Rica, a surprising number of men cosponsor these bills, but women still do so 3 times more often. The model predicts that almost 45% of men will cosponsor at least one women's issue bill, but 85% of women will sign at least one women's issue bill, all else held constant. In the Colombian Chamber of Representatives, women are 8 times more likely than men to sponsor women's issue bills, and in the Senate, they are over 100 times more likely to do so, all else being equal.

In Colombia, this partly reflects the fact that women's issue bills were more often individually sponsored than cosponsored. Eight percent of women in the Chamber of Representatives (three women) cosponsored women's issue bills

TABLE 4.6. Explaining Bill Cosponsorship Patterns on Women's Issues (cosponsored bills)

	Argentina	Colombian Chamber	Colombian Senate	Costa Rica
Gender	1.37**	2.09**	4.80**	1.10**
	(.24)	(.72)	(1.85)	(.21)
Ideology	.57	−6.56	11.21	−.27
	(.31)	(3.76)	(9.12)	(.22)
Related committee	.52*	3.07**	−24.85**	.01
	(.25)	(1.15)	(3.79)	(.20)
Legislative experience	.03	−.10	−1.01	.08
	(.09)	(.32)	(.85)	(.20)
Urban district	.51*	14.07**	—	.20
	(.20)	(.87)		(.19)
Plurality party	−.48	2.91*	26.56**	−.22
	(.29)	(1.43)	(5.60)	(.22)
Chamber president	−14.68**	−16.67**	1.81	.54
	(1.06)	(1.08)	(1.54)	(.30)
Total bills sponsored	.03**	.17**	.29**	.01**
	(.01)	(.06)	(.12)	(.004)
Congress dummy	−.68**	−2.62	−4.88**	.57**
	(.20)	(1.46)	(2.84)	(.19)
Constant	−2.06**	−22.66**	−32.24**	−1.53**
	(.31)	(1.83)	(6.31)	(.44)
N	503	304	181	114
X^2	446.03**	1196.22**	14.52	112.94**
Alpha	.47	5.74	5.54	.01

Negative binomial estimates with robust standard errors clustered around the legislator in parentheses.
$^*p < .05$, $^{**}p < .01$

compared to less than 1% of men sponsoring these bills. Five percent of women in the Senate cosponsored women's issue bills compared to 1.2% of men. Viviane Morales (Partido Nacional Cristiano) and Yolima Espinosa (Partido Liberal) sponsored two different bills together in the 1994–1998 congress—one to increase penalties for sexual harassment and another to create a quota law. In the 1998–2002 congress, Liberal Party representative Leonor Gonzales Mina sponsored two women's issue bills with Senator Piedad Córdoba.

One reason that women are more likely to cosponsor women's issue legislation is that they often seek out other women as cosponsors. One Argentine deputy mentioned in an interview with me that she intentionally courted other women to support a gender equality bill that she sponsored. She said she did not just want signatures but wanted cosponsors who would be committed to the bill. As a result, she sought women only. "I chose from a list of female deputies who I knew were going to defend it; not just sign it and do nothing more" (Augsburger 2006). In Argentina, three of the most active initiators of women's rights legislation during 1999 were Elisa Carrió, who sponsored 6 bills on women, Miriam Curletti, with 5 bills on women, and Margarita Stolbizer, who sponsored 5 on women. The only one of these bills that became law was a major piece of legislation on women's health—the Sexual and Reproductive Health Law (Law 25.673 of 2002). It was cosponsored by Deputies Carrió and Curletti, who overcame significant objections from the Catholic Church and successfully defended the bill on the floor of the Chamber of Deputies.[19]

In terms of cosponsorship of bills that fall into traditional women's and men's domain thematic areas, the only country that exhibits marginalization of women is Argentina (table 4.7). Female deputies are significantly more likely to cosponsor bills on education and health (borderline significant at $p = .07$) and are less likely to cosponsor economic bills, fiscal affairs bills, and agriculture bills (borderline significant at $p = .09$). Substantively, the effects are not huge but still notable. For example, women sponsor 1.3 times as many education bills as men and two-thirds as many economic bills. The effects for health, fiscal affairs, and agriculture are similar. In Costa Rica, the only thematic area in which women cosponsor significantly fewer bills than men is agriculture, an issue on which they also place lower priority

TABLE 4.7. Explaining Bill Cosponsorship on Women's Domain and Men's Domain Issues in Argentina

	Children	Education	Health	Economy	Agriculture	Fiscal Affairs
Gender	.59	.36*	.29	−.37**	−.37	−.45*
	(.31)	(.15)	(.16)	(.10)	(.22)	(.19)
Ideology	.61	.10	−.85*	−.26	.79*	−.09
	(.51)	(.27)	(.35)	(.20)	(.38)	(.32)
Related committee	.67*	1.53**	1.23**	−.01	1.18**	.50**
	(.31)	(.15)	(.23)	(.09)	(.17)	(.15)
Legislative experience	−.02	.12*	−.02	−.02	−.19**	.03
	(.10)	(.06)	(.06)	(.03)	(.06)	(.05)
Urban district	.11	.10	−.32	−.15	−.98**	.30*
	(.27)	(.15)	(.17)	(.09)	(.16)	(.15)
Plurality party	.29	.20	−1.15**	−.15	−.02	−.66**
	(.38)	(.20)	(.24)	(.14)	(.25)	(.23)
Chamber president	−14.40**	1.54**	−12.53**	−17.85**	−13.41**	−17.62**
	(1.10)	(.25)	(1.04)	(1.01)	(1.05)	(1.03)
Total bills sponsored	.03**	.03**	.03**	.05**	.04**	.04**
	(.01)	(.01)	(.01)	(.01)	(.01)	(.01)
Congress dummy	.64*	−.05	.68**	−.08	.77**	−.01
	(.28)	(.14)	(.21)	(.08)	(.17)	(.14)
Constant	−3.07**	−1.82**	−2.06**	.14	−.97**	−1.31**
	(.39)	(.24)	(.26)	(.14)	(.21)	(.20)
N	503	503	503	503	503	503
X^2	295.62**	215.23**	467.28**	527.51**	426.66**	508.34**
Alpha	1.12	.36	.23	.38	.82	.40

Negative binomial estimates with robust standard errors clustered around the legislator in parentheses.
*$p < .05$, **$p < .01$

than men. These patterns existed prior to the adoption of gender quotas and still persist. The only significant difference in the cosponsorship patterns of Colombian senators and representatives is among senators' cosponsorship of agriculture bills. No female senators cosigned any agriculture bills, whereas 15 male senators did.

The cosponsorship findings reinforce the conclusion drawn in the previous section that women do represent women through bill initiation behavior. Women are more likely to represent women's issues than men in almost all chambers by cosponsoring women's issue bills. The cosponsorship findings also provide evidence of women's marginalization in Argentina. Not only do women not cosponsor bills on men's domain issues to the same extent as men, they are more likely to cosponsor social issue bills. When it comes to cosponsoring legislation, male party leaders and male representatives may be corralling women into bill sponsorship behavior that reflects traditional gendered divisions of labor. In contrast, little marginalization of women in cosponsorship is evident in Colombia or Costa Rica. This may be due to the fact that cosponsorship is less common in those countries, and it may occur because it is far easier for legislators to marginalize women by not asking them to cosign legislation than it is to keep them from initiating bills on their own.

Debating Bills in the Legislature

Sponsoring bills is an important part of the policymaking process. But once bills are on the legislative agenda, they need legislators to support and defend them as they work their way through the policymaking process. One way that representatives do this is through legislative debates. These generally occur in committees and on the floor of the legislature. In this section, I examine the extent to which female and male representatives differ in the frequency of debating in both of these forums.

Building from the theoretical framework in chapter 1, I test three specific hypotheses. First, women's shared historical experiences of subordination and the priority that they place on representing women should make it more likely that female legislators will participate in debates on women's rights issues than will male legislators. The gendered legislative environment in which women operate, however, may make it more difficult for women to participate in debates on a wide range of political issues and may limit their debate participation over all. Male voices may overwhelm female voices during these debates, such that only the most confident and vocal women speak out, or male chamber presidents may overlook women's desire to speak in debates. Thus, the second hypothesis is that female legislators should be less likely to participate in debates (regardless of issue) than male legislators. Also following from this logic of marginalization, the third hypothesis is that female legislators should be more likely to debate on traditional women's domain issues and less likely to debate on traditional men's domain issues.

Existing research has found that women are much more likely than men to participate in parliamentary debates on women's issues (Broughton and Palmieri 1999; Walsh 2002; Taylor-Robinson and Heath 2003; Chaney 2006; Catalano 2008; Childs 2008). Taylor-Robinson and Heath (2003) examined congressional debates on women's issue bills in Honduras and found that women are more likely to participate in debates that focus on women's rights and children and family issues. Similarly, Chaney (2006) examined plenary debates in the National Assembly of Wales and found that female representatives initiate, intervene in, and participate in debates on women's issue topics, specifically domestic violence, child care, and equal pay issues, more than male representatives.

Research on women's participation in legislative debates on issues that are not related to gender equality, however, reports mixed findings. Some work has found that women's voices are often obscured in both committee and floor debates (Skard and Haavio-Mannila 1985; Kathlene 1994; 1998). In an oft-cited article on the U.S. Congress, Lyn Kathlene (1994) wrote about significant gender differences in the committee participation of female members of Congress. Women hold the floor for less time than men, initiate and engage discussion less often than men, and interrupt less often than men. She attributed this phenomenon to marginalization of women's voices in the legislative arena. Other studies have found few differences in men's and women's debating styles or patterns. Chaney (2006) found that women and men participate with similar frequency in plenary debates on the full array of topics discussed in the Welch assembly. Broughton and Palmieri (1999) examined gender differences in parliamentary debates over euthanasia in Australia and found that women and men were equally likely to participate in the debates, but they do report that the content of women's speeches was different from men's.

Debating in Committees

One question on the survey of legislators asks about the frequency with which representatives participate in committee debates.[20] Committee debates are an opportunity for legislators to signal their support for or against legislation. Analyzing survey responses reveals that gender differences in legislators' self-perceived committee debate participation are few. The only country where significant gender differences emerged is Costa Rica, where women are much more likely speak in committee debates than men, after accounting for the ideology of the legislator, age, marital status, education level, prior occupation, legislative experience, prior office-holding experience, ambition, and district urbanness (see appendix C for variable coding details).[21] Figure 4.1 shows that the statistical model predicts almost one-quarter of female deputies in Costa Rica speak in committee debates "very often" compared to 6% of men. Almost 90% of women are predicted to

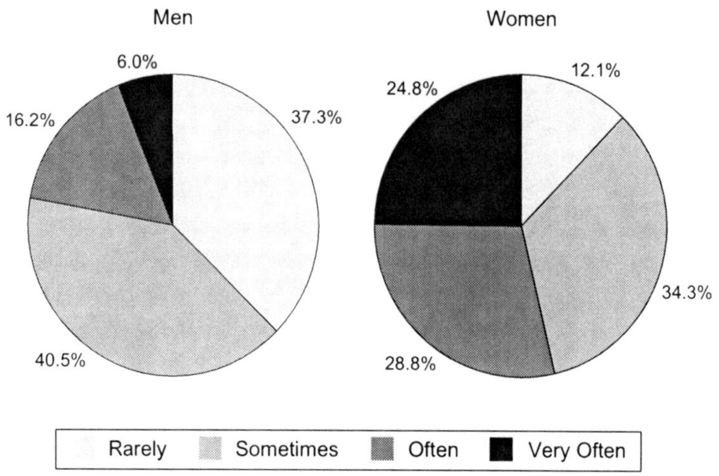

FIGURE 4.1. Frequency of Speaking in Committee Debates in Costa Rica

participate at least "sometimes," whereas only around 60% of men are estimated to participate at least that often. Clearly, women in the Costa Rican Assembly express their support for or against legislation in the policymaking process. This is not mirrored in Argentina or Colombia, however. In neither of these countries are women significantly different from men in the frequency with which they report participating in committee debates.

Debating on the Floor

I also asked legislators about the frequency with which they participate in floor debates. Similar to the findings for committee debates, only a few significant gender differences exist after accounting for relevant control variables (see appendix C). Those differences occur only in Argentina, where women report more frequent participation in floor debates than men do. Figure 4.2 shows that whereas only one-fifth of men are predicted to speak "very often" during floor debates, over half of women are. Over 90% of women are predicted to speak "very often" or "often" compared to only about 65% of men. This finding emerges after accounting for the fact that more ambitious and experienced legislators speak in floor debates more often.

One downside of using self-reported debate behavior is that it assumes representatives can accurately gauge their participation. This may be a difficult assumption to maintain. However, analyses of self-perceived participation are important and revealing on their own. That women perceive such high levels of debate participation

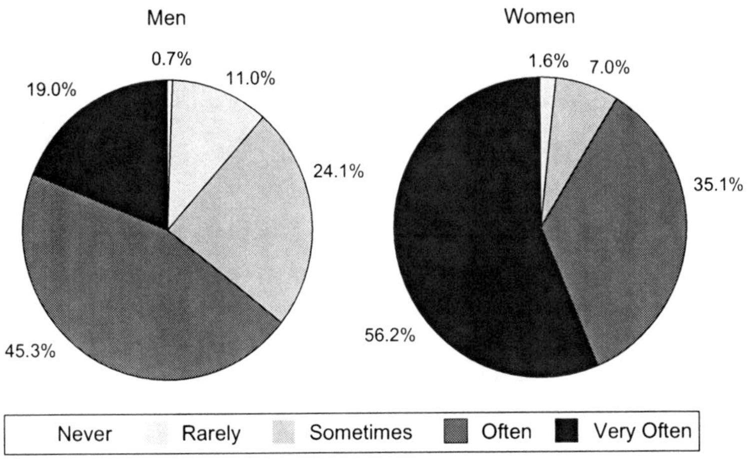

FIGURE 4.2. Frequency of Speaking in Floor Debates in Argentina

for themselves signals a confidence that other studies have overlooked or concluded does not exist because women have not been found to participate as much. Women may still get marginalized in debates and not perceive it, but they do have a confidence about their legislative work that can undermine efforts by male legislators or party leaders to marginalize them in legislative debates.

Finally, I asked legislators about the frequency with which they participate in debates on legislation dealing with specific types of issues. In general, women and men do not perceive different degrees of participation across issues. Statistical models (not shown) predict that women and men speak on behalf of health, education, worker's rights, and economic legislation with similar frequencies. Results are borderline statistically significant for agriculture issues in Argentina and Costa Rica, where women participate in debates slightly less often than men on agriculture bills. However, in the last chapter, we saw that this was an issue that women felt was less important.

Women do participate more often than men in Argentina and the Colombian lower house when debates focus on women's issue legislation. Figure 4.3 shows that the statistical models predict that 75% of women participate "very often" or "often" in Argentina compared to slightly less than 50% of men. In the Colombian Chamber, 80% of women claim to participate "very often" compared to only 24% of men. In the other two legislatures, the effects of gender do not attain statistical significance. This further underscores the findings on bill sponsorship that women represent women's issues through their policymaking efforts. Women not only sponsor legislation in this area more often than men, but they defend this legislation in debates more than men do.

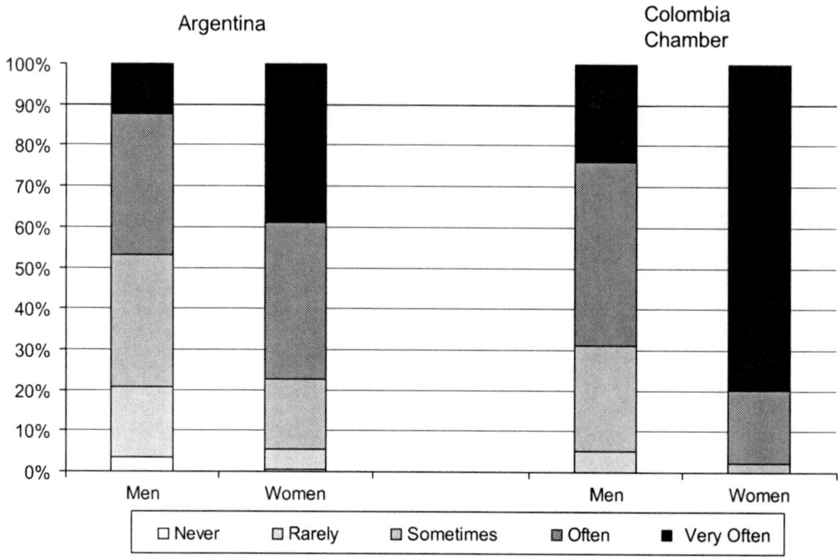

FIGURE 4.3. Frequency of Speaking in Floor Debates on Behalf of Women's Issues

Conclusion

Descriptive representation of women in national legislatures in Latin America does have an impact on policymaking. Women are more likely than men to individually sponsor and cosponsor women's issue bills in Argentina, Colombia, and Costa Rica and defend these bills in floor debates in Argentina and the Colombian lower house. Women are not only placing higher priority on women's issues in their political preferences, but they are bringing forth important women's rights policies, such as gender quotas for legislative elections or domestic violence protections for women, which may not have been introduced or passed had female legislators not been part of the policymaking process. As former Argentine deputy María José Lubertino (2003, 10) writes, "Many laws—such as those on violence and reproductive health in the provinces—would not have been passed had there not been women parliamentarians committed to these issues." Women are getting issues onto the legislative agenda that otherwise would not receive the same amount of attention from male legislators.

Evidence of marginalization of women does appear in some cases, however. Despite Argentine legislators having similar issue preferences on education, health, economics, and fiscal affairs issues, women are more likely to cosponsor legislation on education and health bills (borderline significant) and less likely to individually sponsor and cosponsor bills on economics and fiscal affairs. Women are working with other legislators, often women, to introduce policy on issues traditionally considered women's domain issues and are not sought out as cosponsors for legislation traditionally considered in the "men's domain." In the Colombian Senate, women are more likely to sponsor health bills and are less likely to sponsor agriculture and foreign affairs bills. This does not occur in floor debates on issues in these areas, however. As I argued in chapter 1, a likely reason for this disparity in issue preferences and behavior may be a gendered legislative environment that continues to divide issues into the women's domain and the men's domain.

In contrast to what I theorized in chapter 1, these findings do not fully support the theory that formal representation mediates substantive representation of women. That hypothesis suggests that party-centered systems, such as in Argentina and Costa Rica, will have greater marginalization of women than personalistic systems, such as in Colombia. It also argues that gender quotas could exacerbate women's marginalization. The findings from this chapter, however, show that marginalization of women occurs only in bill sponsorship in Argentina and not in Costa Rica. Because both countries have party-centered systems and quotas, we would expect marginalization in both cases if these institutions mattered. Instead, the divergent findings may reflect the limited control that party leaders in Costa Rica actually have over deputies' bill sponsorship behavior. Deputies in Costa Rica sponsor a large number of bills, many of which focus on pork in the district, and they sponsor many more bills on their own than they cosponsor with other deputies. These factors make it difficult for leaders to have much influence over deputies' bill initiation patterns. This does not mean that marginalization of women does not occur, just that it is not reflected very strongly though bill sponsorship in Costa Rica. It also is not evident in legislators' perceptions of their participation in legislative debates. If anything, women perceive greater roles for themselves in debates than men do, particularly when the topic is women's issue bills.

Women's policymaking is an important measure of substantive representation. Female representatives in Argentina, Colombia, and Costa Rica do represent women's issues through policymaking, and their presence is clearly important for that. As Argentine deputy Elisa Carrió (2002, 5–6) noted, "The representation of women's voices, interests, perspectives and values in decision-making is a necessary condition for the effective observance of women's human rights." Marginalization of women does appear in Argentina, and the Colombian Senate to a lesser degree, but not in all legislatures or in the pattern that formal representation would suggest. This does not mean, however, that women have attained full representation in the legislative chamber. The area of substantive representation in which party leaders and male representatives have the most influence on their female colleagues—committee assignments and leadership posts—has not yet been assessed. The following chapter tackles women's representation in committees and leadership.

5

Taking Charge

Leadership and Committees

On July 20, 2005, Claudia Blum was elected president of the Colombian Senate, becoming the first woman to hold the top leadership post in the Congress. It was a months-long, hard-fought battle between Blum and her *uribista* colleague, Luis Guillermo Vélez, who conceded the party nomination to her only 2 hours prior to the official vote on the floor of the Senate. She was elected with 83 of the 102 votes in the Senate. Her success shows that, despite their overall low numbers in the legislature, women have made some progress attaining positions of political power in the Colombian Congress. This progress has been recent and slow, however.[1] Women first won seats in the Colombian Senate in 1958, but it took almost 50 years before even one reached the top echelon of the congressional hierarchy.

This chapter examines how descriptive representation of women affects substantive representation through committee assignments and leadership appointments. Committees and leadership posts are another part of the process of representation in which female legislators not only have an opportunity to represent women by sitting on women's issue committees but also to represent all constituents by sitting on other important legislative committees, getting elected to committee chairs, and holding chamber leadership positions. Prestigious committees and powerful leadership posts are important legislative resources, however, that male legislators may want to preserve for themselves (Heath et al. 2005). As such, they are a likely site for marginalization of women in substantive representation.

Women in Legislative Leadership

Most legislatures around the world elect an executive board composed of a president, vice presidents, and secretaries to deal with administrative and decision-making tasks for the chamber. These tasks include deciding which bills the legislature will discuss during floor debates, selecting which legislators will speak during those debates, determining which bills go to which committees for study, making committee assignments, creating special committees to study controversial issues or investigate problems within government, appointing staff, and managing relationships with other branches of government. These jobs give the chamber leadership significant power over the functioning of the legislature. Consequently, the choice of which individuals hold these powerful positions is of utmost importance.

Representation of women in legislative leadership is necessary for several reasons. First, it is part of descriptive representation (Pitkin 1967). The number of women in leadership posts should mirror women's numerical representation in the legislative chamber just as women's representation in the chamber should mirror their status as half of the population. Second, their representation serves a symbolic purpose, underscoring that the legislature is diverse, inclusive, and values gender equality (Childs 2004). Relatedly, women's presence in leadership posts makes them highly visible role models for other women, both in the legislature and in society (Childs 2004). Third, women's accession to leadership positions is a mechanism for women to bring greater attention to women's issues in the legislature and work to transform the legislative arena (Phillips 1995; Williams 1998; Young 2000; Lovenduski 2005). Women's inclusion in the legislative leadership gives women direct influence over decision making in congress, which is particularly important when chamber presidents have substantial powers, such as those of appointment and control over the legislative agenda.

In most countries around the world, very few women have been congressional or parliamentary leaders (Rivera-Cira 1993; Reingold 2000; Little et al. 2001; Luciak 2005; Rosenthal 2005; Marx et al. 2007; Saint-Germain and Chavez Metoyer 2008). In Latin America, women have been elected to legislatures in growing numbers over the past 30 years, but it is only in the past few years and only in some countries that they have started to gain access to chamber leadership posts. Further, many of the leadership positions that women have held are the less powerful positions of vice presidents or secretaries. As the cases of Argentina, Colombia, and Costa Rica illustrate, women's access to chamber leadership does not mirror their representation in the legislative chamber (table 5.1).[2] The following subsections analyze women's participation in chamber leadership from the country's transition to democracy (or 1974) through 2006.

TABLE 5.1. Number of Women in Chamber Leadership Positions

	President	Vice Presidents	Secretaries	Pro-secretaries	Women in Chamber(%)
Argentina Lower House					
1983–1997	0	0	—	—	9.8[a]
1997–1999	0	1	—	—	28.9
1999–2001	0	0	—	—	29.2
2001–2003	0	0	—	—	30.7
2003–2005	0	3	—	—	32.7
Colombian Chamber					
1974–1978	0	0	—	—	6.7
1978–1982	0	0	—	—	3.9
1982–1986	0	0	—	—	2.8
1986–1990	0	1	—	—	6.2
1991–1994	0	0	—	—	7.5
1994–1998	0	1	—	—	11.7
1998–2002	1	0	—	—	11.6
2002–2006	1	1	—	—	13.0
Colombian Senate					
1974–1978	0	0	—	—	1.0
1978–1982	0	0	—	—	2.0
1982–1986	0	0	—	—	2.0
1986–1990	0	0	—	—	1.0
1991–1994	0	0	—	—	7.8
1994–1998	0	2	—	—	6.1
1998–2002	0	1	—	—	12.7
2002–2006	1	0	—	—	10.4
Costa Rica					
1974–1978	0	0	0	1	7.0
1978–1982	0	1	0	2	8.8
1982–1986	0	0	2	0	7.0
1986–1990	1	0	1	0	12.1
1990–1994	0	2	0	0	12.3
1994–1998	0	2	0	4	15.8
1998–2002	1	2	2	1	19.3
2002–2006	0	0	3	4	35.1

[a]The 1983–1997 period includes seven different congresses. The 9.8% included in this table is the average across the seven congresses. The percentage of the chamber that was female in each 2-year congress was as follows: 4.4 (1983–1985), 4.7 (1985–1987), 4.8 (1987–1989), 6.4 (1989–1991), 5.6 (1991–1993), 14.5 (1993–1995), 28.5 (1995–1997).

Chamber Presidents

The chamber president is usually the most powerful actor in the legislature. In Argentina, Colombia, and Costa Rica, chamber presidents set the legislative agenda, preside over plenary sessions, prepare the congressional budget, ensure that chamber rules are followed, make administrative appointments, and, in Costa Rica and Argentina, make committee appointments, among other administrative tasks. The chamber president is elected by the members of the legislative chamber and is almost always elected from the majority party or majority coalition. In general, the chamber president has significant influence over the legislative process. Very few women have served in this position, however.

In Argentina, no woman has been elected president of the Chamber of Deputies since the return to democracy in 1983. In part, women's access has been restricted by the fact that, formally, the president is elected to a 1-year term, but in practice, the president is replaced only if he or she loses his or her seat in the chamber or if he or she resigns from the leadership post. This has led to very low turnover among chamber presidents. Juan Carlos Pugliese served from 1983 to 1988 and was replaced by Alberto Reinaldo Pierri, who served until 1999, for example. Between 1983 and 2006, the Chamber of Deputies has had only five different presidents.

In Colombia, only two women served as president of the Chamber of Representatives and one woman as president of the Senate from 1974 through 2006. In 2000, Nancy Patricia Gutierrez Castañeda became the first female president of the Chamber of Representatives, having attained the position in a special midyear election that followed the corruption scandal and subsequent resignation of Armando Pomarico Ramos and his vice presidents. However, she served less than the typical 1-year term and was ineligible for another term due to a congressional rule prohibiting reelection of chamber presidents in any 4-year term. The first woman elected president for a full term was Zulema Jattin Corrales, in 2005–2006. As mentioned at the beginning of the chapter, Claudia Blum became the first female president of the Senate in 2005. However, she was not the first woman to aspire to the office. Viviane Morales ran for the presidency in 1999, though she fell short of the majority of votes needed to win.

The presidency of the Costa Rican Legislative Assembly has only twice been held by a woman—Rose Marie Karpinsky (PLN), in 1986–1987, and Rina Contreras (PUSC), in 2000–2001. Karpinsky's presidency coincided with the first year of Oscar Arias' first presidential term (1986–1990). This was not surprising because both were from the PLN and a key part of Arias' political agenda was increasing the participation of women. Yet, it was another 14 years until another woman held the position. Contreras' bid for the presidency in 2000 was interesting in several ways. First, she made public her interest in the position a good 5 months before the election, much earlier than usual. And she made clear right from the start that her being a woman should not be an obstacle to her election: "I have the experience and the determination to occupy the presidency of the Legislative Assembly. The fact that I am a woman, I believe, will not hinder me" (Venegas 2000b). Second, she crossed party lines to seek support from the six PLN women in the Assembly. PLN party leaders opposed the negotiations and refused to allow the women to vote for Contreras in the official chamber vote on May 1, 2000. Although the PLN was the minority party and knew that it did not have enough votes to elect a member of its own party to the presidency, it wanted to ensure full party support for its own candidate. Although the PLN women toed the party line and voted for the PLN candidate, they openly expressed that Contreras' election to the position would be good for women. PLN deputy Isabel Chamorro praised the election of Contreras saying that "this is a good opportunity for a woman to achieve a position almost inaccessible previously," and her party colleague Sonia Villalobos felt that "with her we will be able to negotiate a much needed gender-oriented agenda" (Venegas 2000a).

Other Leadership Posts

In addition to chamber presidents, most legislatures have vice presidents and/or secretaries who serve as part of the chamber leadership. Women have been slightly more represented in these positions than as chamber presidents, but their numbers still lag far behind their representation in the legislature (table 5.1). In Argentina, the *autoridades* are composed of up to three vice presidents who are elected to an annual term. The vice presidents are relatively weak, however. Their primary role is to stand in for the president when he or she is unable to perform the presidential duties. Even though these posts have limited power, only four women have been vice presidents of the Argentine Chamber of Deputies since 1983. The first female vice president was Graciela Fernández Meijide, who served for 2 years (1997–1999) as third vice president. It was not until April 2004 that Encarnación Lozano was elected midterm to serve as third vice president. In 2005, two women were elected to vice presidential positions—Graciela Camaño replaced Lozano as third vice president and Patricia Vaca Narvaja became the first woman to serve as first vice president. Although vice presidents turn over more frequently than presidents in the Chamber of Deputies, annual change in the leadership is still rare, creating obstacles for female newcomers to be vice presidents.

Colombia's *mesas directivas* have two elected vice presidents, but legislative rules require that the largest minority party or movement selects the first vice president whereas the majority party/movement chooses the second vice president.[3] Similar to Argentina, Colombia's vice presidents are relatively powerless, primarily serving as temporary replacements for the president. Women have not been widely represented among the two vice presidencies of the Colombian Chamber of Representatives or Senate. The first woman to hold a vice presidency in the Chamber of Representatives was María Cristina Rivera de Hernández, who was elected to be first vice president in 1988. She followed the unsuccessful bid for second vice president by Betty Camacho in 1986. No woman held a vice presidential post again until 1995 when Isabel Celis Yáñez became first vice president. It was another 10 years until Sandra Velasquez Salcedo was elected vice president in 2005.

In the Colombian Senate, María Cleofe Martínez de Mesa was the first woman to serve as second vice president for 1996–1997, and Consuelo Durán de Mustafa followed her as the first female first vice president in 1997–1998. Isabel Celis Yáñez was elected first vice president in 2001, but she was the last woman to have held a vice presidency through 2006. Despite electing two vice presidents in each chamber every year, women have not reached these positions with any regularity in either the Chamber of Representatives or the Senate.

Costa Rica's *directorio* provides the greatest opportunity for women to hold leadership positions. In addition to the president, there is one vice president, two secretaries, and two pro-secretaries who change annually.[4] This structure creates six leadership posts that change every year, making it possible for 24 of the 57 representatives in the assembly to be in the *directorio* at some point during their 4-year term. However, the powers accorded to the six leaders vary widely. The president and the two secretaries are the more powerful positions, with the vice president and pro-secretaries comprising a shadow leadership of substitutes, who are called upon when the president or secretaries are absent. Although the president has the most responsibility in presiding over plenary sessions, deciding the order or the day, assigning bills to committees, and appointing committees, the secretaries have significant administrative responsibilities, giving them a visible and important role in the chamber. Thus, the question is not just *if* women serve in the *directorio*, but whether they have gained access to Assembly leadership positions with *real* political power (the presidency and secretaries).

Eight women have served as secretaries in the Costa Rican Legislative Assembly since 1974, and five of them only since 1998 (table 5.1). Irene Urpí Pacheco became *segunda secretaria* in 1998–1999, and then Vanessa Castro was *primera secretaria* in 2001–2002. In the 2002–2006 congress, a woman served in one of the two secretary positions for 3 years of the 4-year term. The majority of women's representation in the *directorio*, however, has been in the shadow leadership posts of vice president and the pro-secretaries. Seven women have served as vice presidents, and 12 women have served as pro-secretaries between 1974 and 2006.

As this analysis shows, women have not been well represented in the chamber leadership of any of the three countries. Women have held more leadership posts in Costa Rica than in Argentina or Colombia, but this is deceptive due to the larger number of leadership positions available. Further, women's representation in Costa Rica has often been symbolic because women most often served in the less powerful positions of the shadow directorate. Women have held the top post—the presidency of the chamber—in only two of the three countries, and even then it has been the exception rather than the rule. Signs of change have emerged in recent congresses, with more women serving in leadership in all three countries in the past few years. But overall, women's representation in the chamber leadership has not matched their growing numbers in office over the past 15 years. It also does not appear to have become substantially better or worse since the adoption of gender quotas in Argentina and Costa Rica.

The Role of Gender in Committee Assignments

One of the primary responsibilities of representatives in most legislatures is committee work. Committees are where legislators study bills, amend them, and issue reports to the chamber with recommendations for moving the bill to the next stage of the policy process or tabling it. This gives legislators substantial influence over the policymaking process (Krehbiel et al. 1987), allows them to build expertise in certain policy areas, affords them an opportunity to cater to the interests of their political party and constituents (Shepsle and Weingast 1987), and makes it possible for them to gain power and prestige by sitting on the more influential committees in the legislature (Cox and McCubbins 2005). Because of this, committee assignments, like leadership posts, are a valuable political resource for legislators. This is particularly true in Argentina and Costa Rica, where electoral rules are party centered and chamber presidents and party leaders are instrumental in deciding who will sit on which committees (Jones et al. 2002; Morgenstern 2002). In Argentina, for example, the closed-list proportional representation electoral system combined with federalism encourages legislators to respond to local party leaders, which leads them to sit on committees "mainly to obtain perks and/or additional resources, as well as to be in good standing with the provincial party leadership" (Jones et al. 2002, 658).

In this section, I offer a multivariate statistical analysis of the extent to which gender affects the types of committee assignments that legislators receive. I use data from multiple congresses in Argentina, Colombia, and Costa Rica.[5] In Argentina, the analysis begins in 1983 with the transition to democracy and runs through nine 2-year congresses ending in 2001. In Colombia and Costa Rica, the analysis begins in 1974 and includes eight 4-year congresses ending in 2006. The time-serial nature of this data increases the generalizability of the findings.

Building on the theory articulated in chapter 1, I argue that the gender of legislators affects committee assignments, alongside an array of other determinants. Female legislators in Argentina, Colombia, and Costa Rica should be more likely than men to sit on committees that deal explicitly with women's equality and women's rights issues because of the greater priority that they place on those issues and the fact that they see themselves as representing female constituents and women's groups (see chapter 3). Women's issue committees are a way for female legislators to craft policies that directly affect women and push those issues through the legislative process. Indeed, research on gender and committee assignments in other countries has often found that women are more represented on committees that deal with women's issue policies than are men (Rivera-Cira 1993; Dolan and Ford 1997; Dodson 1998; Arnold 2000; Swers 2001; Towns 2003; Heath et al. 2005; Marx et al. 2007; Zetterberg 2008).

At the same time, however, female legislators are also likely to be overrepresented on committees dealing with compassion issues, such as education and health, and underrepresented on committees traditionally in men's domain, such as the economy, fiscal affairs, agriculture, defense and foreign affairs (Skard and Haavio-Mannila 1985; Thomas 1994; Norton 1995; Dolan and Ford 1997; Little et al. 2001; Towns 2003; Heath et al. 2005).[6] The likely reason for this is marginalization of women by male party leaders or the male-dominated chamber (Frisch and Kelly 2003; Heath et al. 2005). The male-dominated leadership in legislatures has incentives to preserve powerful and prestigious committees for men and sideline female newcomers to committees more traditionally considered women's domain committees. This should be particularly true in Argentina and Costa Rica, where legislators are tightly tied to their political parties and party leaders have significant influence over committee assignments. It may be more evident since 1991 in Argentina and 1998 in Costa Rica when gender quotas were adopted in the two countries (Vincent 2004; Xydias 2007; Franceschet and Piscopo 2008; Zetterberg 2008).

Committees in Argentina, Colombia, and Costa Rica

In this chapter, I examine the committee assignments of legislators from 1974 to 2006 in Colombia and Costa Rica and 1983 to 2001 in Argentina. Appendix D provides a list of the permanent standing committees in Argentina, Colombia, and Costa Rica and their respective policy jurisdictions.[7] To compare committees across countries, I create six categories of committees based on the types of issues they attend to. I classify committees as to whether they are feminist/women's issues committees; committees dealing with issues traditionally considered to be "women's domain," such as social issues committees; or committees focusing on issues traditionally considered to be "men's domain," economics committees, budget and treasury committees, agriculture committees, and foreign affairs committees. Table 5.2 shows the six categories and the specific committees in each country that fall into the categories. In Costa Rica and Colombia, this yields one committee in each category because there are only six and seven committees, respectively, and each has a wide jurisdiction.[8] In Argentina, multiple committees appear in each category because of the large number of specialized committees.[9] For example, social issue committees include the following: Social Assistance and Public Health, Culture, Education, the Elderly, Drug Addiction, Disabilities, and Human Rights.

Importantly, committees in these three countries have varying levels of prestige and power, with the most important and prestigious committees also being those traditionally considered to be in the men's domain.[10] In Argentina, several committees are particularly desirable for parties and legislators, including the Foreign Relations Committee, the Budget and Treasury Committee, and the Agriculture and Ranching Committee (Jones et al. 2002). In Costa Rica, the Treasury Committee is widely considered to be the most powerful committee in the chamber (Heath et al. 2005). In both Colombian chambers, the Constitutional

TABLE 5.2. Classification of Legislative Committees

	Women's Issues Committees	Social Issues Committees	Economics Committees	Budget/ Treasury Committees	Agriculture Committees	Foreign Affairs Committees
Argentina	Family, Women, Children, and Adolescents	Social Assistance and Public Health	Economics and Regional Development	Budget and Treasury	Agriculture and Ranching	Foreign Relations
		Culture (1993)	Commerce	Finance	Maritime Issues, Fishing, and Ports (1993)	Defense
		Education	Economy (1987)		Energy	
		Elderly (1993)	Small Business (1997)		Mining (1987)	
		Drug Addiction (1987)	Industry		Natural Resources	
		Human Rights (1993)	Mercosur			
		Disabilities (1997)				
Colombia	none	Committee 7—Social Issues	Committee 3—Economics	Committee 4—Budget	Committee 5—Agriculture	Committee 2—Foreign Relations
Costa Rica	(special committee only)	Social Issues	Economics	Treasury	Agriculture, Fishing, and Natural Resources (1982)	Government and Administration

Years in parentheses indicate the year the committee was created.

(Committee 1), Economics (Committee 3), and Budget (Committee 4) committees are considered the most important because they focus on policies of top priority in the country that are frequently part of the president's agenda (Kline 1977; Pachón Buitrago 2003).

Argentina is the only country with a standing committee designated solely to deal with women's issues—the Family, Women, Children, and Adolescents Committee. In Costa Rica and Colombia, women's issues are subsumed under social issues committees. Women's issues are explicitly listed as one of the issues those committees are responsible for, but there is no "ordinary standing committee" that focuses only on women's concerns. In 1999, Costa Rica created a women's committee, but it is a "special standing committee" rather than an ordinary standing committee, meaning that it has different rules and functions than the six ordinary committees. The committee has fewer members, meets less regularly than ordinary committees, and has responsibilities beyond studying and reporting on bills.[11] Thus, the committee has fewer policymaking powers than the six ordinary committees but compensates for this with research and reporting responsibilities. Colombia created a special bicameral committee for women in 2006, under the leadership of a woman chamber president, but that is outside the time frame of this study's analysis.

Legislators get on committees through different mechanisms in different legislatures. In Argentina, the chamber president formally appoints committees but informally follows the recommendations of party leaders, who choose which legislators they want to sit on which committees. Party leaders often use committee assignments as a way to enforce discipline among party members (Jones et al. 2002; Mustapic 2002). In Costa Rica, the Assembly president formally assigns legislators to particular committees, but informally, legislators express a preference for a particular committee to their party leaders and the president. These preferences are part of the decision-making process but by no means fully determine committee memberships. Factors such as seniority, favor within the party, and even gender can interfere with who gets which committee assignments, particularly when it comes to the most powerful and prestigious committees.

Colombian Senate and Chamber of Representatives committee assignments occur through chamber elections. Parties present slates of candidates for each of the committees, and legislators win seats based on a formula of electoral quotients. Party or faction leaders do play a role in committee assignments by officially presenting the candidate slates for election, but ultimately, those lists emerge out of negotiations among faction or party members themselves and are simply coordinated by the leaders (Pachón Buitrago 2003). These rules informally lead to legislators expressing their preferences within parties and negotiating lists at the party level, and given the amount of preelection negotiating that occurs, elections are often rubber stamps on decisions made earlier. However, there have been cases in which lists that were expected to pass were changed during voting and legislators who thought they would be on one committee ended up on another.

In all three countries, committee assignments are a combination of the preferences of individual members of congress and negotiations among legislators, parties, and coalitions. Individual legislators often have preferred committee assignments and have the opportunity to express these to party leaders and to other legislators.[12] However, the limited number of assignments available and the power of party leaders, chamber presidents, and informal negotiations among legislators, who are mostly men, mean that legislators do not necessarily get their preferred assignment. Instead, legislator preferences mix with the needs of the chamber and the party such that the assignments legislators end up with may partly reflect their preferences but also are shaped by legislative rules and the leadership. Because party leaders, chamber presidents, and the chamber as a whole have the final say in assignments, committee memberships ultimately reflect the decision making of those groups. This opens the door for systematic marginalization of women in committee assignments by the male-dominated legislature.

Other Determinants of Committee Assignments

Committee assignments are one of the first decisions that a new congress makes, and it is a decision on which numerous factors, other than gender, have influence. Specifically, committee assignments depend on various characteristics of legislators, characteristics of the district a legislator represents, and chamber rules for committee composition. In the analyses below, I control for these alternative explanations for committee assignments to ensure that they do not explain gender differences in committee membership.

Three of the control variables are the same ones used in the last chapter on policymaking—ideology (coded on a 5-point scale from left to right), legislative experience (the number of terms a legislator has served including the current one), and urban district (urban = 1 and rural = 0). Ideology is important because legislators from leftist political parties may be more likely to sit on committees dealing with social issues, for example, where they can act on their priorities to provide citizens with better healthcare and greater access to education. Legislators with more experience often receive deference to their committee preferences because of their seniority in the chamber. They also may be more likely to sit on more powerful and prestigious committees in the legislative chamber. Seniority is certainly a key consideration in determining committee assignments in the United States (Matthews 1960; Fenno 1973; Frisch and Kelly 2006), though it may be less prominent in Latin America where legislative turnover is high from one congress to the next (Jones et al. 2002). Characteristics of a legislator's district influence committee assignments because legislators are elected to represent the interests of their constituents. Legislators from rural districts, for example, may be more likely to sit on agriculture committees so that they can influence policies that affect significant portions of their district. Where literacy rates are particularly low, which tends to correlate with rural districts, legislators may seek out social committees so they can push through legislation that will improve education in their district. If unemployment is high in a district, as it often is in rural districts, legislators from that district may sit on economics committees to work on bringing jobs and other economic benefits to their constituents.[13]

Chamber rules that define the structure of the committee system and outline who makes committee assignments also influence committee assignments. One important rule for committee assignments in some legislatures is that committee seats must be distributed among political parties in proportion to the number of seats the party holds in the chamber. This rule exists in Argentina and Colombia but not in Costa Rica. Costa Rican opposition legislators often cry foul if the party distribution of committees diverges significantly from that of the chamber, but no rule requires this. To account for the proportionality rule, I control for the percentage of seats held by the legislator's political party in the chamber.

Finally, I control for the number of committees on which legislators sit, which varies in some legislatures. The more committees on which a legislator sits, the greater the likelihood that the legislator will be on any given committee. In Colombia, every legislator sits on one committee for the entire 4-year term. In Argentina and Costa Rica, the number of different committees on which a legislator sits can vary. In Argentina, legislators can sit on more than one committee at any given time for the 2-year congress. In Costa Rica, legislators sit on only one standing committee at a time, but committee assignments change annually.[14] To measure this effect, I control for the number of committees on which a legislator sits in the Argentina and Costa Rica analyses. In Argentina, I measure the number of assignments a legislator has in any given 2-year term. In Costa Rica, the variable measures the number of *different* committees on which a legislator sits in the 4-year term (up to four).

Findings

In tables 5.3–5.6, I present multivariate logit models[15] that estimate the probability that a legislator will sit on different types of committees in each country.[16] Most relevant for this study is how gender influences committee assignments after controlling for the effect of other influences on committee composition. The tables reveal that gender does affect committee assignments; however, there is variation across countries.

Argentina is the only country with a committee whose jurisdiction is specific to women, children, and family issues, and, as table 5.3 shows, women are significantly more likely to sit on this committee than men. Just as women place greater priority on women and women's issues than do men (chapter 3), they also emphasize these issues by being more likely to sit on the women's issue committee. However, they also have a higher probability of receiving social committee assignments and are significantly *less* likely to be represented on committees that focus on issues traditionally considered to be men's domain despite having similar preferences for these issues (chapter 3). Figure 5.1 shows the substantive size of these gender gaps in committee memberships with a calculation of the predicted probability that men and women will get assigned to the different types of committees.[17] A large gap is evident for women's issue committees. The model predicts that 27% of women will sit on the women's issue committee compared to only 2% of men. An even larger gap, however, exists for social committees. The predicted proportion of women who are likely to sit on social committees in Argentina is 65% compared to only 25% for men. Clearly, women are much more likely to get assigned to social committees than are men, and their estimated representation on the committee is twice as large as their numerical representation in the Chamber of Representatives.

Figure 5.1 also shows that women are not getting assigned to traditional men's committees in equal proportions to men in Argentina. The largest gap is on economics committees. The statistical model predicts that only 19% of women

TABLE 5.3. Determinants of Committee Assignments in Argentina

	Women's Issues	Social	Economics	Budget	Agriculture	Foreign Affairs
Gender	3.56**	1.71**	−1.03**	−1.20**	−.47*	−.92**
	(.31)	(.17)	(.20)	(.31)	(.19)	(.27)
Ideology	−.05	−.01	.14	.05	.03	.06
	(.38)	(.24)	(.20)	(.27)	(.23)	(.27)
Legislative	−.01	−.13*	−.17**	.18**	−.09*	.23**
experience	(.11)	(.06)	(.06)	(.07)	(.06)	(.06)
Number of	.38**	.25**	.33**	.26**	.36**	.27**
committees	(.07)	(.04)	(.04)	(.05)	(.04)	(.05)
Urban district	.11	.21	−.24*	−.06	−.90**	.50**
	(.23)	(.13)	(.12)	(.16)	(.13)	(.15)
Party	−.003	−.001	.005	.002	−.003	.002
delegation size	(.007)	(.005)	(.004)	(.005)	(.004)	(.005)
Constant	−4.21**	−2.07**	−1.75**	−2.37**	−1.20**	−2.73**
	(.40)	(.26)	(.22)	(.30)	(.23)	(.30)
N	2254	2254	2254	2254	2254	2254
X^2	216.15	190.05	132.35	67.94	135.20	96.05

Logit coefficients with robust standard errors clustered around the legislator in parentheses. Congress dummies not reported.

*$p < .05$, **$p < .01$

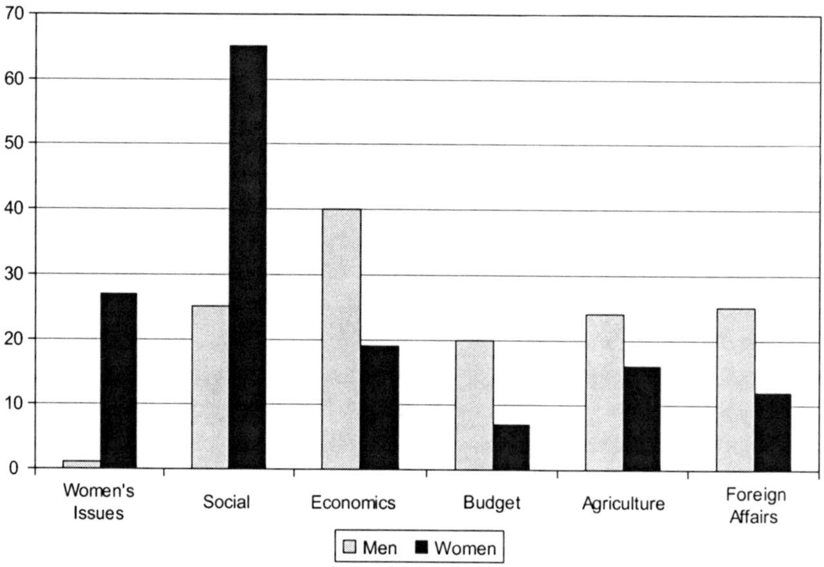

FIGURE 5.1. Predicted Percentage of Male and Female Legislators Assigned to Different Types of Committees in Argentina

will sit on economics committees whereas 40% of men will. The smallest, but still statistically significant, gender difference is for agriculture committees: only 16% of women receive these assignments compared to 24% of men.

Women are winning office in record numbers in Argentina and are representing women by sitting on the Women, Children, and Family Committee. But, they also dominate areas of legislative work along traditional gender lines. Women are not being fully incorporated into the legislative arena in terms of the committees on which they sit. As Deputy Marcela Bordenave asserts, "We have voice, the vote, freedom of expression, but this does not carry over into areas that are not considered women's spaces . . . still they don't consider women for areas such as defense, management of the budget, or distribution of funds within our own party" (Instituto Social y Político de la Mujer n.d.). Deputy Silvia Augsburger (2006) recognizes that a double standard exists for women and talks about the irony of women's success on men's domain issues in some branches of Argentine government but not on committees: "We have female ministers of defense and of the economy in Argentina today. But when you look at the composition of committees, clearly in these themes there is a majority of men and in others (disabilities, family) there is a majority of women."

The theory in chapter 1 suggests that the presence of gender quotas may be one reason that women in Argentina are marginalized in their committee assignments. Quotas may generate a backlash from male representatives who want to minimize women's political power (Vincent 2004; Bauer and Britton 2006; Xydias 2007; Franceschet and Piscopo 2008; Zetterberg 2008). I tested this hypothesis by analyzing the models in table 5.3 during the prequota (1983–1991) and postquota (1991–2001) periods. During the prequota period, women were significantly more likely to sit on social committees and significantly less likely to sit on economics committees, but no significant differences emerge in their presence on budget, agriculture, or foreign affairs committees. After quotas were adopted, however, women became significantly less likely to sit on budget, agriculture, and foreign affairs just as they were less likely to sit on economics committees. In other words, the models in the postquota period look very similar to those reported in table 5.3. This provides some empirical evidence that quotas may hinder women's ability to be equal and effective representatives of all constituents in systems with gender quotas.[18] Quotas may, in fact, offer increased incentives for party leaders to marginalize female representatives. Interestingly, this contrasts with the perception held by some female deputies in Argentina. Recently elected deputy Graciela Rosso (2006), for example, sees significant change in women's access to a diverse array of committees since the quota law was passed in 1991: "Before, women were more on social committees and men were more on economics, politics, and legislative committees. Now it is more varied. It has changed because women have begun to involve themselves

TABLE 5.4. Determinants of Committee Assignments in the Colombian Chamber of Representatives

	Social	Economics	Budget	Agriculture	Foreign Affairs
Gender	.01	−.33	−.21	.72*	−.12
	(.34)	(.31)	(.33)	(.30)	(.34)
Ideology	−.51	−.03	.65*	−.24	.06
	(.30)	(.30)	(.28)	(.31)	(.26)
Legislative experience	−.19	−.03	.20**	−.15*	−.09
	(.11)	(.10)	(.08)	(.13)	(.12)
Urban district	.87*	.56*	−1.10**	−.55*	−.20
	(.33)	(.26)	(.19)	(.24)	(.24)
Party delegation size	−.007	.005	.009*	−.0004	−.006
	(.005)	(.005)	(.005)	(.005)	(.006)
Constant	−2.82**	−2.16**	−.79**	−1.46**	−1.55**
	(.46)	(.38)	(.32)	(.41)	(.40)
N	1386	1386	1386	1386	1386
X^2	19.12	7.61	58.91	16.59	3.75

Logit coefficients with robust standard errors clustered around the legislator in parentheses. Congress dummies not reported.
$^*p < .05$, $^{**}p < .01$

TABLE 5.5. Determinants of Committee Assignments in Colombian Senate

	Social	Economics	Budget	Agriculture	Foreign Affairs
Gender	.78	−.50	−.17	−.28	−1.03
	(.43)	(.62)	(.48)	(.62)	(.77)
Ideology	−.87*	−.39	.63*	.35	−.005
	(.42)	(.42)	(.39)	(.47)	(.41)
Legislative experience	−.10	.14	−.005	−.28*	.04
	(.15)	(.12)	(.09)	(.13)	(.11)
Urban district	.54	.93	−1.15**	.06	.14
	(.61)	(.67)	(.43)	(.57)	(.86)
Party delegation size	−.004	.008	.006	.005	−.013
	(.008)	(.008)	(.007)	(.008)	(.008)
Constant	−2.28**	−2.83**	−.52	−2.20**	−1.77*
	(.71)	(.79)	(.51)	(.73)	(.93)
N	794	794	794	794	794
X^2	14.79	9.72	17.44	10.15	6.10

Logit coefficients with robust standard errors clustered around the legislator in parentheses. Congress dummies not reported.
$^*p < .05$, $^{**}p < .01$

in themes on which men had more authority . . . The idea that issues were more masculine than feminine; this phase is out of date in our country. Women are involved in all themes." Clearly, her perception does not match the empirical reality for women in the Argentina Chamber of Deputies.

The picture of women's representation looks very different in Colombia. Gender affects only agriculture committee assignments in the Chamber of Representatives and has no effect on committee assignments in the Senate (table 5.4 and table 5.5). As mentioned earlier, Colombia does not have a standing committee that focuses exclusively on women's issues, so it is impossible to know whether women are representing women through committee assignments in Colombia. However, the analysis does reveal less marginalization of women than in Argentina. Women and men are equally likely to sit on social, economics, budget, and foreign affairs committees, all of which are issues on which women and men place equal priority, as discussed in chapter 3. Gender differences do emerge for the agriculture committee, but on this committee, women are *more* likely than men to hold seats. Most of this is driven by the fact that large numbers of women sat on this committee in the 1970s and early 1980s. In the 1974–1978 Chamber of Representatives, 42% of female representatives sat on the agriculture committee, and in 1978–1982, it was 71%. After 1982, women's overrepresentation on this committee diminished significantly.

In Colombia, it appears that women are not getting marginalized through committee assignments. This is similar to what Dolan and Ford (1997) found in U.S. state legislatures in the early 1990s. There, women were still committed to promote women's interests on women's issue committees, but they were also "expanding their areas of expertise and influence to include financial and business concerns" (Dolan and Ford 1997, 144). Indeed, Colombian senator Piedad Córdoba views women as making progress in gaining access to legislative resources but also recognizes that this progress is limited: "Women have served as vice president of the Congress, and have chaired commissions, just as they have come to occupy ministries traditionally assigned to men, such as foreign relations, foreign trade, national planning, and mines and energy, in addition to the more traditionally female ones such as education, health, labor and justice, but always to only a minimal degree" (Córdoba Ruiz 2002, 5).

Gender differences in Costa Rican committee assignments are similar to those of Argentina but are smaller and are not significant across all thematic areas.[19] As table 5.6 shows, women are more likely to sit on the social committee and are less likely to be represented on the budget committee. However, there are no significant differences for the economics, agriculture, and government (foreign affairs) committees.[20] Figure 5.2 illustrates the substantive effect of gender on all of these committees. Although 48% of women are predicted to sit on the social committee at some point in their 4-year term, only 22% of men are. For the budget committee in Costa Rica, the model predicts that 43% of women will sit on this committee at some point during their term compared to 61% of men. The statistical model also predicts gaps that favor men for economics and agriculture, but they are not statistically significant. The gender gap for the government committee actually favors women slightly, but again, this gender difference is not statistically significant.

TABLE 5.6. Determinants of Committee Assignments in Costa Rica

	Social	Economics	Budget	Agriculture	Government
Gender	1.23**	−.34	−.77**	−.73	.45
	(.34)	(.33)	(.29)	(.39)	(.32)
Ideology	−.28	.21	−.24	−.01	.09
	(.21)	(.21)	(.21)	(.24)	(.20)
Legislative experience	−.17	−.06	.03	.07	−.05
	(.25)	(.24)	(.24)	(.33)	(.19)
Number of committees	1.00**	1.04**	1.00**	.58**	.82**
	(.15)	(.15)	(.15)	(.17)	(.14)
Urban district	.07	.27	.14	−.76**	−.38
	(.22)	(.22)	(.21)	(.26)	(.21)
Party delegation size	−.01	.02*	.03**	−.01	−.0004
	(.009)	(.01)	(.01)	(.01)	(.008)
Constant	−2.03**	−3.27**	−3.13**	−1.73*	−1.95**
	(.57)	(.62)	(.57)	(.72)	(.52)
N	457	457	457	343	457
X^2	57.55	70.96	77.06	32.60	53.75

Logit coefficients with robust standard errors clustered around the legislator in parentheses. Congress dummies not reported.
$^*p < .05$, $^{**}p < .01$

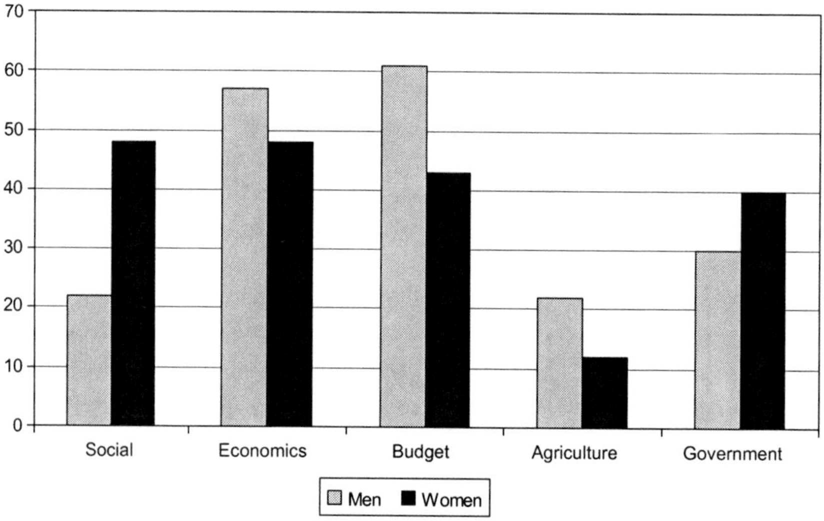

FIGURE 5.2. Predicted Percentage of Male and Female Legislators Assigned to Different Types of Committees in Costa Rica

In Costa Rica, women are somewhat less marginalized than in Argentina but more marginalized than in Colombia. Women are overrepresented on the social issues committee and are underrepresented on the budget committee, which, as noted earlier, is the most important and most desired committee in the Assembly.

Gender differences did not exist in the preferences of legislators for these issues, as described in chapter 3. The presence of gender differences in committee assignments has been noted by female deputies in Costa Rica themselves. Epsy Campbell Barr points out that "participation of women on the Treasury Committee has been very limited, not only because women members are scarce, but also because it deals with issues from which women have consciously and/or unconsciously been excluded" (Campbell Barr 2004, 23). She suggests that because committees deal with issues such as budgets and economics, from which women have traditionally been excluded, the male leadership does not view women as likely candidates for these committees. Although some marginalization appears in Costa Rica, it is not evident across all types of committees. Women are winning seats on other committees in similar numbers to men, and consequently, gaining the opportunity to attend to the needs of their districts.

A second set of analyses (not shown) disaggregates the Costa Rica models into two time periods, prequota (1974–1998) and postquota (1998–2006), to determine whether gender differences in committee assignments are limited to the postquota period when party leaders might have greater incentives to marginalize women (as in Argentina). In the prequota period, the results are very similar to what is presented in table 5.6. Significant differences exist for social committees on which women are more likely to be members and for budget committees on which women are less likely to sit. No differences exist, however, for economics, agriculture, or government committees. In the postquota period, women are still significantly more likely to sit on social committees but are no longer less likely to be marginalized on budget committees. They do become significantly less likely to sit on agriculture committees, but because agriculture is a policy area on which female representatives place less priority, their smaller presence is more likely to reflect their preferences than marginalization. Thus, quotas do not increase marginalization of women in Costa Rica. If anything, the influx of women after the passage of the gender quota law has equalized women's access to committees somewhat.

Examining the special women's committee in Costa Rica reveals that female representatives in Costa Rica are representing women and women's issues. Figure 5.3 shows the representation of women on the *Comisión de la Mujer*, the special women's committee in Costa Rica. In the 8 years since its creation, the committee has been more than half women, and in most years, there has been only one man. Women also dominate the leadership of this committee with the president and secretary being female every year. The committee was created through the efforts of female deputies who wanted to create a forum for discussing gender inequality concerns and to consolidate the study of bills on women's issues in one committee rather than dispersing them among other committees. Rina Contreras (1999, 56) pointed out that the committee is not just a committee but a forum for discussions of gender in the chamber; it is a link to other committees and government agencies with a goal to ensure that

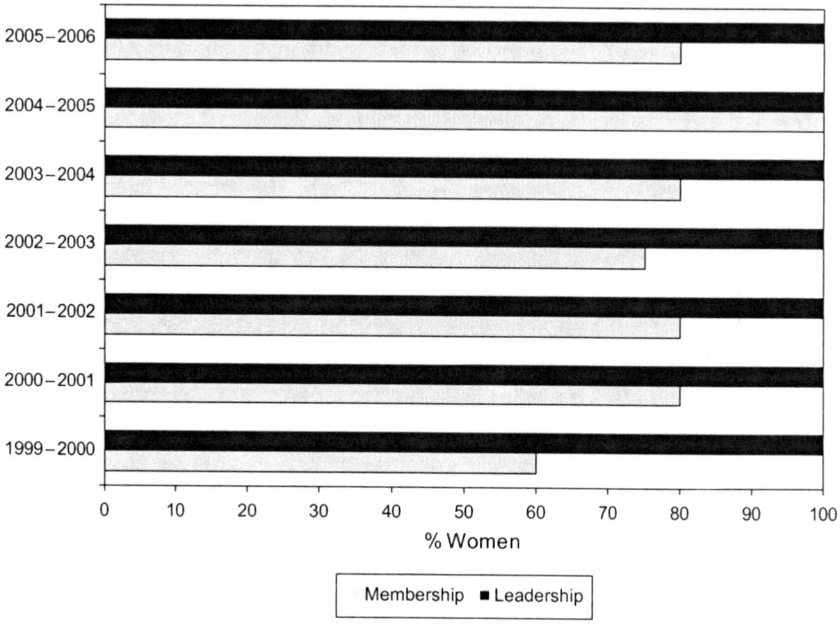

FIGURE 5.3. Gender Composition of Costa Rica Special Women's Committee since Inception (Note: The special women's committee in Costa Rica has five members, but in 2002–2003, it had only four members. It has two leadership positions: president and secretary.)

the government "responds appropriately to the social reality that confronts women" in Costa Rica. Women in the chamber viewed the creation of this committee as an opportunity for them to bring greater political attention to women's issues, and, consequently, they have maintained the majority of the seats on the committee since its creation on November 8, 1999. The large presence of women on the special committee for women provides evidence that women are representing women.

The multivariate analyses in this section show that the role that a legislator's gender plays in committee assignments is above and beyond the effects of a legislator's ideology, seniority, constituency, and chamber rules. These other factors have some effect on committee assignments, but, most important for this study, they do not answer the question of why women are more or less likely to sit on certain committees. Gender differences persist after accounting for the fact that women may be more likely to get elected from left-leaning parties, may have less legislative experience than men, may be more likely to represent urban districts, and may sit on different numbers of committees than men. Differences also occur across countries with the most evidence of women's marginalization occurring in Argentina and the least in Colombia. These findings support the theory that women are more likely to represent women and women's issues than men and that marginalization of women is a likely reason that women in some countries are more likely to sit on women's domain committees and less likely to sit on men's domain committees than men.

Women in Committee Leadership

The final question that this chapter answers is whether the gender of legislators affects the likelihood that they will get committee leadership posts and whether it affects the types of committees on which they serve as leaders. Because of women's preferences for women's issues and their high levels of representation on women's committees demonstrated above, women are likely to seek out leadership posts on women's issue committees to further their representation of women. Women's access to leadership has proven to be particularly important for representing women because women in leadership have been found to bring more of a feminine and "integrative" style to leadership (Rosenthal 1997, 1998) and to continue promoting women and women's rights once there (Little et al. 2001).

Yet, women should also seek leadership posts on other committees to facilitate representation of their district and party. This may not happen, however, if the male-dominated legislative arena marginalizes women through committee leadership. In theory, committee leadership positions are valuable legislative resources that give legislators extensive influence over policymaking. They also increase the prestige of representatives, which they can use as political fodder for reelection or future political careers. Leadership posts are resources that male representatives may want to hold onto and use to promote their own political careers. Yet, not all committee leadership positions are created equal. In some legislatures, committees have several leadership posts, such as a chair, vice chair, and secretaries. Whereas the chair may carry significant political weight, the other positions may be symbolic and carry little real political power or prestige. Similarly, some committees are much more powerful than other committees, and leadership on these more powerful committees is likely to be more important than on other committees. As a result, male legislators and party leaders have several options to preserve their own access to committee leadership posts and prevent women from gaining significant power on committees. The most extreme form that marginalization of women could take is preventing women from accessing any committee leadership positions. A second form would be making room for women in committee leadership as vice chairs or secretaries but limiting their access to committee chairs. Finally, marginalization of women may occur in the types of committees on which women serve as leaders. Women may be more likely to be leaders of women's issue committees and social issue committees but kept out of leadership on the committees traditionally considered men's domain or those that are viewed as the most prestigious committees in the legislature. In the following analysis, I examine whether any of these patterns of women's committee leadership exist in Argentina, Colombia, and Costa Rica.

Existing literature on gender and committees has not spent a significant amount of time studying access to committee leadership, but the small amount of research in this area does suggest that women are disadvantaged in this legislative activity (Skard and Haavio-Mannila 1985; Dolan and Ford 1997; Rosenthal 1998; Reingold 2000; Swers 2002; Rodríguez 2003; Rosenthal 2005; Saint-Germain and Chavez Metoyer 2008).[21] Research from the United States, for example, has found that very few women have served as chairs of committees in the U.S. Congress (Swers 2002) and that women have not been represented as committee chairs in state legislatures in numbers proportional to their representation in state legislatures (Rosenthal 1998; Reingold 2000; Rosenthal 2005). In Latin America, studies also suggest that women are not gaining access to committee leadership positions. In Nicaragua, Saint-Germain and Chavez Metoyer (2008) found that women served as committee presidents in 17% of the assembly's committees, but this was the highest proportion of any Central American legislature. In Mexico, Rodríguez (2003, 145) argued that "women [in the Senate and Chamber of Deputies] are largely relegated to the less influential positions" serving as committee chairs on less important committees or those traditionally in women's domain. In contrast, Zetterberg (2008) showed that female legislators in two Mexican state legislatures are no less likely than men to serve as committee chairs, taking their committee preferences into account. He did point out, however, that women were less likely to express a preference for sitting on economics and fiscal affairs committees.

Committee Leadership in Argentina, Colombia, and Costa Rica

The rules for making committee leadership assignments are critical for understanding the likelihood that women will participate in this legislative activity. In Argentina, Colombia, and Costa Rica, committee members elect their own leaders. In Argentina, each committee has a president, up to two vice presidents, and up to five secretaries who are elected to serve a 2-year term. In Colombia, each committee has a president and a vice president who must be from different political parties and are elected to a 1-year, nonrenewable term. In Costa Rica, each committee has a president and a secretary elected for 1 year. Whereas leadership posts are filled via committee elections in all three countries, party leaders in Argentina and Costa Rica have significant influence over who wins those elections. The majority party (or majority coalition) leaders usually determine who they will nominate to the leadership posts in advance of the election and can ensure that the party's slate of candidates wins because of its majority on the committee. Thus, party leaders and chamber presidents often use committee leadership positions as a reward for legislators who toe the party line. In Colombia, parties have less control over their members. This compounded with the rules requiring the presidency and vice presidency of the committee to be shared by the two largest parties and the prohibition on reelection means that leadership is shared pretty widely among committee members.

Findings

Table 5.7 presents the results of a set of cross-tabulations of gender and committee leadership positions.[22] Data were available for the entire 1983–2001 period in Argentina but were available only from 1990 in Costa Rica and 1994 in Colombia.[23] The table shows the percentage of each type of leadership position and each category of committee that is female by country.

The first three rows of the table show the overall representation of women in committee leadership positions and reveal that women often have been elected to committee leaderships in numbers comparable to their representation in the legislative chamber. In Argentina, Colombia, and Costa Rica, women have served as presidents of legislative committees in proportion to their legislative representation, and they have been vice presidents and secretaries of committees in numbers sometimes *greater* than their representation in the chamber. In Argentina from 1983 to 2001, for example, 12% of committee presidents and 14.6% of those in the Chamber of Deputies were female.[24] Almost 19% of vice presidential and secretarial posts were held by women. Similarly, in Costa Rica, women comprised 22% of the Assembly from 1990 to 2006 but held 30% of committee secretarial posts and 25% of the presidencies. At first glance, it appears that women are not underrepresented in committee leadership positions.

However, disaggregating committees by their policy jurisdiction reveals that women and men are leaders on very different types of committees (table 5.7).[25] In Argentina, women have been overrepresented in leadership on the women's committee and social committees and underrepresented on economics, budget, and foreign affairs committees, particularly in presidential posts. On the women's issue committee, 82% of the vice presidential and secretarial posts have been held by women and the president of the committee has been a woman in every congress since 1985.[26] Silvia Augsberger talks about how and why she became secretary of the Women and Family Committee during the 2003–2005 congress: "It was my preference, and since [other committee members and I] began to talk about participation and divided the work among ourselves, I had the aptitude and wanted to hold an important position on this committee. Also, in my political work I am developing work specifically on this theme. So it was two things—a personal and collective decision. My party also had an interest in occupying a space on this committee."

Women have also been significantly overrepresented as vice presidents and secretaries of social committees—37% of those posts have been held by women

TABLE 5.7. Women in Leadership (percentages)

	Argentina (1983–2001)	Colombian Chamber (1994–2006)	Colombian Senate (1994–2006)	Costa Rica (1990–2006)
Chamber average	14.6	12.0	10.0	21.5
Committee vice presidents/ secretaries	18.9*	7.3	7.5	29.6*
Committee presidencies	12.1	11.4	6.6	25.0
Women's committees				
% seats	61.4	—	—	—
% vice presidency/secretary	82.1*	—	—	—
% presidencies	100.0*	—	—	—
Social committees				
% seats	30.1	13.8	16.7	40.6
% vice presidency/secretary	37.0*	12.5	11.1	50.0
% presidencies	24.3	18.2	20.0	53.3
Economic committees				
% seats	9.9	10.2	8.0	19.6
% vice presidency/secretary	9.0	8.3	18.2	14.3
% presidencies	0*	0	0	20.0
Budget committees				
% seats	6.1	12.0	7.0	15.0
% vice presidency/secretary	7.9	9.1	9.1	33.3*
% presidencies	0	0	0	0*
Agriculture committees				
% seats	12.4	10.0	5.3	5.7
% vice presidency/secretary	14.0	0	0	14.3
% presidencies	18.4	10.0	0	0
Foreign affairs committees				
% seats	7.3	6.6	2.7	23.1
% vice presidency/secretary	4.6	12.5	0	37.5
% presidencies	0	0	0	46.7*

Cross-tabulations with an asterisk (*) denoting whether the chi-square is statistically significant at the 90% level (*$p < .10$).

compared to 30% overall representation of women on those committees. In the presidencies of social committees, women have been slightly underrepresented—only 24% of presidential posts have been filled by women. On traditional men's domain committees, women have served as vice presidents and secretaries, but as of 2001, no women had ever served as president of an economics committee, budget committee, or foreign affairs committee. Not only are women not getting assigned to men's domain committees, but the few women who are on the committees are not getting elected president of the committee.

In Costa Rica, women's disproportional representation in committee leaderships is most evident for social committees where they are slightly overrepresented and budget and agriculture committees where they are underrepresented. Just over half of the secretarial and presidential posts on social committees have been held by women, whereas 41% of the social committee membership has been female. On the budget committee, almost 33% of the secretaries have been women but not a single woman has served as president of that committee. Similarly, 14% of agriculture committee secretaries have been women but no woman has served as president. Women are becoming leaders of an array of committees in Costa Rica, but most of these leadership positions are among the far less powerful secretaries rather than as presidents.[27]

In Colombia, women have been slightly overrepresented on leadership of social committees and slightly underrepresented on traditionally men's domain committees, but none of these differences are statistically significant. What is notable, however, is the relative absence of women in most committee presidencies. In the Chamber of Representatives, no women had served as president of the economics committee, budget committee, or foreign affairs committee through 2006. The pattern is even worse for women in the Senate, where the only committee that has had a female president is the social committee. The higher probability that all legislators have of serving in committee leaderships due to the rules prohibiting reelection to these posts has not helped women become committee leaders. Part of the explanation is that their overall representation on men's domain committees is small, just as in the chamber as a whole, but their complete absence from committee presidencies also suggests that the male-dominated legislative chamber may be marginalizing women in committee leadership. Negotiations among legislators to prepare slates of candidates for committee leadership positions are ignoring the women who serve on these committees, or if they do include them, it is as vice president. This may also be exacerbated by the rule requiring that different parties hold each post. This makes it difficult to promote gender diversity because a party has only one position to fill.

This analysis of committee leadership in Argentina, Colombia, and Costa Rica clearly shows that the question of women and committee leadership is more nuanced than just whether women serve as committee leaders. The problem for women in leadership in the three countries is not that they have not held committee leadership positions but that they have not been *presidents of traditionally male-dominated committees*. Women have been vice presidents and secretaries of economics, budget, and foreign affairs committees in all three countries, but they have only rarely won election to the presidency of any of these committees. No women have been presidents of the economics or foreign affairs committees in Argentina or Colombia, and not a single woman has held the presidency of a budget committee in any of the four chambers. These patterns existed in the pre- and postquota periods in Costa Rica, suggesting that quotas have not exacerbated this effect there, and have only been slightly more evident in postquota Argentina.

Women have been largely overlooked as power players on committees in all three countries for nearly 30 years.

Conclusion

This chapter shows that women's descriptive representation has led to increased substantive representation of women and women's issues in the form of women being more likely to sit on women's issue committees. In both of the countries that have women's issue committees (Argentina and Costa Rica), women are the large majority of the committee's members and hold nearly all of the leadership posts. The higher priority that women place on these issues translates into assignments to and leadership posts on these committees. On one hand, this reinforces the findings from the last chapters that women are bringing new issues to the political arena and working to promote gender inequality policy through their committee work. On the other hand, however, it underscores that issues of gender inequality are still considered "women's issues" and should be dealt with by women. Male legislators in all three countries think that women's equality is an important priority (see chapter 3), but very few male legislators are promoting these issues on women's issue committees.

However, women are not representing nonwomen-specific constituencies to the same extent that men are in Argentina, Colombia, and Costa Rica. Despite the finding from chapter 3 that men and women place equal priority on most other constituent groups and political issues, this has not translated into gender equality in access to important legislative resources, such as leadership and committees. Instead, women in these legislatures are underrepresented in chamber leadership, in some cases disproportionately overrepresented on women's domain committees and underrepresented on men's domain committees, and kept out of committee presidencies on men's domain committees. The extent to which women are marginalized in committee and leadership behavior, however, varies across countries. In the most extreme case, Argentina, almost no women have reached the top posts of the chamber leadership, and consequently, they have little influence over the legislative arena. Women's representation on committees in Argentina reflects a very traditional model of representation. Women congregate on committees that focus on the private sphere issues that have traditionally defined their political roles (i.e., social issues) and are largely kept off of men's domain committees that deal with public sphere issues. This has been particularly true since quotas were adopted in 1991. Once on these women's domain committees, women do win leadership posts. They do not get elected to the presidencies of men's domain committees, however. Despite increased numbers of women in the chamber in recent years, little evidence suggests that women are making their way into positions of power within the legislature.

In Costa Rica, women have been more successful getting into leadership positions and gaining representation on men's domain committees than women in Argentina, but they are not represented in chamber leadership and have not gained substantial access to the most powerful committee—the Treasury Committee. Women have been represented in the chamber leadership, but their representation has been limited largely to the shadow directorate that serves a symbolic role rather than having real political power. Women have sat on more diverse committees than in Argentina, but they are overrepresented on social committees and underrepresented on the budget committee. Women's underrepresentation on the budget committee appears to have abated in recent years with the adoption of gender quotas, but women are still overrepresented on social committees despite having political preferences similar to men's on social issues. Finally, they are significantly underrepresented among budget committee presidents. No woman has ever been president of the budget committee. Although gender divisions are not as extensive as they are in Argentina, Costa Rica still exhibits evidence of marginalization of women.

Women in Colombia also have not gained access to leadership, but their representation across committees has been more proportional to their still small numbers in the legislature. Only a few women have been president of the Chamber of Representatives or Senate, and women have not achieved positions of power as presidents of most men's domain committees. However, they do get representation on legislative committees across policy jurisdictions. Women are no more likely than men to sit on social committees and no less likely to sit on economics, agriculture, budget, or foreign affairs committees. Their presence on these committees, however, is small which may make it difficult for them to effect policy in all issue areas. Even though women are winning seats on a diverse array of committees, their presence has not led to election to committee leadership posts. Very few women have served as presidents or vice presidents of committees other than the social committee.

The patterns of gender differences in chamber leadership, committee assignments, and committee leadership posts in Argentina, Colombia, and Costa Rica suggest that formal representation of women may play a mediating role in the extent to which women are marginalized in Latin America. The party-centered systems, Argentina and Costa Rica, reveal greater marginalization of women than Colombia's personalistic system. Gender quotas, however, only appear to have an exacerbating effect on women's marginalization in Argentina's committee assignments. In general, few changes in the leadership and committee assignment patterns of legislators occurred in these countries after the adoption of quotas.

Returning to the full picture of women's representation, women's descriptive representation directly affects substantive representation through committee assignments. However, it both increases substantive representation of women and decreases it. On one hand, women are more likely to sit on women's issue committees, working to bring issues that directly affect women to the legislative arena and craft policy that will improve women's lives. On the other hand, however, women in office are marginalized in chamber leadership, access to diverse committees, and committee leadership such that they do not have influence over all policy issues or over the legislative process. Descriptive representation of women in Latin America is a double-edged sword.

6

Working in the District

Home Style

Representatives are most recognized for the legislative work that they do while in the capital—specifically, policymaking. Another important aspect of the job, however, is working in the district—also known as *home style*. Fenno (1977) developed the concept of home style to refer to nonpolicy activities that representatives do aimed primarily at generating votes and that frequently occur in one's electoral district rather than in the capital. He suggested that there are three "ingredients" of home style—allocation of resources to the district, presentation of self, and explanation of "Washington" behavior.[1] *Allocation of resources* refers to the way that representatives direct political resources, such as staff or time, toward constituents in the district. *Presentation of self* refers to how representatives show constituents who they are and try to leave positive impressions with their constituents. It is about what representatives do for their constituents, specifically constituency service and casework, and the image they present to constituents through nonverbal cues. Finally, *explanation of legislative behavior* refers to how legislators explain the work they do in the legislature to their constituents back home in the district.

Although Fenno (1977) conceptualized home style in the context of the U.S. Congress, others have extended research on home-style activities to other countries and shown that home style is an important aspect of a representative's job in many legislatures. Cain, Ferejohn, and Fiorina (1983) looked at constituency service activities in Britain relative to the U.S. Congress in one of the first comparative studies of home style. Buck and Cain (1990) examined not just constituency service but ways that members of the British Parliament generate visibility by attending local functions and constituent group meetings, building relationships with the press, and working with their local party organization. Anagnoson (1983) extended the study of home style to New Zealand, where MPs work in single-member districts under parties with very tight party discipline. Still others have looked at home style in the Nordic states (Esaiasson 2000), Ireland (Wood and Young 1997), Canada and Australia (Halligan et al. 1988; Heitshusen et al. 2005), and even Latin America (Taylor 1992; Ingall and Crisp 2001; Crisp and Desposato 2004).

The importance of home style as a legislative activity makes it a key part of research on the relationship between formal, descriptive, and substantive representation. It is an activity that female representatives may find particularly useful for representing women because they can interact directly with female constituents and promote a gender agenda. It is also an activity through which women can reach other constituents to show them that they do not just represent women but are representatives of all constituents. They can promote their varied political agenda by giving press conferences or doing interviews with the media, they can hold district meetings with diverse groups (farmers, fisherman, union workers, etc.), and they can do casework for citizens needing assistance with an array of problems (not just women's equality issues), among other things. However, it is also an activity that male party leaders could use to marginalize women's growing political influence. Parties could use home-style activities as compensation for women whom they may exclude from other political activities, such as sponsoring key pieces of legislation, holding leadership posts, or sitting on prestigious committees.

In this chapter, I use the survey of legislators in Argentina, Colombia, and Costa Rica to analyze how formal and descriptive representation of women affects substantive representation focusing on Fenno's (1977) three categories of home style. The analyses reveal that female legislators do represent women through home style, often expending more effort on activities on behalf of women and women's issues than men. At the same time, women in all three countries use home-style activities to represent all constituents just as men do. Marginalization of women is not particularly apparent in this area of legislative work.

Home Style in Latin America

Legislators have many reasons for allocating resources to the district, presenting themselves in certain ways, and carefully explaining their legislative work to constituents. One reason is a personal interest in interacting directly with constituents. For example, some scholars have argued that representatives do constituency service because they take satisfaction in helping constituents solve problems (Anagnoson 1983; Thomas 1992). Another reason is that one's home style can make or break efforts to get reelected. In personalistic systems, casework, discussing legislative work with the press, or speaking publicly on behalf of constituents facilitates credit claiming and generates name recognition for representatives that can be invaluable during elections (Cain et al. 1983; Buck and Cain 1990; Wood and Young 1997). In party-centered systems, participating in home-style activities allows representatives to build relationships with local party elites who may be responsible for candidate nominations within the party or with party elites at the national level who rely on representatives to generate electoral support for the party as a whole (Anagnoson 1983; Taylor 1992).

In Argentina, Colombia, and Costa Rica, legislators regularly participate in home-style activities; however, the incentives for representatives to work in the district vary across the three countries. In Colombia, home style looks much as it does in the U.S. Congress. Representatives and senators allocate resources to the district, are concerned with how they present themselves to constituents, and explain their legislative behavior carefully because they must garner support for their own reelection bids. Because electoral rules give parties very little weight in the Colombian political system, representatives and senators must forge their own networks of constituency support. This is particularly important in the Senate, where all representatives are elected from a single nationwide district and senators cultivate specific geographic constituencies to ensure their reelection (Ingall and Crisp 2001; Crisp and Desposato 2004).

In contrast, Costa Rican representatives are prohibited from running for immediate reelection so they have little incentive to focus on home-style activities. Yet, research has found that cultivating constituent support is still an important part of deputies' jobs in Costa Rica (Taylor 1992; Carey 1996). This is because parties recognize the importance of creating tight ties between parties and constituents and instruct their deputies to allocate resources to the district, present themselves to constituents as representatives of the party, and explain to constituents how they promote the party's platform in the legislature. Costa Rica has a closed-list proportional representation electoral system with multimember districts. After elections, parties carve out parts of districts (aka *bailiwicks*) and assign specific legislators to these bailiwicks, effectively creating a single-member district system (Taylor 1992; Carey 1996). Individual deputies are then responsible for a specific geographic constituency and are charged with doing home style for this bailiwick. If they fail, parties can hold the individual deputies directly responsible. The incentive for doing home style is different in Costa Rica, but the outcome is similar—home style is an important part of a deputy's job. Representatives in Argentina also participate in home style but do so for different reasons. One, it is an effort to please party leaders and ensure a place on the party's ballot in the next election. Two, Argentina's federal system creates a very strong local party organization that connects representatives to their districts more tightly than it would in a unitary system (Jones et al. 2002).

Incentives for cultivating votes through home-style activities exist in all three countries, and these incentives motivate both male and female representatives. However, legislators in Colombia concentrate on home-style activities to ensure their own political future whereas representatives in Argentina and Costa Rica do this to ensure their party's future and their own future within the party. Do these varying incentives lead to different patterns of home style among male and female legislators in the three countries? More specifically, are women more likely to represent women through their home-style activities, and do the different incentives for representatives to do home style lead to different patterns of marginalization of women in the three countries?

Theorizing Gender's Effect on Home Style

As home-style activities became recognized as an important part of legislative work, gender and politics scholars began to examine how female representatives do home style and whether women differ from men in this area of legislative work (Diamond 1977; Thomas 1992; Richardson and Freeman 1995; Friedman 2000; Reingold 2000; Childs 2004; Saint-Germain and Chavez Metoyer 2008). Research on legislator gender and home style is relatively sparse, but that which does exist (primarily from studies of U.S. legislatures) suggests that gender influences the way representatives relate to constituents in their districts. For example, several studies of constituency service in the United States found that female legislators spend more hours on constituency service than men do (Thomas 1992) and receive more casework requests than male legislators (Richardson and Freeman 1995). This is echoed by Saint-Germain and Chavez Metoyer (2008, 164) who interviewed a female representative in Honduras who felt that "women deputies were more often sought out than male deputies for solving the personal problems of constituents." In contrast, however, Reingold (2000) found no gender differences in constituency service patterns among male and female representatives in Arizona and California. In regard to relationships with female constituents, more specifically, Thomas (1992) found that women target different parts of the constituency than men, particularly sectors that have been underserved in the past, such as women. Female representatives in Central America also report using their time in the district to interact with women and women's groups and learn about which issues they can take to the legislative arena in the form of policy (Saint-Germain and Chavez Metoyer 2008, 165).

These findings, however, shed little light on why differences exist and whether they are universal or conditioned by the legislative environment. Building from the theoretical model introduced in chapter 1, I argue that female representatives should be more likely to do home-style activities on behalf of women and women's issues for two reasons. One is that female representatives seek female constituents' electoral support. They may feel a special obligation to represent women or have a personal interest in working on behalf of women, who have previously been overlooked by representatives, and so intentionally emphasize interactions with female constituents (Thomas 1992, 1994; Franceschet and Piscopo 2008). The second reason is that female constituents may seek out female representatives when they have problems on which they want a representative's assistance (Childs 2004). In multimember electoral districts—which Argentina, Colombia, and Costa Rica have—constituents can choose which of the representatives from their district they want to approach with casework requests. Female constituents may feel that a female representative is more trustworthy, more sympathetic, more approachable, or more likely to share their point of view, and this too could lead to greater representation of women by women.[2]

I also argue, however, that marginalization of women in home-style activities is likely, particularly in Argentina and Costa Rica, where gender quotas and party-centered electoral rules may provide particularly strong incentives for marginalizing women. Home style focuses on aspects of a representative's job that are directly related to constituents and how the representative interacts with and presents him or herself to constituents. These activities are inherently "feminized" because they draw on qualities that are often considered to be more feminine than masculine, such as caring for constituents, solving problems, listening, and cooperating (Reingold 2000). Although some research suggests that women may be more likely to do this type of work because it draws on these traits that women have (Thomas 1992; Childs 2004), chapter 3 showed that female representatives in Argentina, Colombia, and Costa Rica place no greater priority than male representatives on doing constituency service, providing pork to the district, or giving public speeches. If women prioritize these activities to the same extent that men do, then female legislators should be no more likely than men to participate in these kinds of activities.

Yet, differences may occur as a result of male legislators and party leaders marginalizing female representatives. In Argentina and Costa Rica, strong party leaders have the ability to encourage women to spend more time on what the masculinized legislature may view as more "feminine" activities while pushing men to represent the party through what it may view to be the more influential tasks of lawmaking and leadership. Marginalization of women through home-style activities is less likely in Colombia, where party leaders have little control over representatives' efforts to generate electoral support and where representatives must use home style to ensure their own reelection. Both men and women have the same incentives for allocating resources to the district, focusing on their *presentation of self*, and explaining their legislative successes to their constituents, and they should be equally likely to do these things to ensure their future political careers.

Of course, the gender of a legislator is not the only thing that determines how representatives relate to their constituents. Other characteristics of legislators, characteristics of their electoral districts, and priorities of legislators affect representatives' home-style patterns, and these factors may obscure or explain the gendered nature of home-style behavior. For example, the way that legislators perceive their job, specifically the importance that they place on constituency service and certain constituencies, could explain why some representatives work on behalf of those constituencies more than others or why they do constituency service more than other legislators do (Fenno 1977; Clarke 1978; Fenno 1978; Studlar and McAllister 1996; Wood and Young 1997). Similarly, the demography of electoral districts (Richardson and Freeman 1995), their socioeconomic status (Studlar and McAllister 1996), and their proximity to the capital (Studlar and McAllister 1996; Saint-Germain and Chavez Metoyer 2008) could influence the demand for special projects in the district or requests for casework, affecting how representatives interact with constituents.

Legislative experience, political experience, and political ambition also could influence the extent to which representatives focus on home-style activities (Ingall and Crisp 2001). More senior legislators who are politically well known have less need to engage in home-style activities to increase their visibility, and parties may prefer to place these legislators in the most powerful and prestigious jobs in the legislature instead. Those who aspire to reelection or higher office have greater incentive to interact with constituents to generate electoral support and try to please the party by focusing on home-style activities. Finally, personal characteristics of legislators, such as their educational background (Clarke 1978), ideology, age, religious affiliation, and occupation (Thomas 1992) may affect home-style behavior. A number of studies of constituency service, for example, argue that liberal legislators may be more likely to conduct casework than conservative legislators because of their social agendas and the fact that most of their members are lower class or working class rather than middle-upper class (see Clarke 1978, for an exception; Cain et al. 1983; Richardson and Freeman 1995; Wood and Young 1997; Heitshusen et al. 1999).[3]

In the following sections, I present the results of multivariate statistical analyses of gender's effect on various home-style activities in Argentina, Colombia, and Costa Rica. I analyze several activities under each of Fenno's categories of home style—allocation of resources, presentation of self, and explanation of legislative behavior. I draw on questions from the 2001–2002 survey of legislators in Argentina, Colombia, and Costa Rica to estimate the effect of a legislator's gender on these activities after controlling for other influences on constituency-centered behavior, specifically, a legislator's ideology, age, marital status, educational background, previous occupation, legislative experience, prior political experience, political ambition, the urbanness of the legislator's district, and the importance a legislator places on female constituents or constituency service activities (see appendix C for details on control variables' coding). This chapter presents a combination of tables with the full statistical models, figures that show predicted probabilities of gender's substantive effects estimated from the statistical models, and discussion of the statistical results in the text.[4]

Allocation of Resources

The way in which representatives allocate resources toward their constituents is a key part of home style. Fenno (1977, 890–891) notes that

> the congressman's decision about how much time he should spend physically at home and his decision about how much of his staff he should place physically in the district are decisions which give shape to his home style. Of all the resources available to the House member, the scarcest and most precious one, which dwarfs all others in posing critical allocative dilemmas, is his time. Time is at once what the member has least of and what he has the most control over. When a congressman divides up his time, he decides by that act what kind of congressman he wants to be.

Drawing on the importance of a legislator's "time" as an indicator of home style, I assess the allocation of resources in Argentina, Colombia, and Costa Rica in three ways—frequency of visiting the district, frequency of attending public events in the district, and frequency of participating in interest group activities in the district.

Visiting the District

The amount of time that legislators spend in the capital versus in their district varies across the three countries. In Costa Rica, many constituents travel to San José, where legislators regularly hold office hours with the explicit purpose of meeting with constituents. Although some legislators have district offices, most spend Monday through Friday of their workweek at the Assembly and work in their districts only on weekends or when the Assembly is on break. This is quite different from Colombia and Argentina. Most members of the Colombian Congress are in Bogotá only Tuesday through Thursday when committees meet and floor sessions are held. In addition, legislators receive a weekly plane ticket to encourage them to return to their districts. Argentine legislators spend even less time at Congress, usually only 1 or 2 days a week, while putting in the majority of time at their district offices.

The survey of legislators asked representatives a question about how frequently they visit their district in a given (nonelection period) month. Respondents could choose from a 5-point scale ranging from "never" to "very often." A statistical analysis of the effect of gender on responses to this question, controlling for other determinants of visiting the district, reveals that women in Argentina and the Colombian Chamber of Representatives are more likely than men to spend time in the district but are no different than men in how often they travel to the district in the Colombian Senate or Costa Rican Legislative Assembly.[5] Figure 6.1 shows the predicted probabilities for the frequency with which the average male and female legislator will visit the district in the two cases where gender is statistically significant. In both Argentina and the Colombian Chamber, the model predicts that almost all female representatives visit the district "very often." Men, in contrast, spread across the "very often" and "often" categories. They still spend time in their districts but report that they do so a little less frequently than women.

Marginalization of women by the male-dominated political party in Argentina may be one reason for these gender differences. Deputies' travel schedules are

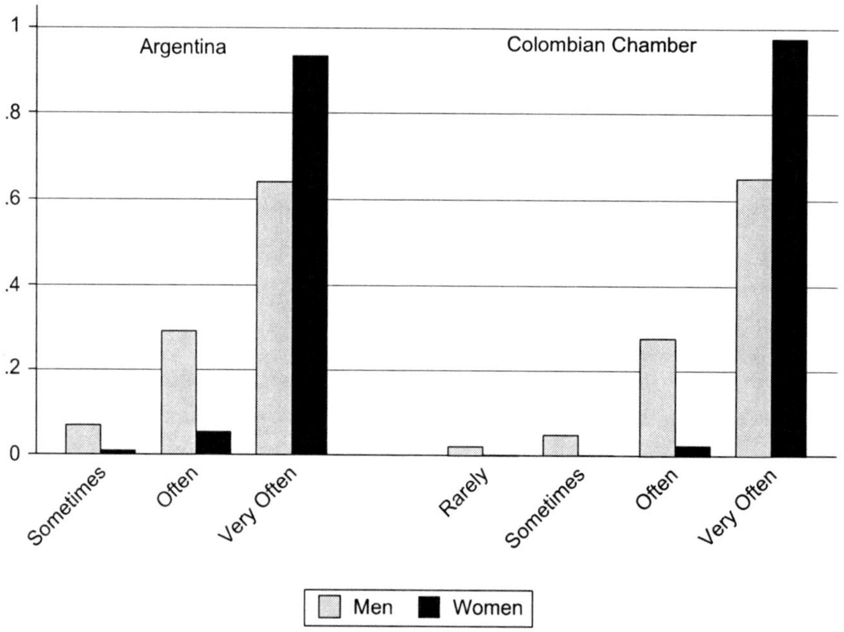

FIGURE 6.1. Predicted Probability that Legislators Visit Their District

partly dictated by their parties, as described by *Partido Justicialista* deputy Juliana di Tullio:

> With working on ten committees, the truth is that I don't have as much time [for visiting the district] as I would like. Specifically, because of my political work and my party affiliation, I not only go to my electoral district but also to the rest of Argentina. I belong to a national movement. My political boss is the President of the nation and we have a political movement called the Movimiento Evita and it is part of the Frente para la Victoria del Pueblo. As a part of the national board of this movement, I have to visit all of the provinces of Argentina, not just my electoral district. (di Tullio 2006)

The presence of gender differences in Colombia, however, weakens the theory that marginalization of women is responsible for the differences because it is not a party-centered system. Instead, it suggests that something else may explain the differences in district visits. One explanation may be that women return to their districts for reasons other than work—to see their families—and this makes them more likely to visit the district in countries where these trips are logistically more difficult. Social norms make it less acceptable for women than men to leave their families for long periods of time; consequently, female representatives may feel a need to return home more frequently than men. Because some districts are geographically far from the capital in Argentina and the Colombian lower house, traveling between the district and the capital is time consuming, and family responsibilities may be an incentive that leads women to visit more frequently. In Costa Rica and the Colombian Senate, visiting the district is logistically easier. Traveling to remote districts in Costa Rica requires little time compared to Argentina and Colombia, and thus almost all legislators (male and female) return to their districts very frequently. The Colombian Senate is elected via a single nationwide district of 100 seats, meaning that the entire country is every legislator's district. Here, "visiting the district" can be done in the capital or its surrounding communities without long trips to remote parts of the country.

Attending Public Events in the District

Another way that legislators allocate resources to the district is by spending time participating in public events and rallies put on by constituents, city governments, or local branches of the political party. Cinthya Hernández, a UCR deputy in Argentina's Chamber of Deputies, describes what she does in her district: "Meetings with non-governmental organizations and with the people in the party committee that I represent. More than creating a physical presence, the committee is the part of the party that you represent. You go there to tell them what you are doing, to listen to the people, and to hear requests for assistance" (Hernández 2006).

A statistical analysis of responses to the survey question about how frequently legislators attend public events in the district during an average month reveals no significant gender differences in any of the four legislatures (models not shown).[6] In Argentina, Colombia, and Costa Rica, women and men are equally likely to say that they frequently attend public events. In the Colombian Senate, more ambitious legislators are more likely to attend public events than less ambitious legislators are, and in Costa Rica, deputies who place higher priority on their electoral district are more likely to participate in events. In Argentina and the Colombian Chamber of Representatives, legislators with prior careers as lawyers and businesspeople were more likely to participate in public events. However, the gender of the legislator had no significant effect.

Participating in Interest Group Activities

Participating in events such as rallies, celebrations, conferences, or invited dinners sponsored by interest groups is another important aspect of home style. Interest groups often pressure legislators to participate in their activities in an effort to capture a legislator's attention and boost the cachet of the group. Legislators themselves also have an incentive to interact with local constituent groups—they can be sources of policy information and expertise, they provide opportunities for legislators to cultivate support among specific constituencies, and they are potential allies for representatives in other aspects of their legislative work. The specific groups with which legislators interact, however, is also an important part of home style because it sends signals to constituents about whom a representative associates with.

Statistical models of the survey question asking respondents how frequently they participate in meetings or activities sponsored by professional groups, environmental groups, agricultural groups, and unions reveal that male and female legislators in Argentina, Colombia, and Costa Rica are similar in the types of groups with which interact (models not shown).[7] They attend meetings and activities sponsored by professional groups, environmental groups, agricultural groups, and unions with very similar frequency. Gender differences do emerge, however, in how often they attend meetings and activities with *women's* groups. As table 6.1 shows, women are significantly more likely to participate in meetings and activities sponsored by women's groups in Argentina, Costa Rica, and the Colombian Chamber of Representatives. They are also more likely to do so in the Colombian Senate, but the difference is only borderline statistically significant at the 0.90 level, meaning we can be only 90% confident (rather than the more acceptable threshold of 95%) that the statistical model's estimate is generalizable beyond the

TABLE 6.1. Frequency of Participating in Meetings or Activities Sponsored by Women's Groups

	Argentina	Colombian Chamber	Colombian Senate	Costa Rica
Gender	.97**	1.25***	.90*	1.73***
	(.47)	(.39)	(.56)	(.62)
Priority on women constituents	.54**	.45**	.70***	.86**
	(.23)	(.21)	(.24)	(.39)
Ideology	−1.02	.60	−.42	−.25
	(.68)	(.49)	(.73)	(.39)
Age	.03	.01	−.02	.03
	(.02)	(.02)	(.02)	(.02)
Married	−.02	.61	.40	−.10
	(.62)	(.47)	(.52)	(.61)
Education	.09	−.003	.06	−.01
	(.25)	(.16)	(.23)	(.24)
Feeder occupation	−.25	.17	−.46	.13
	(.39)	(.27)	(.39)	(.37)
Legislative experience	−.08	−.05	.15*	−.23
	(.27)	(.10)	(.09)	(.57)
Prior political experience	.95	−.16	.44	.88**
	(.69)	(.69)	(.63)	(.41)
Political ambition	.71	.93**	−.34	.18
	(.50)	(.41)	(.38)	(.46)
Urban district	−.19	.13	—	.15
	(.35)	(.23)		(.39)
N	49	84	52	38
X^2	34.76***	35.83***	27.35***	38.99***

Ordered probit estimates with robust standard errors in parentheses.
$^*p < .10$, $^{**}p < .05$, $^{***}p < .01$

survey sample. Importantly, gender is significant even after controlling for the fact that the legislators who place higher priority on women as a constituency are more likely to participate in these meetings. This suggests that female representatives are more likely to do this for other reasons, such as a personal interest in these groups, viewing members of women's groups as potential supporters, or drawing policy expertise from these groups.

Substantively, the differences are quite large. In Argentina, the model predicts that almost 70% of female representatives participate in women's group activities "often" or "very often" while less than one-third of men do, all else being held at its mean or mode. The difference is even larger in the Colombian lower house. Eighty-four percent of women are predicted to attend women's group sponsored meetings or activities "often" or "very often" compared to only 43% of men. In the Colombian Senate, the model predicts that 81% of women participate in women's group activities "often" or "very often" compared to 55% of men. Forty-five percent of women are predicted to do so "very often," whereas only 16% of men are predicted to participate in activities that frequently. The gender gap is the most substantial in Costa Rica. The statistical model from table 6.1 predicts that almost 90% of female representatives interact with women's groups "very often" or "often," whereas only 37% of men do. None of the men or women in Costa Rica, however, report that they "never" do so. In all three countries, both men and women claim to spend at least some time attending women's group meetings or participating in activities that they sponsor. Women are likely to do this more frequently than men, however.

Presentation of Self

The way that legislators present themselves to constituents is a key part of their efforts to maintain existing electoral support and garner more of it. Representatives can do this symbolically and substantively. Symbolically, they do this through nonverbal cues generated by their actions or through their mere presence in the legislature (Fenno 1978). Actions are symbolic when they are designed to generate emotive responses, such as trust and support, among the represented. Legislators themselves can be symbols to the extent that they are role models or examples for others in society who might aspire to similar offices. Substantively, they present themselves to constituents through "service to the district" (Fenno 1978, 101).

Constituency service refers to work that representatives do on behalf of individual citizens or groups of citizens. It includes casework performed on behalf of individual constituents, assistance for constituency groups with specific problems or concerns, and project work aimed at benefiting a large spectrum of constituents. Constituency service often involves meeting with constituents who come to legislators' offices either in the capitol or in the district to express concerns about issues or policies, taking up casework requests from individual constituents or groups of constituents who need help negotiating the government bureaucracy, or working on small projects, such as helping to complete a housing project or offering small education grants.

Although constituency service is an aspect of legislative work that is often overlooked by scholars in favor of policymaking, it is an important part of substantive representation that provides benefits to both constituents and legislators. Constituency service attends to the problems of constituents, inspiring greater support for representatives and generating votes at election time. Although the expectation of electoral advantage is a common motivation for conducting constituency service, such service can also benefit legislators through policy. Pleasing constituents by conducting service gives legislators leeway to adopt policy positions that at times might be unpopular with constituents (Cain et al. 1987). In addition, spending time with constituents and working to solve their problems makes legislators more aware of constituents' policy concerns and brings the policy agendas of legislators and constituents into closer congruence. As chapter 3 showed, many representatives in Argentina, Colombia, and Costa Rica think that constituency service is an important part of their job. Across the four legislatures, an average of 65% of legislators feel that "helping constituents with personal problems with the government" is "important" or "very important." It is a higher priority, however, for legislators in Argentina and Costa Rica than in Colombia. Eighty percent of deputies in Argentina and 74% of Costa Rican respondents see it as "important" or "very important," but only 55% of Colombian legislators saw it that way.

The survey of legislators included four questions that assess substantive and symbolic ways that representatives present themselves to the district—the amount of time they spend doing constituency service, the extent to which they do constituency service on behalf of women, the types of casework requests they receive, and whether they view themselves as role models for certain groups. The following sections analyze each of these dimensions of the presentation of self.

Time Spent on Constituency Service

In Argentina, Colombia, and Costa Rica, legislators spend varying amounts of time meeting with their constituents and doing service on behalf of individuals in their district.[8] Electoral rules in Colombia provide the strongest incentives for legislators to cater to their constituents and seek "personal votes," and in fact, they do more constituency service in the Colombian Chamber of Representatives. Representatives spend an average of 24 hours per week with constituents, and survey responses ranged from 1 to 134 hours a week.[9] In the Senate, however, the average is just 20 hours per week with a range from 0 to 72, which is quite similar to the amount of time that legislators in the less personalistic systems of Argentina and Costa Rica spend working with constituents. In Argentina, they spend between 0 and 72 hours per week on constituency service, with an average of 19. In Costa Rica, they spend an average of 21 hours per week on constituency service with some deputies spending as few as 2 hours per week working with constituents whereas others claimed to spend up to 70 hours a week on constituency service. Clearly, constituency service is common in all four legislatures, despite the fact that Colombian legislators think it is less important.

Table 6.2 presents the results of statistical models estimating the effect of gender on the number of hours that legislators do casework or constituency service with constituents in an average week.[10] The models show that statistically significant gender differences in the time spent on constituency service are rare, and where they do exist, women are estimated to spend *less* time on constituency service than men. In the Colombian Senate, the model predicts that men will spend 25 hours per week on constituency service whereas women will spend only

TABLE 6.2. Number of Hours Spent on Constituency Service in an Average Week

	Argentina	Colombian Chamber	Colombian Senate	Costa Rica
Gender	–.50	.28	–.92**	–.10
	(.32)	(.28)	(.29)	(.18)
Ideology	.35	.05	.26	–.13
	(.30)	(.31)	(.53)	(.17)
Age	.03**	–.01	–.02**	.01
	(.01)	(.01)	(.01)	(.01)
Married	–.50*	–.79**	.72**	–.66***
	(.29)	(.33)	(.29)	(.17)
Education	–.51***	–.20	.06	.01
	(.15)	(.14)	(.14)	(.14)
Feeder occupation	.24	.11	–.12	.22
	(.22)	(.17)	(.21)	(.20)
Legislative experience	–.67***	.15	.08	.27
	(.22)	(.13)	(.05)	(.35)
Prior political experience	–.39	.51	1.37***	–1.03***
	(.60)	(.51)	(.32)	(.31)
Political ambition	.60**	.51*	–.19	.27
	(.24)	(.30)	(.29)	(.24)
District is the capital	–.66***	–.12	—	–.95***
	(.21)	(.28)		(.28)
Constant	4.28***	3.56***	1.78**	3.38***
	(1.21)	(1.00)	(.82)	(.90)
N	43	81	47	41
X^2	41.26***	17.34*	46.50***	38.69***
Alpha	.28	.44	.36	.27

Negative binomial estimates with robust standard errors in parentheses.
$^{*}p < .10$, $^{**}p < .05$, $^{***}p < .01$

11 hours working with constituents. This difference, and the lack thereof in Argentina, the Colombian Chamber, and Costa Rica, exists after accounting for other influences on the amount of constituency service that legislators do. For example, being married has a negative effect on the amount of time legislators spend working with constituents in all cases except the Colombian Senate. Having a personal life that could conflict with the time a representative can spend out in the district when he or she is home for a visit leads to less time spent on constituency service.

Overall, these findings provide little evidence that women are marginalized into spending more time on constituency service, particularly after accounting for the array of other reasons that legislators do constituency service. Just as women placed no higher priority on constituency service, they are no more likely to get pushed into this area of work either. The only exception is the Colombian Senate, where women do constituency service *less* often than men. This may be due to competing demands on their time because they are women and there are so few women in the legislature. It also could indicate some degree of marginalization precisely because building networks and electoral support among constituents is so important to legislators' careers. Because the entire country is one electoral district in the Senate, technically all legislators compete for the same constituents. This puts pressure on legislators to compete with one another for constituency service, which could marginalize women. Alternatively, constituents may be more likely to seek out male representatives when they have 100 legislators to select from and so few are women.

Constituency Service on Behalf of Women

In addition to the overall amount of time that legislators spend on constituency service, the distribution of time spent with male versus female constituents is revealing. It shows whether female legislators act on the priority that they place on women as a constituency and whether female constituents feel more represented having a woman in office and seek her assistance with political problems. To determine whether female legislators are more likely to spend time doing constituency service for female constituents and male legislators spend more of their time working with male constituents, the survey asked legislators to report the percentage of their constituency work that is for female citizens and for male citizens. The possible range was 0 to 100, with most legislators in each chamber reporting a division of 50/50. In Argentina, 75% of respondents said they spent an equal amount of time working with male and female constituents. In Colombia, 45% of representatives spent equal time with men and women and 54% of senators did. In Costa Rica, 59% did constituency service on behalf of men and women equally.

The remaining legislators, however, reported spending disproportionate amounts of time with male and female constituents. Some representatives in Argentina reported spending as little as 30% of their time with female constituents, whereas others spent as much as 90% with women. The range was similar in Costa Rica, where deputies reported a female/male ratio of time that ranged from 25/75 to 70/30. In Colombia, the disparity was much larger. In the Chamber of Representatives, some legislators said they spend as little as 20% of their constituency service efforts on behalf of women and one legislator claimed to do all of his constituency service with women. In the Senate, the range was from 5% to 80%.

In three of the four legislatures, the gender of the legislator partly explains variation in time spent with female constituents (table 6.3). In Argentina, Costa Rica, and the Colombian Senate, female representatives spend significantly more time with female constituents than male representatives do. The effect of gender is also positive in the Colombian Chamber of Representatives, but it does not quite reach statistical significance ($p = 0.14$). The size of the gender differences is quite similar across the three countries—approximately 8 percentage points. For example, in Argentina, the model predicts that the average male representative

TABLE 6.3. Percentage of Time Spent on Constituency Service on Behalf of Women

	Argentina	Colombian Chamber	Colombian Senate	Costa Rica
Gender	7.49**	5.80	9.89*	8.65**
	(3.21)	(3.85)	(4.90)	(3.63)
Priority on women constituents	—	4.31***	2.44	−.20
		(1.59)	(2.92)	(2.91)
Ideology	−9.15**	−2.10	−5.71	2.99
	(4.18)	(3.67)	(8.14)	(3.06)
Age	.11	−.07	−.05	.18
	(.14)	(.15)	(.22)	(.14)
Married	−1.41	5.76**	−1.22	−.01
	(2.97)	(2.66)	(5.17)	(2.94)
Education	−1.84	−2.11	−.70	.14
	(1.62)	(1.79)	(2.65)	(1.40)
Feeder occupation	.57	2.53	−2.25	−2.84
	(2.14)	(2.55)	(3.88)	(3.02)
Legislative experience	5.15**	−1.95	.25	−5.03**
	(2.10)	(1.32)	(1.14)	(1.95)
Prior political experience	4.44	5.07	15.31	−2.36
	(4.18)	(4.29)	(12.86)	(2.47)
Political ambition	.73	1.21	1.19	8.00**
	(2.46)	(2.75)	(6.76)	(3.00)
District is the capital	−4.60*	5.40	—	−.77
	(2.71)	(3.51)		(3.95)
Constant	36.67***	33.90***	29.11	44.20***
	(12.40)	(12.24)	(26.81)	(13.85)
N	45	80	47	38
R^2	.52	.20	.25	.39

Negative binomial regression estimates with robust standard errors in parentheses.
*$p < .10$, **$p < .05$, ***$p < .01$

spends 50% of his constituency service efforts with female constituents whereas female representatives will spend 58% of their time with female constituents. In the Colombian Senate, the average male representative is estimated to spend near-equal time with male and female constituents, but women focus 61% of their constituency service on female constituents.

Although these results do not reveal whether this results from female representatives choosing to focus more on constituency service for women or female constituents seeking out female representatives with their problems and concerns, it is likely a combination of the two. Some representatives that I interviewed emphasized that casework starts with constituents who send letters with requests for assistance or go to the representative's local office to get his or her staff's help with problems. Others saw constituency service more as a way to be knowledgeable about the problems of their constituents and sought out meetings with constituents to learn about their concerns. Argentine deputy Juliana di Tullio said her role on the board of the PJ's *Movimiento Evita* meant that she "gathers together the worries that women have. I am the depository of the concerns of the majority of women. I know the problems of women and this is reflected in my work in the chamber. . . . A deputy should echo the debate that society generates because this is the vehicle for our actions" (di Tullio 2006).

Although the gender of the legislator has no independent effect on doing constituency service for women in the Colombian Chamber, the views that representatives have of women as a constituency is a strong determinant of the actual time spent doing constituency service on women's behalf. Those who place a higher priority on female constituents also spend more time doing constituency service for women.[11] This variable does not matter, however, in the other countries.[12] Thus, most legislators view women as an important constituency to serve. Yet, there is a stronger link between female representatives and female constituents in Argentina, the Colombian Senate, and Costa Rica, than between male representatives and female constituents.

Types of Casework Requests

Casework is a way for legislators to interact directly with their constituents by helping them resolve problems that they or a group they belong to have with government agencies. Legislators in Argentina, Colombia, and Costa Rica receive requests from constituents to help with a wide variety of issues and concerns. Table 6.4 shows the various types of casework requests that legislators receive and the percentage of legislators who claimed to get these requests. The most common request was for assistance with jobs—28% of the top three requests that legislators received were related to employment. Constituents oftentimes were seeking help in finding a job or seeking a legislator's intervention to get an employer to rehire them. The large proportion of requests for employment assistance is not surprising because unemployment rates reached 18.3% in Argentina in 2001 and 19.5% in Colombia in 2000.

Another common request that legislators received was from individuals with other financial problems—9.4% of the requests were for economic assistance. Legislators reported constituents seeking their help obtaining welfare services from the government, economic grants and loans, and sometimes direct requests for money. High levels of poverty in countries spur these types of requests. Other casework requests asked for help with educational loans and grants, health services, housing assistance, food donations, personal favors such as recommendations, contacts, passports, and visas, and intervention in legal matters. In Colombia, where a civil war still rages, a common concern was human rights violations.

A few gender differences do exist in the extent to which legislators do casework on these different issues (models not shown).[13] In Costa Rica, for example, female legislators report conducting casework on issues related to health care more frequently than male legislators do, and in the Colombian Chamber of

TABLE 6.4. Frequency of Casework Requests in the Four Legislatures

Casework Type	Legislators Who Received Casework Requests[a]	
	n	%
Employment	229	28.0
Public projects	99	12.1
Economic problems	77	9.4
Health	61	7.5
Education	59	7.2
Personal favors	41	5.0
Legal issues and government processes	39	4.8
Housing	36	4.4
General social assistance	35	4.3
Communities and groups	29	3.5
Legislative concerns	25	3.1
Security	17	2.1
Corruption concerns	12	1.5
Public services	12	1.5
General information	10	1.2
Business concerns	6	0.7
Agriculture	5	0.6
Senior citizens	5	0.6
Public positions	4	0.5
Human rights	4	0.5
General help or support	4	0.5
Equality	3	0.4
Environment	2	0.2
Food	2	0.2
Children	1	0.1
Total	817	100

[a] Legislators could provide up to three of their most common casework requests.

Representatives, women work on environmental issues more frequently than men do. In Argentina, women do casework on poverty issues more often than do men, but in the Colombian Chamber, female representatives work on poverty issues *less* often than their male counterparts. In Argentina, Costa Rica, and the Colombian Chamber, female representatives focus on legal issues with their constituents more often than do men, but in both Colombian chambers, women work on employment issues with their constituents less often than men. No gender differences emerged in the areas of education or tax-related casework. The variety of issues on which gender differences emerge and the fact that they do not correspond to the issues on which gender differences existed in issue preferences in chapter 3 suggests that women are not being marginalized into working on cases traditionally in women's domain while men tackle traditional men's domain cases.

The findings do support, at least partially, the theory that female representatives represent women's issues in their casework more than male representatives.

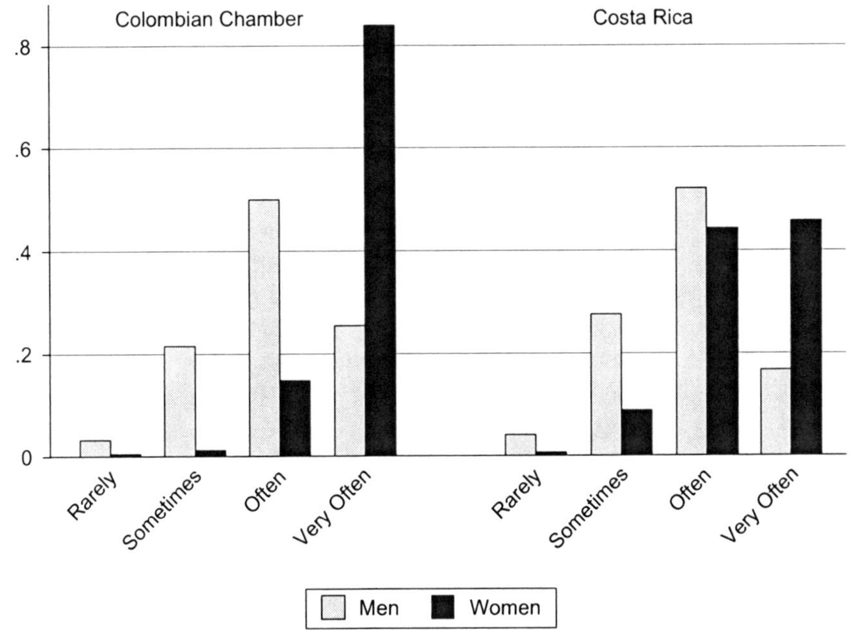

FIGURE 6.2. Predicted Probability that Legislators Do Casework Related to Women's Issues

This may involve, for example, dealing with petitions for assistance with sexual harassment cases or a request from a woman wanting assistance getting elected to a post in her municipality. Figure 6.2 shows predicted probabilities emerging from statistical models that reveal significant differences between male and female representatives in the Colombian Chamber and Costa Rica on the frequency with which they do casework on women's issues.[14] In Colombia, women are more likely to report doing casework on women's issues "very often" whereas men fall into the categories of "sometimes, often, and very often." In Costa Rica, more men than women say they do casework on women's issues "sometimes," but more women than men do casework on women's issues "very often." Gender differences were not significant in Argentina, once the priority that legislators place on women as a constituency was controlled. However, without this variable, significant differences did exist. This implies that female representatives in Argentina do more casework on women's issues than do men, but it is a direct result of women placing a higher priority on women as a constituency.

Legislators as Role Models

Representatives symbolically present themselves to their district in two ways. One is by acting in ways that make citizens feel they are trustworthy, responsive, and hardworking, which can generate greater electoral support as a result. Another way is by being role models for the electorate. The idea of legislators as role models is particularly relevant in literature on underrepresented groups. One of the primary arguments is that it is important to elect more women and minorities to office because they set examples and are role models for members of those groups in society (Phillips 1995). By holding office, they generate feelings among young members of those groups that they too can aspire to and achieve public office (Burrell 1997; Childs 2004). The symbolic act of being a role model is one way representatives present themselves to the district and generate electoral support. Specific to women, the presence of women in positions of political power sets an example for women and girls in society that politics is not "just a man's game" (Phillips 1995; Burrell 1997; Mansbridge 1999; Swers 2001). Although all legislators serve as role models to some extent, women in particular carry the burden of being examples for other women. As Swers (2001, 172) writes, "Women must be elected to provide role models for other women and to demonstrate that politics is not only a male domain."

In Argentina, Colombia, and Costa Rica, nearly all female representatives recognize this burden. Table 6.5 presents the average percentage of legislators in each chamber who see themselves as role models for women.[15] Of the women surveyed in the Colombian Chamber of Representatives, all but 1 (93%) see themselves as role models for women. In the Colombian Senate and the Costa Rican Legislative Assembly, all of the women surveyed said that they view themselves as role models for women. Argentina had 5 of 20 women who did not consider themselves examples for women, but 75% do see themselves as role models for women. Interestingly, in all three countries, many men also see themselves as role models for women. Yet, significantly fewer do so than women. In Argentina, 48% of men consider themselves role models for women, and 45% do so in Costa Rica. The percentages are higher in Colombia—64% in the Chamber of Representatives and 60% in the Senate.

Women viewing themselves as role models and recognizing the importance of women's presence in office, more generally, was also evident in interviews with women in the three countries. Isabel Chamorro, a PLN deputy in the 1998–2002 Costa Rican Assembly, noted that "women [in society] depend on us. The role

TABLE 6.5. Percentage of Legislators Who See Themselves as Role Models for Women

	Women	Men	*p*
Argentina	75	48.5	.06
Colombian Chamber	93.3	64.9	.03
Colombian Senate	100	60.5	.02
Costa Rica	100	45.1	.01

Bivariate cross-tabulations with *p*-values from a chi-square test for statistical significance.

that we play is important for the future representation of women in the congress" (Chamorro 1999). Sonia Picado, a PLN deputy from 1998 to 2002, has been a role model throughout her career, being the first female dean of the law school at the University of Costa Rica, the first female ambassador to the United States, and the first female president of the PLN. She said, "I think that just by being here I am sending a message to other women that we can do it. I think that throughout my whole career I have had to make decisions for women that this can be done" (Picado 1999). Deputy Silvia Augsburger in Argentina speaks of the symbolic role women play in politics, more generally: "That Michelle Bachelet can be president of Chile, independent of whether she does well or poorly, I believe that it is good symbolically to demonstrate that a woman can be president of Chile. So, my daughter says that when she grows up, she wants to be president, not a ballerina or a teacher. She can choose what she wants to be because symbolically she sees that women can hold these positions" (Augsburger 2006). Women in Argentina, Colombia, and Costa Rica near universally recognize the symbolic importance of their presence in politics.

Explanation of Legislative Activity

The third and final dimension of home style is the way in which representatives explain their legislative activity to constituents in their district. Relaying information to constituents about the way representatives are doing their jobs, the successes they have had in office, and the goods and services they have produced for the district is critical to ensuring ongoing electoral support from constituents. Fenno (1977, 1978) examined representatives' explanation of legislative activity by describing and classifying the actual verbal styles that legislators use. Another way to assess how representatives explain their behavior is to focus on the mediums through which legislators reach constituents and the frequency with which they use them. Three ways that representatives do this are giving public speeches, making public presentations, and speaking to the press.

Statistical models explaining variation in each of these three activities reveal that male and female legislators in Argentina, Colombia, and Costa Rica do not differ much in the extent to which they explain their legislative activities to constituents back home in their districts (models not shown).[16] However, one statistically significant gender difference that does emerge is in giving public speeches in the Colombian Chamber of Representatives. Here, women are significantly more likely to give public speeches than men even after adjusting for the priority that legislators place on this activity. The statistical model predicts that 81% of female representatives give public speeches "frequently" or "very frequently" whereas only 52% of men give speeches that often (figure 6.3). In none of the other legislatures, however, do women and men differ significantly from

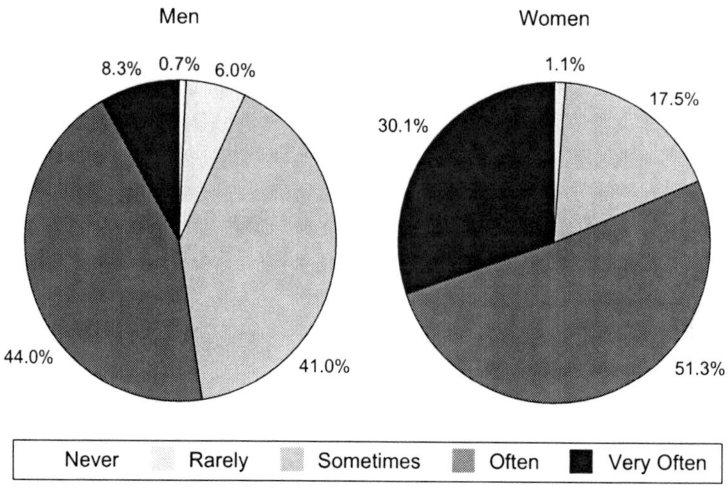

FIGURE 6.3. Frequency of Giving Public Speeches in the Colombian Chamber of Representatives

one another in the frequency with which they give public speeches. Also, no significant differences exist in how often legislators give public presentations in any of the three countries.

Significant differences do emerge in Argentina and Costa Rica in how often female and male legislators speak to the press. The effect of gender is different in the two countries, however (figure 6.4). In Argentina, women speak to the press more often than men do. In Costa Rica, they do so less often than men. Eighty-seven percent of female deputies in Argentina are predicted to speak to the press about their work "often" or "very often" compared to 66% of male deputies. Men are more likely than women to respond that they speak to the press "sometimes"—26% of men are predicted to fall into the "sometimes" category, whereas only 11% of women are. In Costa Rica, the model predicted that 60% of women will speak to the press only "rarely," whereas men fall rather equally into the "sometimes," "often," and "very often" categories of frequency. Importantly, these differences existed after controlling for the priority that legislators place on speaking publicly among other factors.

These findings lend little support to the theory that women are marginalized in their explanations of legislative activity. Despite Argentina and Costa Rica both having party-centered systems that should facilitate marginalization, Argentine deputies speak with the press more often than men, whereas Costa Rican deputies speak less often than men. Similarly, little marginalization is expected in Colombia, but women in the Chamber of Representatives give public speeches more often than men do. Across the three countries, some gender differences emerge in

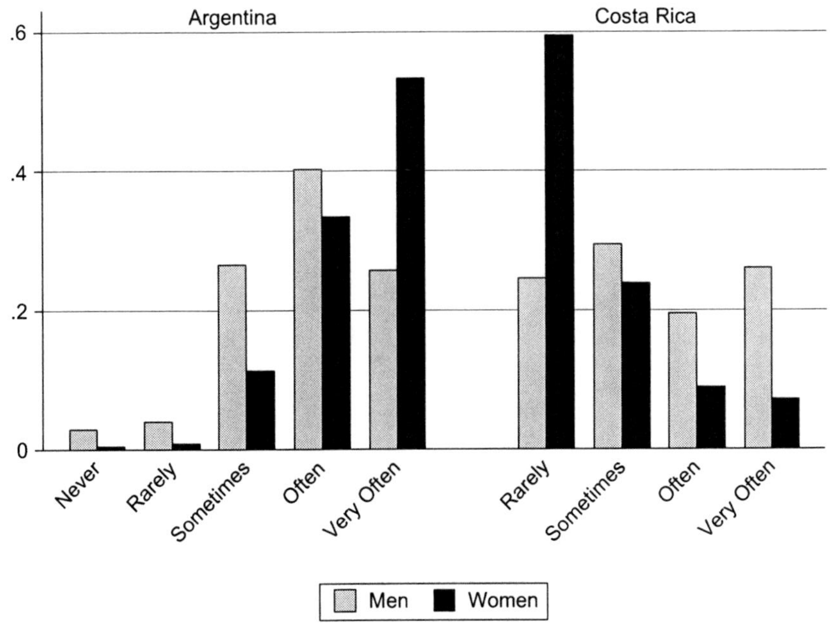

FIGURE 6.4. Predicted Probability that Legislators Speak with the Press

how legislators explain their activities but they do not offer systematic evidence of parties or male legislators marginalizing women.

Conclusion

Although policymaking is widely considered to be the most important part of a legislator's job, representatives also build relationships with constituents in their electoral districts. It is through their interaction with constituents that they learn what issues and problems are most important to citizens and that they work to generate electoral support for themselves and their political parties. Substantive representation is about policymaking, or as Fenno (1978) referred to it in the context of the U.S. Congress, "hill style." But, it is also about the nonlegislative activities done on behalf of constituents, or "home style." Previous chapters have shown some degree of marginalization of women in policymaking, committee assignments, and leadership posts in the legislatures of Argentina, Costa Rica, and Colombia. This chapter shows, however, that marginalization of women does not occur consistently in legislators' home styles. In Colombia, where legislators are dependent upon strong constituent support for their political careers and party marginalization of women through home-style activities is difficult to begin with, women and men are quite similar in how they allocate resources to the district, present themselves to constituents, and explain their legislative work. As expected, few gender differences exist in home-style activities. They are also uncommon in Argentina and Costa Rica. Party leaders and male legislators may not have as much power over how legislators allocate resources, present themselves, and explain legislative behavior as electoral rules would suggest, or they may not view these activities as gendered. Either way, it is clear that they do not marginalize women into spending more time on these activities. Women use home style just as men do to allocate resources, present themselves, and explain their legislative activity to constituents in their district. Home style is a tool for women to represent their parties and a wide array of constituents.

When male and female legislators do exhibit differences in their home-style behaviors, it most often involves representing women, women's groups, and women's issues. Having female representatives in office gives female constituents greater options for getting their demands heard and their cases taken up by legislators. In Argentina, Costa Rica, and the Colombian Chamber of Representatives, female representatives are more likely to participate in meetings, rallies, and other activities sponsored by women's groups. In Argentina, Costa Rica, and the Colombian Senate, female legislators do more hours of constituency service on behalf of female constituents, and in Costa Rica and the Colombian Chamber of Representatives, they do casework on behalf of women's issues more often than men do. In all four countries, almost all women view themselves as role models for women in society. Importantly, all of these differences occurred after accounting for the priority that legislators place on women as constituents. Legislators who view women as an important constituency to represent are often more likely to do home style on behalf of women, but even after accounting for the fact that women tend to be more likely to feel this way, gender matters. Just as women represent women's issues in the policymaking process and in their committee work, they promote women and women's issues in their home-style activities. Women in these national legislatures clearly represent women.

7

Symbolic Representation

Evoking Support for the Political System

The election of women to political office has important consequences for representative democracy. As the preceding chapters showed, the presence of women in national legislatures increases substantive representation of women in Latin America by generating greater attention to women's rights and equality issues. This occurred in various areas of legislative work, such as bill sponsorship, committee membership, discussing women's issues on the chamber floor, and even interactions with constituents and interest groups. In addition to the substantive contributions that women make in Latin American politics, women's representation may also have symbolic effects. In other words, it may affect the way citizens, both men and women, feel about their democracies. Women's representation is a symbol of the inclusiveness of the political system that sends signals to citizens that can generate positive feelings about elected government.

The notion that women's representation symbolically affects citizens is rooted in Pitkin's (1967) vision of symbolic representation—that representation itself is a symbol that can produce emotional responses among the represented. Most often, symbolic representation is tied to descriptive representation. For example, the presence of women campaigning for and winning political office sets an example for women and girls in society who may, in turn, begin to view politics more favorably and as an arena open to their participation (Phillips 1995; Kittilson 2005; Wolbrecht and Campbell 2007). In addition, the increasingly representative nature of electoral institutions and policy outputs may affect symbolic representation.

For example, the adoption of gender quotas in many developing countries has been driven, in part, by a desire to enhance the legitimacy of representative democracy (Htun and Jones 2002; Krook 2004; Araújo and García 2006; Krook 2006; Marx et al. 2007; Krook 2009). Quotas are symbols of gender equality, representativeness, and inclusiveness that can lead citizens and international observers to view a country's democracy in a more positive light. Similarly, political and economic performance can be symbols of how well government is working and generate positive or negative feelings toward government (Mishler and Rose 2001). The passage of women's issue policies may symbolize political support for women and women's equality, making citizens, particularly women, feel better about their government (Schwindt-Bayer and Mishler 2005). As these examples illustrate, formal representation, descriptive representation, and substantive representation can shape symbolic representation (Pitkin 1967).

In this chapter, I return the analysis to the regional level and examine the extent to which formal, descriptive, and substantive representation of women influence the way citizens feel about government in fourteen Latin American democracies. I examine the effect it has on citizens, regardless of gender, and whether women's representation has a stronger effect for female citizens in particular, using data from the Latin American Public Opinion Project's (LAPOP) 2006 Americas Barometer. This chapter illustrates that women's representation has important symbolic consequences for democracy in Latin America.

Measuring Symbolic Representation

Symbolic representation is not about the extent to which representatives or representative bodies are symbols, but instead, it is about the feelings or attitudes that representation generates among constituents (Pitkin 1967, 97; Lawless 2004). This can be measured in a variety of ways, but here I focus on three categories of attitudes about government—satisfaction with democracy, perceptions of government corruption, and institutional trust. These three aspects of symbolic representation assess citizen affect and evaluations of democracy, though they do so in different ways. Democratic satisfaction, for example, is a general assessment of how pleased citizens are with the way their democracy functions and is a very common measure of mass attitudes (Anderson and Guillory 1997; Lijphart 1999; Norris 1999; Anderson et al. 2005; Farrell and McAllister 2006; Aarts and Thomassen 2008). It indicates the legitimacy that citizens attribute to their government and provides an overarching indicator of citizens' feelings about the actual performance of their government. Satisfaction with democracy is often thought to correlate with the stability of democracy, which is particularly important in new democracies such as those in Latin America (Lagos 2001).

The second set of attitudes is citizen perceptions of corruption. Corruption is a common problem in many Latin American democracies that can have important consequences for the stability of democracy, the functioning of democracy, and citizen views of democracy (Seligson 2002; Anderson and Tverdova 2003; Canache and Allison 2005; Seligson 2006). Attitudes about corruption give an indication not of how much corruption actually exists in a country but of how much corruption citizens *perceive* in their country. Perceptions of corruption are likely to be influenced by how citizens feel about their government (Davis et al. 2004; Canache and Allison 2005). If citizens are positively inclined toward government, then they may perceive less corruption regardless of whether or not it actually is less.

Finally, institutional trust assesses how citizens feel about specific democratic institutions. Many scholars argue that institutional trust is vital to the stability and consolidation of democracy (see, for example, Mishler and Rose 1997). Without it, democracies may struggle to consolidate and eventually fail. There are many dimensions of institutional trust, however. In this chapter, I focus on trust in the legislature, specifically, and trust in the entire national government. These two are particularly important for assessing the effect of women's representation on institutional trust because they include the two government institutions in which women have made the most visible gains in politics—the legislature and the executive branch.

Satisfaction with democracy, political trust, and corruption perceptions are important for representative democracy because they can influence government effectiveness, the way representatives act, the way citizens operate within the system, and a government's overall stability. Governments with strong support from citizens can operate without having to regularly convince citizens of its efforts (Mishler and Rose 1997). When citizens are more trusting of government, they give political leaders the flexibility to focus on longer-term goals such as good governance through programmatic policy production rather than short-term goals such as reelection through the generation of pork (Mishler and Rose 1997). Democratic satisfaction and trust also allow governments to make mistakes or suffer downturns without fear of democratic breakdown. Determining what affects symbolic representation is important because it helps to create better governance, stronger citizen participation, and greater democratic stability.

Another question related to measuring symbolic representation is who the subjects of symbolic representation are. Symbolic representation focuses on the emotional or psychological reaction of the represented to government, but what "the represented" refers to is not always clear. It may mean all citizens, but it may also refer to more specific groups such as registered voters, geographic constituencies, or social constituencies. In this study of women's representation, I classify "the represented" in two ways—all citizens and women, specifically. I ask two related questions about how formal, descriptive, and substantive representation affect symbolic representation.

One is whether improving women's representation has symbolic effects on all citizens, both men and women, and the second is whether it has disproportionately large effects on women in society (Lawless 2004). Some research suggests that making electoral institutions more women-friendly, improving the gender representativeness of legislatures and executives, and passing more women-friendly policy will have positive effects on both male and female citizens (Lawless 2004; Schwindt-Bayer and Mishler 2005; Atkeson and Carrillo 2007; Karp and Banducci 2008; Kittilson and Schwindt-Bayer 2008). Men, just like women, may see increased representation of women as an indication of greater social representativeness and inclusiveness of government, more generally, and feel better about their democracy. On the other hand, women's formal, descriptive, and substantive representation may have a disproportionately larger effect on women in society (High-Pippert and Comer 1998; Atkeson 2003; Atkeson and Carrillo 2007; Ulbig 2007; Wolbrecht and Campbell 2007; Reingold and Harrell forthcoming). Because gender friendly electoral rules, the increased presence of women in office, and the passage of women's issue policies directly target women, these factors may make women in society feel that they are more included and represented in government but generate resentment among men who may not see the need for greater women's representation. In this chapter, I focus on both the overall effect that women's representation has on citizens and whether it has disproportionately different effects on women's symbolic representation and men's symbolic representation.

The theory driving this chapter argues that greater formal, descriptive, and substantive representation of women will improve citizens' perceptions of representative democracy. That said, I do not expect that women's representation has led to dramatic changes in citizen views of representative democracy or that it will counter the overall decline in satisfaction with democracy and institutional trust that many countries in the world, including Latin American countries, have seen over time (Dalton 1996). What I do expect, however, is that women's representation can play a small role in mediating this decline. Specifically, I do not test a longitudinal effect for women's representation within countries. Instead, I test whether citizens in countries with greater representation of women view their governments more positively than those in countries with less representation of women. Overall levels are likely to still be low in all countries, but some countries may have higher levels than others. This may, in part, be due to women's representation.

Data and Methods

This chapter presents a region-wide analysis of 14 Latin American democracies.[1] The primary source of data is the 2006 Americas Barometer conducted by the Latin American Public Opinion Project (LAPOP) at Vanderbilt University.[2] I measure each of the four dimensions of symbolic representation with four separate questions on the Americas Barometer. To measure citizen satisfaction with democracy, I use the question that asks, "In general, would you say that you are very satisfied, satisfied, dissatisfied, or very dissatisfied with the way in which democracy functions in this country?" The responses are coded 1 to 4 from "very dissatisfied" to "very satisfied."[3] The question that measures corruption asks, "Taking into account your own experience or what you have heard, corruption among public officials is (1) very common, (2) common, (3) uncommon, or (4) very uncommon?" The questions for citizen trust in the legislature and government simply ask respondents "to what extent do you trust the National Congress [or Central Government]?" and asks them to respond on a 1 to 7 scale from "not at all" to "a lot."

To analyze symbolic representation, I use both respondent-level data and country-level data (i.e., multilevel data).[4] However, to provide an initial look at how citizens feel about their democracies, table 7.1 aggregates the survey responses for each question by country to show the average percentage of respondents who are satisfied with democracy, feel that corruption is common, trust the legislature, and trust government. It also presents the size of the gender gap in women's and men's attitudes toward government and whether the gap is statistically significant. The table reveals that wide variation exists across Latin American countries in how citizens feel about government. In 2006, only about half of the citizens in Latin America were satisfied with their democracies. Citizens were least satisfied with democracy in Paraguay, where only 20% of respondents were "very satisfied" or "satisfied" with democracy. Citizens were most satisfied with democracy in Uruguay, where 80% of respondents said they were "very satisfied" or "satisfied" with their democracy. The large majority of people in Latin America, 79%, view corruption as "very common" or "common" in their countries. The country where the largest number of citizens thought corruption was extensive is Guatemala, where 91% of respondents felt this way. Bolivia had the smallest proportion of citizens who perceive of corruption as common, but still, 68% of respondents think corruption is common.

Overall, well under half of the citizens in Latin American countries have confidence in their national legislatures and governments—37% and 43%, respectively. Across countries, trust in legislatures and governments varies widely. Peruvians and Paraguayans are least trusting of their legislature and government. Less than 20% of citizens in both countries responded in the highest three categories of trust in the legislature, and only 24% and 28%, respectively, trust the central government as a whole. The most trusting citizens are in Uruguay and Mexico. In Uruguay, 58% of respondents trust the legislature and 63% trust the national government. Fifty-seven percent of Mexicans trust in the legislature and the same percentage trust the national government. Chileans also rank near the top on both measures, with 44% trusting the legislature and 57% trusting the central government.

TABLE 7.1. Citizen Attitudes toward Government

Country	Democratic Satisfaction		Corruption		Trust in Legislature		Trust in Government	
	Mean	Gender Gap	Mean	Gender Gap	Mean	Gender Gap	Mean	Gender Gap
Uruguay	80	−2	75	3	58	0	63	−4
Bolivia	60	−4*	68	−1	35	−1	—	—
Chile	59	−2	71	−2	44	3	57	6*
Colombia	59	1	80	−2	39	1	53	1
Costa Rica	59	1	84	−2	42	1	47	4
Venezuela	59	−3	88	−1	44	−1	49	−4
Mexico	52	5*	75	−6*	57	1	57	3
El Salvador	47	1	72	−6*	43	−1	49	8**
Panama	47	−3	77	−1	37	−1	39	1
Nicaragua	43	−4	88	0	28	3	27	3
Brazil	42	−3	79	1	30	−3	42	−6*
Guatemala	41	3	91	−1	30	−1	32	0
Peru	37	5*	86	−5*	18	2	24	3
Paraguay	20	−3	—	—	19	−1	28	−6*
Region average	51	−.01	79	−.02**	37	0	43	.01*

The gender gap calculation subtracts men's average responses from women's average responses.

Democratic satisfaction = percentage of respondents who are "very satisfied" or "satisfied" with their democracy. Corruption = percentage of respondents who think corruption among public officials is "very common" or "common." Trust in the legislature = percentage of respondents who trust in the legislature (top three categories from seven-category response scale). Trust in the government = percentage of respondents who trust the central government (top three categories from seven-category response scale). The trust in government and corruption questions were not asked as part of the surveys conducted in Bolivia and Paraguay, respectively.

Statistical significance tests are chi-square tests for the individual countries and *t*-tests for difference of the region averages.*$p < .05$, **$p < .01$

The table also reveals important information about the extent to which a gender gap exists in citizen views of government in Latin America. Only a small amount of research has been conducted on gender gaps in political participation or political attitudes in Latin America, and none of it examines democratic satisfaction, corruption perceptions, or political trust (Morgan et al. 2008; Desposato and Norrander 2009). Overall, gender differences in attitudes toward government are quite small. For democratic satisfaction, only Bolivia, Mexico, and Peru have statistically significant gender gaps and the direction of the gap varies. In Bolivia, women are less satisfied with democracy than men, but in Mexico and Peru, they are more satisfied than men. Only three countries have significant gender gaps in how citizens perceive of corruption—Mexico, El Salvador, and Peru—and in all three women think the government is less corrupt than do men. No significant gender differences emerge in trust in the legislature but several gender gaps exist for trust in the government. In El Salvador and Chile, more women than men trust government (a gap of 8% and 6%, respectively), but in Brazil and Paraguay, fewer women than men are trusting of government (a gender gap of 6% in each country). The overwhelming similarity in how women and men view government provides initial evidence that women's formal, descriptive, and substantive representation may have similar effects on men's and women's symbolic representation.

Measures of Women's Representation

I use several variables to measure formal, descriptive, and substantive representation. Similar to chapter 2, I measure formal representation as the use of gender quotas and the proportionality of electoral rules.[5] As of 2006, half of the countries in this study (7 of 14) had a gender quota—Bolivia, Brazil, Costa Rica, Mexico, Panama, Paraguay, and Peru (table 7.2).[6] The presence of a gender quota measures institutional support for women's representation. It sends signals to citizens about how representative their democracy is, makes them feel better about their government, and encourages a belief that they have an opportunity to participate (Zetterberg 2009). Senator Luz María Sapag of Argentina emphasized the symbolic role that quotas can play: "I believe that the system of quotas has lowered the obstacles for women to occupy political spaces and maybe opened the possibility to more women who previously did not see politics as a space for development. I perceive great support from the people for participation of women in politics. I suppose that comes from our greater sensibility. And, especially I feel great support from women" (Sapag 2006).

The second measure of formal representation is electoral disproportionality. Latin American lower chambers or unicameral legislatures all use proportional representation (PR) or mixed PR-SMD rules, making useless the

TABLE 7.2. Descriptive Statistics on Formal, Descriptive, and Substantive Representation

Country	Gender Quota	Electoral Disproportionality	Percentage of Legislature Female	Percentage of Laws on Women's Issues
Bolivia	Yes	4.00	16.92	1.26
Brazil	Yes	3.00	9.00	1.25
Chile	No	6.82	15.00	4.67
Colombia	No	5.58	9.63	3.17
Costa Rica	Yes	7.53	38.60	1.70
El Salvador	No	1.62	16.67	1.47
Guatemala	No	7.75	13.33	0.54
Mexico	Yes	4.74	24.60	2.42
Nicaragua	No	3.26	21.73	0.00
Panama	Yes	14.06	16.66	2.33
Paraguay	Yes	8.50	10.00	0.25
Peru	Yes	13.95	28.33	1.75
Uruguay	No	1.32	12.24	3.03
Venezuela	No	10.91	17.36	1.12

All data are observed for the election or legislative term immediately prior to the 2006 Americas Barometer survey.

dichotomous distinction between proportional and majoritarian systems that is common in studies of how institutions affect citizen views of democracy (Anderson and Guillory 1997; Aarts and Thomassen 2008). Instead, I measure the *degree* of proportionality of electoral rules using the least squares index of electoral disproportionality calculated for the election immediately prior to the 2006 Americas Barometer survey (Gallagher and Mitchell 2008). More disproportional electoral rules signal to citizens that government does not value representativeness and political inclusiveness, which may generate feelings of frustration among citizens with their representative democracy. The proportionality of electoral rules in the 14 Latin American democracies varies widely, as shown in table 7.2. In the election just prior to the 2006 survey, the most proportional countries were Uruguay (index = 1.32) and El Salvador (index = 1.62). The least proportional were Panama and Peru, with disproportionality indices equaling 14.06 and 13.95, respectively.

To measure descriptive representation, I use two variables. The first is the percentage of the legislature that was female in 2006 (IPU 2006). As chapter 1 described, the presence of women in office may have an important effect on citizens' view of democracy by making the legislature more representative. Particularly for women, seeing individuals in office who "look like" them may make them feel that they are more represented than when women are largely absent from the legislative arena. Regardless of whether the women actually do anything to benefit women, their mere presence could have a symbolic effect on the electorate. Indeed, some studies of political engagement and participation have found that citizens in countries or districts with female representatives are more engaged in politics than those with less female representation (Hansen 1997; Norris and Franklin 1997; Sapiro and Conover 1997; High-Pippert and Comer 1998; Atkeson 2003; Atkeson and Carrillo 2007; Wolbrecht and Campbell 2007; Karp and Banducci 2008; Desposato and Norrander 2009; Reingold and Harrell forthcoming). In the 14 Latin American democracies under study here, women's legislative representation varied from a low of 9% in Brazil to a high of 39% in Costa Rica (table 7.2).

Also an indicator of descriptive representation of women, but quite distinct from women's *legislative* representation, is women's representation in other parts of government such as the executive branch (Lawless 2004; Atkeson and Carrillo 2007). In 2006, one country—Chile—had a female head of state. To distinguish women's legislative representation from executive representation, I included a variable measuring whether or not the country had a female chief executive. Essentially, this variable is a dummy variable for Chile so the variable must be interpreted carefully and tentatively. However, it may offer some leverage for future studies when women have greater representation in the executive branch. I also tested the role played by women's representation in presidential cabinets with a variable measuring the percentage of the cabinet that was female in 2006.[7] This variable is not included in the main models presented below because of the need to preserve degrees of freedom at the country level, but I discuss the results of models with this variable throughout the chapter.

Finally, substantive representation of women may affect how the public feels about its government. As I have shown in this book, there are many ways to assess substantive representation of women. For the purpose of this chapter, however, I need a single measure of substantive representation that is clear and visible to citizens. Following my earlier study with Mishler (2005, 409), I measure substantive representation as policy responsiveness—"the extent to which representatives enact laws and implement policies that are responsive to the needs or demands of citizens." Due to data limitations, our measure of policy responsiveness focused on the presence of gender equality in a limited number of policy areas—political rights, social rights, national maternity leave policy, and marriage and divorce laws—to determine whether simply having more gender equality policies implies greater citizen trust in the legislature. Somewhat surprisingly, we found little effect.

In this chapter, I focus on whether the passage of women's issue policies in a much broader range of issue areas generates more positive responses from citizens. Specifically, I collected data on the laws that the national legislature passed in the congress immediately prior to the 2006 Americas Barometer survey and calculated the percentage of laws that focused on women's issues.[8] As table 7.2 shows, these laws compose less than 5% of laws in Latin American countries. It ranges from 0 in Nicaragua to 4.7% in Chile.[9] Measuring women's policy passage in this way allows a test of whether governments that pass more policies that target women produce citizens who feel more represented by their government. It also tests what other studies have often assumed to be the case but have not directly tested—that women in office will produce more policy outputs which together (or in turn) makes people feel more satisfied with democracy (Phillips 1995; Karp and Banducci 2008).

Other Explanations for Citizen Attitudes

Studies of mass attitudes have identified a range of factors that affect how citizens feel about their governments, such as demographics, political interest, views of the economy, and the nature of a country's democracy. To isolate the effect of women's representation from these other possible explanations, I control for these factors in this chapter's analyses. Specifically, I control for the effect of key demographic factors that the Americas Barometer survey measured and are commonly found to affect citizen views of representative democracy—gender, age, religion, education, and marital status.[10] These demographic controls account for the fact that women, older citizens, those affiliated with conservative religions, those with higher education levels, and married citizens may have different political attitudes.[11]

In addition to these demographics, a respondent's level of political interest and perception of the country's economic performance are likely determinants of citizens' views of their representative democracy (Farrell and McAllister 2006). Citizens with greater political interest pay more attention to the news and to what governments are doing, and are more likely to be critical of the government's performance. Research has long reported a strong link between economic performance and citizen views of government (Hibbing and Patterson 1994; Mishler and Rose 1997; Dalton 2004). When the economy is doing well (or is perceived to be doing well by the people), citizens feel better about their political leaders and governments, more generally. When the economy is doing poorly, citizens blame their political leaders and feel frustrated with how their government functions. In the analyses below, I use two questions from the Americas Barometer that measure political interest and perceptions of economic performance.[12]

In addition to these individual-level variables, I control for a country-level variable that assesses the nature of the country's democracy—the number of years that a country has been democratic.[13] Several studies focusing on the developed world have found that length of democracy is related to citizen views of democracy, with citizens in older democracies being more satisfied with government than those in newer democracies (Norris 1999; Farrell and McAllister 2006; Aarts and Thomassen 2008). Yet, in a region of democracies that transitioned very recently, it may be that citizens in the older democracies become less positive about their governments as the euphoria from the transition itself wears off (Lagos 2001). Over time, positive feelings about democracy may decline as citizens become disillusioned with it.

The remainder of this chapter examines each of the four measures of symbolic representation—democratic satisfaction, perceptions of corruption, trust in the legislature, and trust in the government—in turn theorizing the specific effects that women's representation should have on citizen attitudes toward government and then discussing the results of the statistical analyses. The conclusion brings these findings together, drawing overarching conclusions about how formal, descriptive, and substantive representation affect symbolic representation of women.

Democratic Satisfaction

A large body of research exists that tries to explain variation in citizen satisfaction with democracy across countries. Most research focuses on how cultural, structural, institutional, and contextual factors affect citizen satisfaction with democracy. Cultural and structural accounts, for example, focus on explaining varying levels of satisfaction with democracy among citizens drawing on their socioeconomic status, education levels, age, ideology, religious preferences, and social capital (Hibbing and Theiss-Morse 1995; Nye et al. 1997; Inglehart 1999). Institutional accounts, in contrast, have found that consensus-based political systems and preferential voting systems foster satisfaction with democracy (Anderson and Guillory 1997; Lijphart 1999; Norris 1999; Anderson et al. 2005; Farrell and McAllister 2006; Aarts and Thomassen 2008). Studies emphasizing contextual variables have found that characteristics of the political environment—such as recent economic and political performance, corruption levels, "democraticness," and the age of democracy—affect citizen satisfaction with democracy (Nye et al. 1997; Klingemann 1999; Miller and Listhaug 1999; Anderson and Tverdova 2003; Anderson et al. 2005; Aarts and Thomassen 2008).

Very little research, however, has examined how women's representation could affect citizen satisfaction with the functioning of democracy. I argue that women's representation may affect satisfaction with democracy because it can send signals to citizens that government values representativeness and the participation of diverse groups. Aarts and Thomassen (2008), for example, examined how formal institutions affect citizen satisfaction with democracy and found that citizens are more strongly affected by institutions that embody representativeness than institutions that emphasize accountability. In this way, women-friendly electoral institutions, such as more proportional rules and gender quotas, could send cues to citizens about the representativeness of the election process and increase citizen satisfaction with democracy. Women's descriptive representation may also signal greater democratic satisfaction. Some research on the relationship between gender and political participation argues that the presence of women as candidates or in office shapes political behavior by providing symbolic cues that women can compete for and win public office (Sapiro and Conover 1997; Atkeson 2003; Atkeson and Carrillo 2007; Wolbrecht and Campbell 2007; Karp and Banducci 2008). Karp and Banducci (2008) extend this line of thinking to political attitudes and show that women's presence explains attitudes toward democracy as well. Lastly, legislatures that actually produce more policy on women's issues may also send signals that government is representative of women and boost citizen satisfaction with democracy.

Table 7.3 reports the results of statistical models analyzing the effect of women's formal, substantive, and descriptive representation on citizen satisfaction with democracy in Latin America. Because the dependent variable, satisfaction with democracy, is an ordinal 4-point scale, the most appropriate model is a partial proportional odds model that estimates the probability that a respondent will be in a given category as compared to others.[14] The model produces three sets of estimates for the different categories of the dependent variable—one for "very dissatisfied" with democracy, one for "dissatisfied" with democracy, and one for "satisfied" with democracy. "Very satisfied" is the baseline, and consequently excluded, category. The interpretation of the statistical results is a bit counterintuitive because the model estimates the likelihood that respondents will *not* be in the

TABLE 7.3. Explaining Citizen Satisfaction with Democracy

	Interaction Model			Noninteraction Model		
	Very Dissatisfied	Dissatisfied	Satisfied	Very Dissatisfied	Dissatisfied	Satisfied
Formal Representation						
Gender quota	−.251	−.251	−.251	−.253	−.253	−.253
	(.270)	(.270)	(.270)	(.239)	(.239)	(.239)
Disproportionality	−.084**	−.064	−.049	−.063**	−.055**	−.032
	(.039)	(.040)	(.042)	(.029)	(.023)	(.033)
Descriptive Representation						
Female president	−.905*	−.722**	−.288	−.841**	−.724**	−.309
	(.490)	(.374)	(.497)	(.497)	(.378)	(.485)
% legislature female	.042**	.007	−.027	.050***	.014	−.011
	(.020)	(.016)	(.017)	(.017)	(.011)	(.016)
Substantive Representation						
Women's issue policies	.429***	.199*	−.105	.368**	.277***	.042
	(.160)	(.105)	(.130)	(.143)	(.089)	(.130)
Interactions						
Gender * quota	−.177	.026	.121	—	—	—
	(.142)	(.094)	(.144)			
Gender * disproportionality	.016	.006	.011	—	—	—
	(.013)	(.013)	(.026)			
Gender * % legislature female	.006	.004	.009	—	—	—
	(.007)	(.005)	(.008)			
Gender * women's policies	−.039	.052*	.100	—	—	—
	(.032)	(.029)	(.069)			
Gender	.086	−.161	−.598***	.156***	.053	−.111
	(.173)	(.137)	(.205)	(.045)	(.051)	(.085)
Age	−.001	.004***	.010***	−.001	.004***	.010***
	(.003)	(.001)	(.003)	(.002)	(.001)	(.003)
Catholic	.013	.061	−.093	.005	.062	−.091
	(.068)	(.047)	(.097)	(.069)	(.047)	(.097)
Education level	−.077	−.133***	−.057	−.078	−.133***	−.056
	(.072)	(.047)	(.040)	(.072)	(.047)	(.040)
Married	.009	.009	.009	.011	.011	.011
	(.033)	(.033)	(.033)	(.033)	(.033)	(.033)
Political interest	.026	.133***	.253***	.024	.134***	.255***
	(.061)	(.038)	(.049)	(.062)	(.038)	(.050)
Perception of economy	.770***	.608***	.449***	.768***	.608***	.447***

continued

TABLE 7.3. (Continued)

	Interaction Model			Noninteraction Model		
	Very Dissatisfied	Dissatisfied	Satisfied	Very Dissatisfied	Dissatisfied	Satisfied
	(.054)	(.065)	(.108)	(.052)	(.065)	(.107)
Years democratic	−.004	.010**	.027***	−.003	.010**	.027***
	(.009)	(.005)	(.008)	(.009)	(.005)	(.008)
Constant	−.139	−2.055***	−4.897***	−.196	−2.163***	−5.123***
	(.323)	(.344)	(.618)	(.311)	(.308)	(.600)

Partial proportional odds estimates with robust standard errors clustered around country in parentheses. Baseline category is "very satisfied."
Respondent $N = 20535$; country $N = 14$
Interaction model chi-square = 87.641
Noninteractive model chi-square = 157.578
$^{*}p < .10$, $^{**}p < .05$, $^{***}p < .01$

current category or any lower category (e.g., "dissatisfied" or "very dissatisfied"), and instead, be in a higher category (e.g., "satisfied" or "very satisfied"; Williams 2006). In other words, a positive coefficient for "very dissatisfied" implies that as the values of the independent variable increase, the likelihood is greater that citizens will *not* be "very dissatisfied" and instead will be more satisfied with democracy. A negative coefficient for "very dissatisfied" means that increasing values of the independent variable lead to less satisfaction with democracy (i.e., a greater likelihood that the respondent *will* be "very dissatisfied" with democracy).

In table 7.3, I present two models. The *interaction model* tests whether the dimensions of women's representation have different effects on female citizens than on male citizens. The *noninteraction model* illustrates the effect of different dimensions of women's representation on all citizens regardless of gender. The interactive model reveals that women's representation does not have significantly different effects on women than on men (most of the interaction terms are not statistically significant). The only interaction term that attains statistical significance at the 0.10 level is the interaction between citizen gender and women's issue policies. The interaction reveals that women's issue policies have a larger effect on women's satisfaction with democracy than on men's satisfaction with democracy. However, calculations of the predicted probabilities that women and men will have varying levels of satisfaction with democracy show very small substantive differences.[15] The overwhelming absence of significant interactions means that if women's representation affects citizens, it affects women and men in similar ways. Consequently, I focus on the noninteractive model in the remainder of this section.

In terms of formal representation, the presence of gender quotas does little to shape citizen support for democracy,[16] but disproportional electoral rules substantially dampen satisfaction with democracy. Specifically, citizens in disproportional

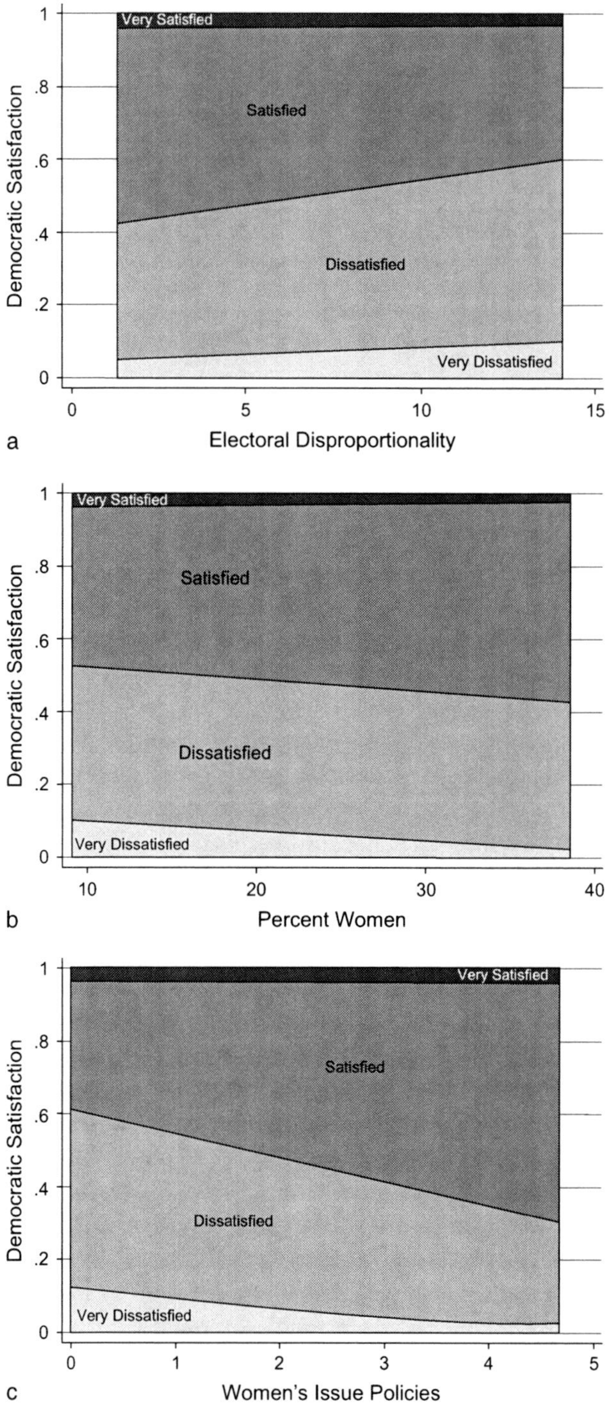
Very Satisfied
Satisfied
Dissatisfied
Very Dissatisfied
Democratic Satisfaction
0
.2
.4
.6
.8
1
0
5
10
15
a
Electoral Disproportionality
Very Satisfied
Satisfied
Dissatisfied
Very Dissatisfied
Democratic Satisfaction
10
20
30
40
b
Percent Women
Very Satisfied
Satisfied
Dissatisfied
Very Dissatisfied
Democratic Satisfaction
0
1
2
3
4
5
c
Women's Issue Policies

systems are less likely to be in the higher response categories than in the "very dissatisfied" and "dissatisfied" categories. Figure 7.1a illustrates the relationship between electoral disproportionality and satisfaction with democracy more clearly. As disproportionality increases from its minimum value in the dataset, 1.32, to its maximum value, 14.06, the predicted proportion of respondents who fall into the "very dissatisfied" and "dissatisfied" categories gets larger. The cumulative proportion of respondents in those categories when disproportionality is at its lowest is 42.5, but it grows to 59.8 when disproportionality is at its highest. At the same time, of course, the proportion of respondents predicted to fall into the "satisfied" category decreases significantly from 53.5 to 37.5. No significant change occurs in the proportion of respondents predicted to be "very satisfied." Citizens in countries where electoral rules are highly disproportional are less satisfied with their democracy than citizens in countries with more proportional electoral rules. This supports the theory that rules that promote representativeness can send signals of inclusiveness to citizens that make them feel better about their representative democracy.

Descriptive representation of women also helps to explain citizen satisfaction with democracy in Latin America. Table 7.3 shows that greater representation of women in the legislature makes citizens more satisfied with democracy. Specifically, as the percentage of women in the legislature increases, the probability increases that respondents will be "dissatisfied," "satisfied," and "very satisfied" as compared to "very dissatisfied." No significant differences exist, however, for the likelihood of not being in the "dissatisfied" and "satisfied" response categories as compared to higher categories, which suggests that the key effect of women's legislative representation is moving citizens out of the "very dissatisfied" category. Again, this can be illustrated more clearly with a graph of predicted probabilities. Figure 7.1b shows that fewer citizens are predicted to be "very dissatisfied" when the percentage of women in the legislature is large compared to when it is small. When legislative representation of women is at its lowest value in the dataset—9% in Brazil—10.5% of citizens are predicted to be "very dissatisfied" with democracy, all else being equal. When legislative representation is at its highest—38.6% in Costa Rica—the model predicts that only 2.6% of citizens will be "very dissatisfied" with democracy. Instead, they are more likely to be "satisfied" with democracy, as can be seen from the slightly larger shaded area for "satisfied" at higher values of women's legislative representation. The substantive effect of women's legislative representation is not huge, but it does support the argument that the mere presence of women in office

FIGURE 7.1. (a) Effect of Electoral Disproportionality on Citizen Satisfaction with Democracy (cumulative probabilities). (b) Effect of Women's Legislative Representation on Citizen Satisfaction with Democracy (cumulative probabilities). (c) Effect of Women's Policy Passage on Citizen Satisfaction with Democracy (cumulative probabilities).

can make citizens feel better about their democracy and lead to higher levels of democratic satisfaction, all else being equal.

In contrast, the presence of a female president makes citizens in Latin American countries less likely to be satisfied with democracy. This effect is probably driven by the fact that this variable is "1" only for the case of Chile, because Chile was the only country with a female president in 2006. It may not be having a female president that dampens satisfaction with democracy in Chile compared to other countries but something else unique about Chile that is captured by this variable. Another way to test the effect of descriptive representation is to measure the percentage of the cabinet that is female. Models with this variable, however, do not reveal any statistically significant effect. Representation of women in the executive branch, below the position of chief executive, has no influence on satisfaction with representative democracy.

Finally, the passage of women's issue policies affects democratic satisfaction in Latin America. Table 7.3 reveals that countries that passed more women's issue laws have citizens that are more likely to be satisfied with democracy. The variable's estimates are significant only in the models for "very dissatisfied" and "dissatisfied," but they do show that the passage of more women's laws decreases the likelihood that citizens will be "very dissatisfied" and "dissatisfied" with democracy. Figure 7.1c shows the substantial size of the effect. The predicted proportion of citizens who are "dissatisfied" and "very dissatisfied" with democracy drops from just over 60% when no women's issue bills are passed to only 30% when almost 5% of the laws passed by the most recent congress were related to women. At the same time, the probability that respondents will be "satisfied" with democracy increases dramatically from 0.354 to 0.658.

The cases of Nicaragua and Chile illustrate this finding nicely. Nicaragua passed no women's issue laws in the 2002–2006 congress, and the majority of citizens reported low levels of satisfaction with democracy in 2006—only 43% were "satisfied" or "very satisfied" with democracy. In contrast, 4.7% of the laws passed in 2002–2006 in Chile were related to women and nearly 60% of citizens were "satisfied" or "very satisfied" with democracy. This pattern has statistical support even after accounting for the fact that Chile had a female president in 2006, has more disproportional electoral rules, has a stronger economy that is viewed more favorably by citizens, and has more educated citizens than Nicaragua. Passing policies that deal with women's issues, regardless of whether women are in the legislature pushing women's issues through the agenda, makes citizens, both women and men, feel better about their representative democracy and contributes to higher levels of citizen satisfaction with democracy.

Perceptions of Corruption

Most research on corruption focuses on the causes of political corruption (see, for example, Rose-Ackerman 1999; Treisman 2000; Gerring and Thacker 2004;

Tavits 2007) and the consequences of corruption for democracy and democratic stability (Seligson 2002; Anderson and Tverdova 2003; Chang and Chu 2006; Seligson 2006). Yet, understanding citizen *perceptions* of corruption and why they vary within and across countries is also important (Davis et al. 2004; Canache and Allison 2005). If citizens perceive of little corruption, regardless of how much corruption is actually taking place, prospects for democracy may remain high. If citizens perceive of extensive corruption, then democracies may have more trouble governing and may face an uncertain future.

Can increased women's representation decrease citizen perceptions of the pervasiveness of corruption in government and, as a result, foster greater democratic legitimacy and stability? Deputy Josefina Abdala of the Argentine Chamber of Deputies believes that women "are more honest. It pleases me to be able to say that 99% of women are honest. I don't mean to say that men are not honest but I believe that there is less corruption among women, for now" (Abdala 2006). Actually, little empirical evidence exists that women indeed are less corrupt than men. However, the myth that women are less corrupt than men is widespread (Goetz 2007). Both women and men alike believe that women have a moral superiority to men that makes them less corrupt, and this greater integrity is thought to transfer into the political arena with women (Goetz 2007). This view of women has led to politicians targeting women for jobs that have been tarnished by corruption. In Colombia, for example, when Nancy Gutierrez Castañeda was elected interim president of the Senate in 1999, some people believed it was partly because being a woman would restore integrity to the Senate after a corruption scandal involving the male leadership. Goetz (2007) pointed out that the argument that women's election may lead to less corruption is unfounded and even detrimental to women's progress in politics because it reinforces the very notions that have long kept women out of politics. Although her concern is justified, she offers only anecdotal evidence to counter recent claims that women are less corrupt than men.

Below, I offer empirical evidence that, in fact, increased women's representation does influence perceptions of corruption among all citizens in Latin America. Regardless of whether women are actually less corrupt than men or not, the prevalence of the myth makes it likely that greater women's representation decreases citizens' perceptions of the pervasiveness of corruption in government. If citizens believe that women are less corrupt than men, then institutions that favor the election of women, a larger presence of women in office, and actual attention to women's issue policies may lead to perceptions of less corruption. Part of this may be a function of the high levels of corruption in the male-dominated military governments that dominate recent Latin American history. If people widely believe that women are less corrupt and more compromising than men, then society might view a legislature with more women as an improvement over the past.

Models 1a and 1b of table 7.4 report the results of statistical models explaining citizen perceptions of the prevalence of corruption in Latin American governments.[17]

TABLE 7.4. Explaining Citizen Perceptions of Corruption, Legislative Trust, and Government Trust

	Model 1a: Corruption	Model 1b: Corruption	Model 2a: Legislative Trust	Model 2b: Legislative Trust	Model 3a: Government Trust	Model 3b: Government Trust
Formal Representation						
Gender quota	.304	.308*	−.138	−.142	−.035	−.069
	(.193)	(.177)	(.102)	(.092)	(.067)	(.059)
Disproportionality	−.037***	−.039***	−.033*	−.030**	−.020	−.028***
	(.014)	(.011)	(.019)	(.015)	(.014)	(.009)
Descriptive Representation						
Female president	.185	.185	−.493***	−.491***	−.332***	−.330***
	(.224)	(.225)	(.165)	(.166)	(.107)	(.107)
% Legislature female	−.016	−.011	.011*	.012***	−.008	−.000
	(.013)	(.011)	(.006)	(.004)	(.005)	(.005)
Substantive Representation						
Women's issue policies	.120*	.119**	.172***	.186***	.158***	.177***
	(.067)	(.056)	(.056)	(.046)	(.039)	(.035)
Interaction Terms						
Gender * quota	.009	—	−.009	—	−.067**	—
	(.045)		(.026)		(.030)	
Gender * disproportionality	−.001	—	.002	—	−.005	—
	(.004)		(.003)		(.005)	
Gender * % legislature female	.003*	—	.000	—	.005***	—
	(.002)		(.001)		(.001)	
Gender * women's policies	−.000	—	.010	—	.012	—
	(.012)		(.010)		(.009)	
Gender	−.013	.046***	.028	.064***	.041	.089***
	(.057)	(.015)	(.039)	(.013)	(.044)	(.018)
Age	−.006***	−.006***	.001	.001	.003**	.003**

	(.002)	(.002)	(.001)	(.001)	(.001)	(.001)
Catholic	.019	.019	.035**	.035**	.032	.033
	(.023)	(.023)	(.017)	(.017)	(.029)	(.029)
Education level	–.143***	–.143***	–.090***	–.090***	–.125***	–.126***
	(.032)	(.032)	(.022)	(.022)	(.029)	(.029)
Married	–.034*	–.033*	–.012	–.012	.019	.019
	(.018)	(.018)	(.023)	(.024)	(.016)	(.016)
Political interest	.017	.018	.127***	.127***	.126***	.126***
	(.017)	(.017)	(.018)	(.018)	(.027)	(.027)
Perception of economy	.115***	.115***	.212***	.212***	.297***	.297***
	(.014)	(.014)	(.036)	(.036)	(.040)	(.040)
Years democratic	.002	.002	—	—	.006**	.006**
	(.004)	(.004)			(.003)	(.003)
Cut1	–.285	–.255	–.091	–.073	.072	.095
	(.270)	(.261)	(.230)	(.219)	(.189)	(.184)
Cut2	.655**	.685***	.311	.328	.446**	.470***
	(.267)	(.260)	(.219)	(.208)	(.175)	(.171)
Cut3	1.615***	1.645***	.745***	.763***	.841***	.864***
	(.244)	(.238)	(.210)	(.199)	(.164)	(.162)
Cut4	—	—	1.291***	1.309***	1.337***	1.360***
			(.201)	(.191)	(.162)	(.160)
Cut5	—	—	1.917***	1.934***	1.893***	1.917***
			(.195)	(.185)	(.160)	(.160)
Cut6	—	—	2.479***	2.497***	2.447***	2.470***
			(.194)	(.184)	(.158)	(.160)
Respondent *N*	19272	19272	20589	20589	18281	18281
Country *N*	13	13	14	14	13	13
Chi-squared	518.45	18267.37	43484.467	2055.664	2434.77	55726.58

Ordered probit estimates with robust standard errors clustered around country in parentheses.
$^{*}p < .10$, $^{**}p < .05$, $^{***}p < .01$

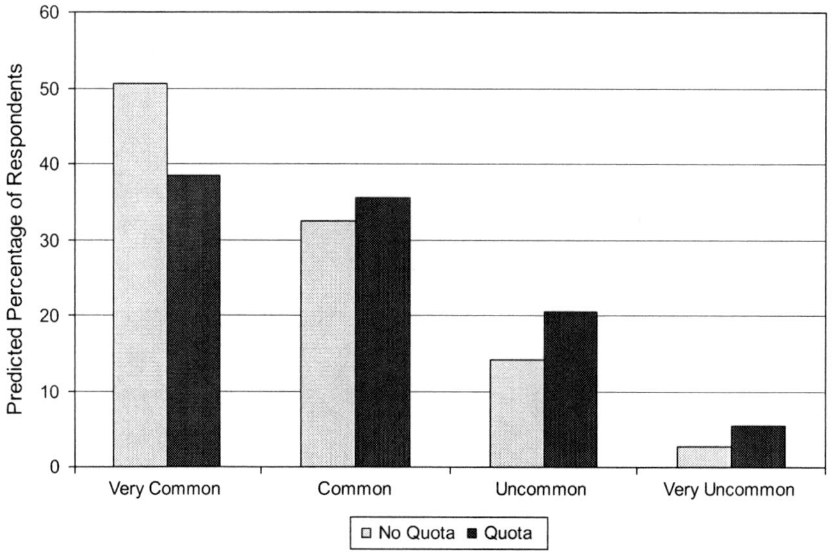

FIGURE 7.2. Effect of Gender Quotas on Corruption Perceptions

Model 1a includes interaction terms that test whether women's representation has different effects on female and male citizens, whereas Model 1b estimates the effect of women's formal, descriptive, and substantive representation on all citizens (no interactions). Recall that high levels of corruption are coded as low levels of the dependent variable (1 and 2), and low levels of corruption have higher values (3 and 4). Consequently, positive coefficients in the table suggest a lower likelihood of respondents perceiving corruption, whereas negative coefficients suggest a higher probability of perceiving corruption.

The only interaction term in Model 1a that suggests statistically different effects of women's representation on women's and men's views of corruption is the interaction between gender and the percentage of the legislature that is female ($b = 0.003$, $p = 0.09$). Yet, calculating the conditional effects and standard errors of women's descriptive representation on women and men reveals no statistically significant differences for women or men. Further, there is no statistically significant gender gap in views of corruption within the range of women's descriptive representation among countries under study (9% of the legislature is female in Brazil, and 38.6% of the legislature is female in Costa Rica).

Model 1b estimates the effect of women's representation on all citizens' corruption perceptions. The model shows that formal and substantive representation of women affect citizen views of corruption but descriptive representation does not. Both the presence of gender quotas and the degree of disproportionality in the country's legislative electoral rules influence how common citizens think corruption is in government. Citizens in countries with a gender quota

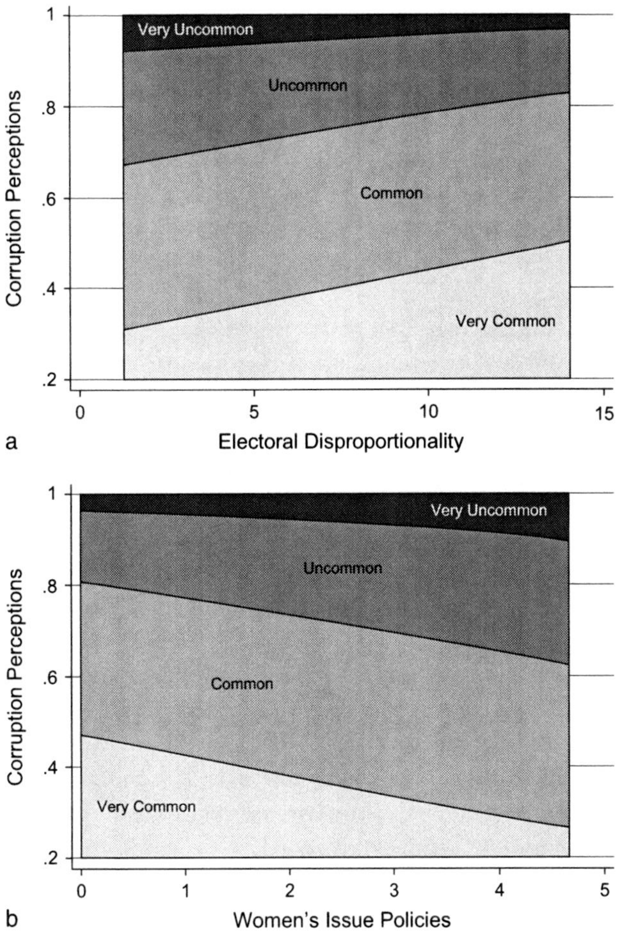

a

b

FIGURE 7.3. (a) Effect of Disproportionality on Perceptions of the Prevalence of Corruption in Government (cumulative probabilities). (b) Effect of Women's Policy Passage on Perceptions of the Prevalence of Corruption in Government (cumulative probabilities).

view government corruption as less common than citizens in countries without quotas.[18] Figure 7.2 shows the predicted proportion of respondents in countries with quotas and without quotas who perceive of varying degrees of corruption in government. Where gender quotas are absent, just over 50% of respondents think corruption is "very common." Where quotas are in place, only 38% of citizens are predicted to see corruption as "very common." The differences are smaller for those who view corruption as "common," "uncommon," and "very uncommon."

Similarly, respondents in countries with more disproportional electoral rules are more likely to feel that government corruption is common. Figure 7.3a shows the substantively strong effect of electoral disproportionality. The predicted proportion of people who think corruption is "very common" increases from 31% at the lowest level of electoral disproportionality to 50% at the highest level. The model predicts that respondents who think that it is "very common" or "common" increases from 67% to 82% as the degree of electoral disproportionality moves from its lowest level to its highest level. Clearly, the use of women-friendly electoral institutions sends positive signals to citizens about government and yields a public that is less likely to think the government is corrupt than when less women-friendly institutions are in place.

In contrast, the two measures of descriptive representation have no statistically significant effect. Citizens in Chile, a country run by a female president, do not perceive of any less corruption than do citizens in other Latin American countries. Similarly, citizens in countries with more women in the legislature are no less likely to feel that the government is corrupt than citizens in countries with fewer women in office.[19] This also holds for representation of women in the cabinet. I tested a model that included the percentage of the cabinet that was female in 2006, but this too had no statistically significant effect (models not shown).

The passage of women's policies also yields a lower probability of perceiving corruption in Latin America. Citizens perceive governments that pass more women's issue laws to be less corrupt than governments that expend less effort addressing women's concerns. Figure 7.3b illustrates this graphically. The percentage of citizens predicted to think that corruption is "very common" is significantly higher (47%) when no women's issue laws are passed than when women's issue laws comprise almost 5% of the laws passed by a congress (26%). Only 19% of citizens are predicted to believe that government corruption is "uncommon" or "very uncommon" when no women's issue laws are passed, but this grows to 38% if women's issue laws are 4.7% of all laws passed. Governments that address women's issues through national legislation make citizens feel that the government is attending to citizen concerns and have citizens who are less likely to think that corruption is rampant in government.

Trust in the Legislature

Perhaps the clearest relationship between the three dimensions of women's legislative representation and symbolic representation should exist when symbolic representation is measured as citizen trust in the legislative body itself. The previous two measures of symbolic representation focused on citizen affect toward two aspects of general government performance. Focusing on how citizens feel about the legislature, specifically, should reveal most clearly how they respond to women-friendly electoral rules, women's presence in the legislature, and the passage of women's policies.

The literature on political trust is extensive (for a review, see Levi and Stoker 2000). Explanations for institutional trust tend to fit one of two theories—cultural or institutional (Mishler and Rose 2001). Cultural explanations focus on citizens' long-standing beliefs and cultural norms and argue that the values citizens hold determine how much confidence they have in political institutions (Almond and Verba 1963; Putnam 1993; Jackman and Miller 1996). Institutional explanations argue that political trust emerges from citizen evaluations of how well governments perform (North 1990; Hibbing and Patterson 1994; Mishler and Rose 1997; Norris 1999). When institutions perform well and produce positive outputs and outcomes, citizens evaluate those institutions positively. When they perform poorly, citizens become frustrated with government institutions and register that frustration as distrust.

Theorizing that women's representation could affect citizen trust in legislatures is relatively new. The reason that it may matter in Latin America is that citizens have grown tired and frustrated with many years of political and economic turmoil. They may associate this turmoil with the male-dominated political environment. Bringing into politics new faces, new parties, new ethnic representation, or more women could bring hope for change to the Latin American public. Indeed, the notion of populism in Latin America refers to political leaders who seek political support from outside traditional political sectors and often promote an agenda of change for the country (Weyland 1996). The election of presidents Alberto Fujimori in Peru, Evo Morales in Bolivia, and Hugo Chavez in Venezuela resulted in part from their ability to generate political support from nontraditional political sectors and their promises of significant political and economic changes. In a similar way, the recent adoption of women-friendly electoral rules, the election of more women to legislatures, and the passage of women's issue policies could signal to constituents a change in the political system. Deputy Graciela Rosso of the Argentine Peronist Party notes that "the people have a perception that women work harder and have more conviction than men. We are less likely to forgo our principles. We make agreements with other politicians but not at the expense of our principles. This gets transmitted to the people" (Rosso 2006). Women's institutions, presence, and policy may represent improvements in how legislatures operate, making citizens feel more trust in the legislature.

Existing findings on the relationship between women's representation and trust in the legislature have been mixed (Lawless 2004; Schwindt-Bayer and Mishler 2005; Ulbig 2007; Zetterberg 2009). Lawless (2004) found little support for a link between women's presence in the U.S. Congress and political trust. Neither male nor female constituents are more likely to approve of Congress or have greater trust in the federal government when they have a female representative or senator or when the percentage of Congress or their state legislature that is female increases. Similarly, Gay (2002) found no support for the idea that greater racial representation in the U.S. Congress affects constituents' perceptions. Ulbig

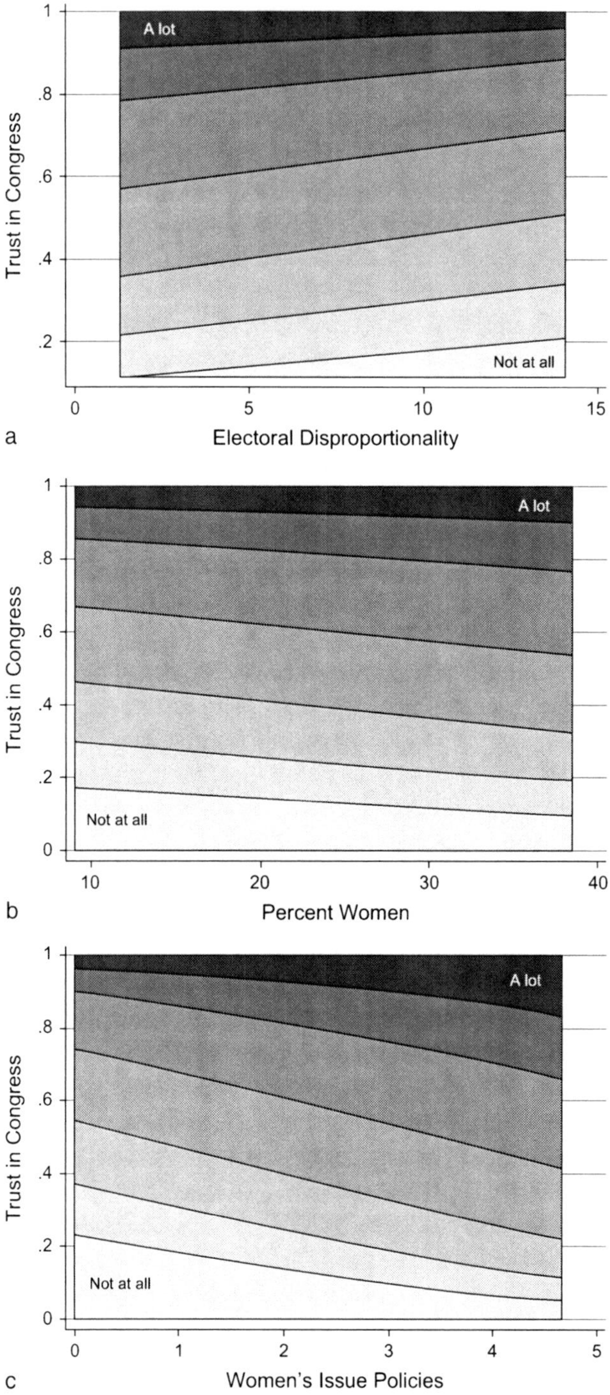
A lot
Not at all
Trust in Congress
1
.8
.6
.4
.2
0
5
10
15
a
Electoral Disproportionality
A lot
Not at all
Trust in Congress
1
.8
.6
.4
.2
0
10
20
30
40
b
Percent Women
A lot
Not at all
Trust in Congress
1
.8
.6
.4
.2
0
1
2
3
4
5
c
Women's Issue Policies

(2007), however, found that women's representation on municipal councils in the United States does lead to women having greater political trust and men having less political trust. In Latin America, Zetterberg (2009) found no empirical relationship between the adoption of gender quota laws and an index combining women's trust in the legislature with their trust in political parties, nor does he find an effect for the presence of women in legislatures. In contrast, my cross-regional comparative study with Mishler (Schwindt-Bayer and Mishler 2005) found that descriptive representation of women in legislatures is linked to higher levels of legislative trust in both men and women. We also found that more proportional electoral systems—an indicator of formal representation of women—enhance legislative trust.

Models 2a and 2b in table 7.4 show the results of statistical models explaining citizen trust in the legislature in Latin America.[20] Again, formal, descriptive, and substantive representation have no significantly different effects on women's and men's trust in the legislature. None of the interaction terms in Model 2a are statistically significant. Instead, women's representation affects citizen trust in the legislature for all citizens, both women and men (Model 2b). The only measure that does not affect citizen trust in the legislatures is the use of gender quotas.[21] All other measures affect both men's and women's trust in the legislature. For formal representation, the more disproportional the electoral system, the less likely citizens are to trust the legislature. In other words, Latin American countries with electoral rules that result in a more proportional distribution of seats to votes and send signals that government prioritizes representativeness have citizens with greater trust in the legislature than countries with less proportional rules. Figure 7.4a shows that as disproportionality increases, the probability that respondents will fall into the three lowest levels of trust gets significantly larger. In the most proportional systems, the predicted percentage of respondents in the lowest three categories is 36%. It increases to 51% in the least proportional systems. At the same time, the proportion of respondents predicted to have the highest three levels of trust gets smaller as electoral disproportionality increases. The predicted percentage of citizens who have high levels of trust in the legislature is 43% in the most proportional systems and only 27% in the least proportional systems. More proportional electoral rules produce citizens who are more trusting in the legislature.

Women's descriptive representation also has a significant effect on trust in congress. Model 2b shows that as the proportion of the legislature that is female

FIGURE 7.4. (a) Effect of Disproportionality on Trust in the Legislature (cumulative probabilities). (b) Effect of Percentage of the Legislature that Is Female on Trust in the Legislature (cumulative probabilities). (c) Effect of Women's Policy Passage on Trust in the Legislature (cumulative probabilities).

increases, the probability that citizens trust the legislature increases as well. Figure 7.4b shows the substantive size of the effect more clearly. When the percentage of the legislature that is female is at its lowest observed value in the dataset, 9% (Brazil), the proportion of respondents who have little trust in the legislature (respond 1, 2, or 3 on the 7-point scale) is 46%. When the percentage of the legislature that is female is at its highest observed value, 38.6% (Costa Rica), the predicted percentage of citizens with little trust in the legislature is only 33%. More citizens trust the legislature in countries where larger numbers of women are elected to the national legislature.

Having a female chief executive, however, decreases trust in the legislature. Citizens in Chile tend to have lower levels of trust in their congress than citizens in the other countries that do not have a female president. This relationship also holds when the model includes a measure of the percentage of cabinet ministers that are female (model not shown). Having more female ministers generates a lower likelihood of high levels of trust in congress. Consequently, electing women to the legislature boosts trust in the legislature, but electing or appointing women in the executive branch dampens legislative trust regardless of how many women are in the legislature.

The empirical analysis also supports the hypothesis that women's substantive representation helps to explain varying levels of citizens' legislative trust in Latin America. The passage of more women's policies leads to a higher probability that citizens will have greater trust in the legislature. As figure 7.4c shows, the effect is quite dramatic. When no women's issue laws are passed by the legislature, as in Nicaragua's 2002–2006 congress, more citizens distrust the legislature (lowest three levels of trust: 1, 2, 3) than trust it (highest three levels of trust: 5, 6, 7). The predicted proportion of respondents who distrust the legislature is 55%, compared to 25% who do have confidence in it. Twenty percent of respondents are predicted to neither trust nor distrust the legislature. When 4.7% of the laws passed by the legislature are women's issue laws, as in Chile's 2002–2006 congress, those predictions more than reverse themselves. Fifty-eight percent of respondents are predicted to trust the legislature, compared to 23% who do not. The proportion that neither trust nor distrust congress remains near constant at 19%. The passage of women's issue policies has a substantial effect on the level of confidence that the public has in the national legislature.

Focusing on symbolic representation as citizen trust in the legislature reveals that citizen trust in Latin American legislatures is shaped, in part, by greater formal, descriptive, and substantive representation of women. Further, women's representation contributes to higher levels of trust among both women and men in society. Although gender quotas have no independent effect, electoral disproportionality, the presence of women in the legislature, and legislative attention to women's issues yields male and female citizens who are more trusting of the legislature than citizens in countries with lower levels of women's representation. Each of these dimensions sends positive signals to the public that generates feelings of being more represented and enhances citizen affect toward the legislature. Of course, as table 7.1 showed, overall levels of legislative trust are low in Latin America and citizens reveal greater frustration toward their congresses than they do trust. But some of the variation in trust across countries appears to be linked to greater representation of women in some Latin American countries. Citizens in most countries are distrustful of legislatures in general, but they are less distrustful in countries that use more proportional electoral rules, elect women to the legislature, and pass women's issue policies. This suggests that improving women's representation could play a role in improving citizen affect toward national legislatures in Latin America.

Trust in the Government

Women's legislative representation is directly linked to legislative confidence, but does it also increase confidence in the national government more broadly? Although trust in legislatures and trust in government are correlated with one another in Latin America ($r = 0.65$), they are not identical. Citizens may think more highly of the president than the congress, and this could improve their level of trust in the overall government as compared to their trust in the legislature. Women's representation also may affect legislative trust and government trust in different ways. On one hand, the measures of electoral institutions, women's numbers in the legislature, and laws passed by congress may not affect government trust in general because they measure aspects of women's legislative representation more specifically. On the other hand, a positive response to increases in women's formal, descriptive, and substantive representation in the legislature could work to increase trust in the overall government as well.

Models 3a and 3b of table 7.4 show how women's representation affects trust in the national governments of Latin American countries. The results are quite similar to those for legislative trust with the exception that gender quotas and the percentage of the legislature that is female appear to have significantly different effects on women and men (Model 3a). Calculating the marginal effects from the interaction terms reveals that quotas have no effect on men's trust in government but they significantly *depress* women's trust in government ($b = -0.10$, $p = 0.06$). The difference between the effect that quotas have on women and men, however, is substantively small (less than 0.05). Descriptive representation also appears to have different effects on women and men (the interaction term for women's legislative representation and gender is statistically significant), but closer examination of the statistical and substantive significance of the interaction reveals this is minimal. Calculating the marginal effects and conditional standard errors revealed that the percentage of women in the legislature does not have significant effects on men ($b = -0.008$, $p = 0.15$) or on women ($b = -0.003$, $p = 0.58$). Even though the interaction terms for gender and quotas and gender and the percentage of the legislature that is female are statistically significant, women's representation has only minimally different effects on women and men.

As a result, I focus on the noninteractive model (Model 3b) and describe the effects that formal, descriptive, and substantive representation have on citizens in general (both women and men) in Latin America. This model shows that the most significant dimensions of women's representation for trust in the government are formal and substantive representation. Formal representation of women, measured as electoral disproportionality and the passage of laws related to women increase the probability of trust in government, just as they did trust in the legislature. Graphs of the predicted effects of these variables look much like those presented above for trust in the legislature (figures 7.4a and 7.4c) so I do not report them again here. The predicted values are still illustrative, however. When electoral rules are at their most proportional level in the dataset (1.32), the predicted proportion of respondents with the lowest three levels of trust is 0.31 compared to 0.44 when rules are most disproportional (14.06). The opposite pattern exists for the highest three levels of trust. When rules are most proportional, the predicted percentage of citizens who have strong trust in government is 50%. When the rules are very disproportional, the percentage is 37%, all else being equal. More proportional rules yield a greater likelihood that citizens will trust government.

For women's policy passage, passing no policies yields predicted probabilities for citizen trust in government of 0.48 in the lowest three levels of trust and a probability of only 0.32 for the highest three levels of government trust. When almost 5% of laws passed are women's issue laws, the probability that respondents will fall into the lowest three levels of trust is 0.20 compared to 0.64 for the highest three levels. Similar to the findings for legislative trust, the effect of passing women's policies on government trust in Latin America is substantial.

Neither the presence of gender quotas nor legislative representation of women has significant effects on governmental trust. This contrasts sharply with the findings for legislative trust in which women's presence in the legislature did matter. Although citizens clearly link women's legislative representation to their trust in the legislature, this does not translate into greater confidence in the central government.[22] This suggests that citizens in Latin America do distinguish among government bodies and allocate different levels of trust across them. Descriptive representation measured as having a female president, however, dampens trust in government. Citizens in Chile are less trusting of government than are citizens in countries without a female president. Citizens are also less trusting of government in countries with more women in the president's cabinet (model not shown). Thus, formal and substantive representation of women increase governmental trust, as hypothesized, but descriptive representation has no effect when measured as women's legislative representation and a negative effect when measured as women's executive representation. Although similar, explanations for legislative trust and governmental trust are clearly different.

Conclusion

The findings from this chapter provide clear and substantial support for the theory that formal, descriptive, and substantive representation are related to symbolic representation. Citizens in Latin America have varying levels of satisfaction with democracy, perceptions of the pervasiveness of corruption, and trust in the legislature and central government. Across countries, these variations are partially explained by women-friendly electoral rules, a larger presence of women holding seats in the legislature, and the passage of laws related to women and women's issues. Specifically, formal representation measured as electoral disproportionality dampens democratic satisfaction, legislative trust, and governmental trust, and contributes to citizens viewing government as more corrupt than in countries with more proportional electoral rules. Similarly, substantive representation of women through the passage of women's issue policies produces citizens with higher levels of democratic satisfaction, legislative trust, government trust, and citizens who perceive of less corruption in government. Descriptive representation, measured as the percentage of the legislature that is female, increases satisfaction with democracy and legislative trust but has no significant effects on perceptions of corruption or governmental trust. Much as the presence of women has been found to increase women's political engagement and participation in politics (Hansen 1997; Norris and Franklin 1997; Sapiro and Conover 1997; High-Pippert and Comer 1998; Atkeson 2003; Atkeson and Carrillo 2007; Wolbrecht and Campbell 2007; Karp and Banducci 2008; Desposato and Norrander 2009; Reingold and Harrell forthcoming), it also affects women's and men's attitudes toward government (Lawless 2004; Schwindt-Bayer and Mishler 2005; Ulbig 2007). Gender quotas, however, do not systematically affect symbolic representation in Latin America, correlating with the results of a recent study of the symbolic effect of quotas in Mexico (Zetterberg 2009).

Also important is that women's representation improves both men's and women's affect toward government and democracy in Latin America. Rather than leading only to increased symbolic representation of women, formal, descriptive, and substantive representation affect symbolic representation of women *and* men. This suggests that the use of more proportional electoral rules, the presence of women, and the passage of women-friendly policies not only sends signals to women that democracy is representative of women but sends more general signals of representativeness and inclusiveness that also make men feel better about their government. This supports some of the recent gender and politics research that finds women's representation has similar effects on men's and women's attitudes and behavior (Lawless 2004; Schwindt-Bayer and Mishler 2005; Atkeson and Carrillo 2007; Karp and Banducci 2008; Kittilson and Schwindt-Bayer 2008). Lindgren et al. (2009) go even one step further to show that women are *better* representatives than men. They found that the policy attitudes of constituents and representatives in India are more in line when the representative is female. Women's representation may not only be good for women but good for representative democracy, more generally.

Although this chapter does not test whether improving women's representation over time leads to greater affect toward government, a time-serial theory is valid and deserves empirical testing. A longitudinal study could provide even stronger evidence that increases in the election of women affect symbolic representation or that variations in the passage of women's policies yield varying levels of symbolic representation. Indeed, improving levels of women's representation in Latin America may be a way to improve the often low levels of citizen satisfaction with democracy, trust in legislatures and governments, and perceptions of government corruption. However, as Argentine deputy Alicia Tate notes, "It will take a long time" (Tate 2006).

Overall, this chapter shows that more proportional electoral rules, the passage of women's issue policies, and the election of women (to a lesser extent), send positive signals to citizens that their governments are representing them and produce citizens who feel better about their government. This underscores that the four dimensions of representation are linked together, as theorized in chapter 1. Chapter 2 showed that formal representation helps to explain descriptive representation, and chapters 3–6 showed that descriptive representation leads to greater substantive representation of women. This chapter shows that all three of these dimensions of representation play a role in explaining symbolic representation. The dimensions of women's representation are indeed interrelated.

8

Conclusion

Women's Representation in Latin American Legislatures

In the past 30 years, the participation of women in politics has increased dramatically in many Latin American countries. Women have been elected president in four Latin American democracies, they have been appointed to ministerial posts in many countries, and their legislative representation has reached unprecedented levels in several countries. Yet, the causes and consequences of women's influx into Latin American politics are still unclear, as are the reasons why some countries lag behind others in legislative representation of women. This book helps to fill this void with a study of women and Latin American legislatures. Framing the study in terms of representation, I argued that women's representation has four interrelated dimensions and that studying all four—and their relationships to one another—is necessary to present a complete picture of the causes and consequences of women's representation in Latin America. I then presented empirical tests of the way in which formal representation shapes descriptive representation of women, formal and descriptive representation affect substantive representation, and formal, descriptive, and substantive representation of women influence symbolic representation. The results of these analyses paint a much more complete picture of women's representation in Latin America than currently exists.

Women's Representation in Latin America

Ultimately, this book shows that women in Latin America are indeed gaining a presence in politics but are not achieving full political power. Thanks in part to the adoption of gender quotas, women have won legislative seats in record numbers in recent years. Wide variation persists across countries, but all democracies have witnessed at least some increase in the number of women in office, and many have substantially improved descriptive representation of women. Inside Latin American legislatures, women are working to represent women and women's issues in the political arena. They place high priority on female constituents and women's issues and promote these priorities in their legislative work. They sponsor bills on women's issues, promote women's issues in legislative debates, sit on and chair women's issue committees, and do home style on behalf of female constituents and women's issues. In society, female citizens (along with male citizens) positively perceive the use of electoral rules that facilitate women's election, the presence of women in office, and the passage of women's policies and respond to women's representation with greater support for representative democracy.

Despite these advances, however, women's substantive representation in Latin America is hindered by the gendered legislative environment that obstructs women's access to real political power. Female representatives rarely hold leadership positions in legislative chambers, and they do not serve as chairs of powerful committees or those traditionally considered to be in men's domain. In some countries, they get marginalized into sponsoring bills on women's domain issues rather than men's domain issues and sitting on committees traditionally considered to be in women's domain rather than getting appointed to the full range of legislative committees. This occurs despite women and men placing similar priority on women's and men's domain issues and is more extensive in Argentina, where formal institutions may be exacerbating it. Women are winning office in larger numbers, representing women, and symbolically effecting representative democracy, but they are not always given the opportunity to represent their constituents fully.

Descriptive Representation of Women

In Latin America, women have been elected to legislatures in increasing numbers over the past 30 years, but their success has been uneven across countries. Although a large literature explaining variation in descriptive representation of women exists, it rarely focuses specifically on Latin America (see, however, Jones 2009). This book shows that the nature of electoral institutions is an important explanation for women's descriptive representation in Latin

America. The use of more proportional electoral rules and the adoption of gender quotas in 12 Latin American countries have led to countries having more women in office than countries without these institutions. More important, however, *strong* quotas—those that mandate larger proportions of the ballot to be female, specific placement of women on the ballot, and enforcement mechanisms—get many more women in office than weaker quotas when they are implemented under quota-compatible electoral rules, such as closed-list proportional representation.

Although some studies have found little to no effect for gender quotas on women's representation (Reynolds 1999; Htun and Jones 2002; Kunovich and Paxton 2005; Tremblay 2007; Schmidt 2008a), this book's findings support the growing body of research that shows that quotas do matter, once the type of quota and political context are taken into account (Caul 1999; Kittilson 2006; Stockemer 2008; Tripp and Kang 2008; Jones 2009; Schwindt-Bayer 2009). The adoption of quotas and the use of more proportional electoral rules have been key mechanisms for generating gender representativeness in a region with limited internal variation in cultural and socioeconomic contexts. Women are still descriptively underrepresented in all Latin American legislatures, but the use of quotas and more proportional rules have brought several countries close to parity.

Substantive Representation

Since the 1970s, the dominant view of women in Latin American politics has been that they are *supermadres.* In her seminal book on women in Latin American politics, Elsa Chaney (1979) found that the experiences of motherhood translated into women's roles in the political sphere and was a defining characteristic of women in Latin American politics. The characterization of women as supermadres has two important implications. One is that women in politics are not so much *feminist* as *feminine.* The other is that women in politics will think and act differently than men because of their experience of motherhood and their gendered roles as homemakers and caregivers. This book counters these arguments. It suggests that women in Latin American politics have changed significantly since Chaney's research in the late 1960s. Women in Latin American legislatures today are driven by feminist concerns with women's equality and women's rights and represent these feminist concerns in office. They are also driven by an interest in representing a wide range of constituents and political issues, not just those that emerge from their traditional gendered roles. They are not always able to do this effectively, but this is likely due to marginalization by the masculinized legislature—not women's preferences. Perhaps a better characterization of women in Latin American politics today is *supermujer* (or superwoman) rather than supermadre. Women are working not only to represent women but to be effective representatives of all constituents.

The Effect of Descriptive Representation on Substantive Representation

Evidence for this new characterization of women in Latin American politics comes from chapters 3–6, which examine how formal and descriptive representation affect substantive representation. First and foremost, the chapters show that female representatives in Argentina, Colombia, and Costa Rica substantively represent women by prioritizing female constituents, women's groups, and women's rights issues more than male representatives and by acting on behalf of these groups and issues more than men.[1] Much like women in legislatures in many regions of the world (see, for example, Thomas 1994; Carroll 2001; Swers 2002; Childs 2004), women in Latin American legislatures do place a special priority on promoting a feminist agenda and are able to translate this priority into legislative action. Specifically, female representatives are more likely than male representatives to sponsor and cosponsor bills on women's issues in all three countries,[2] discuss women's issues in floor debates in Argentina and the Colombian lower house, sit on committees that study women's issue bills in Argentina and Costa Rica, and get elected to leadership positions on women's issue committees in Argentina and Costa Rica.[3] Women in Argentina, Colombia, and Costa Rica also more frequently attend events sponsored by women's groups, spend more time serving female constituents, do more casework related to women's equality issues, and are more likely to see themselves as role models for women and girls in society than male representatives. Both in their issue attitudes and their actions on behalf of women's issues, female legislators tend to see themselves as having a responsibility to represent women and promote women's issues in the legislative process. In this way, the election of women does lead to substantive representation of women in Latin America.

Women in office, however, are not always able to represent nonwomen-specific constituencies to the same extent as men in the three countries due to marginalization of women by the male-dominated and gendered legislative environment. Chapter 3 shows that male and female representatives place similar priority on a wide range of constituents, such as minorities, the poor, environmentalists, business owners, blue-collar workers, professionals, farmers, and fishermen. It also shows that female representatives place similar priority or higher priority on a range of legislative activities (sponsoring bills, sitting on committees, doing constituency service, and giving public speeches and presentations)[4] and that they place similar priority on issues traditionally considered to be in the "men's domain" and the "women's domain."[5] Yet, chapters 4–6 show that women represent these constituents and issues in some of their legislative activities but not all, and that there is variation across countries in the extent to which women represent constituents in their legislative behavior.

Two areas of legislative behavior in which female representatives in Argentina, Colombia, and Costa Rica are able to translate their political preferences into political action are speaking in debates and home style. In all three countries, female and male representatives were similar in their perceptions of how often they speak on the floor on behalf of women's and men's domain issues. They differed only in the frequency of participating in floor debates, regardless of issue area in Argentina, and in committee debates, regardless of issue in Costa Rica. Female representatives also "act for" their constituents similarly to male representatives in their home-style activities. In Argentina, Colombia, and Costa Rica, female and male legislators allocate their time to the district, present themselves to their constituents, and explain their legislative activities in similar ways. Women and men attend events in their district with similar frequency and participate in activities sponsored by various interest groups, such as professional groups, environmental groups, agricultural groups, and unions, with similar frequency. They do constituency service for a similar number of hours (except in the Colombian Senate, where women do less service than men) and report giving similar numbers of public presentations and public speeches (except in the Colombian lower house, where women report doing this more often than men). Some gender differences in home style do emerge in how frequently legislators visit their district, the types of casework they do, and how often they speak to the press, but these differences do not consistently help or hurt women and the differences are not present in any clear pattern across the three countries.

Marginalization of women, however, appears in other legislative activities and varies across countries. This is apparent in the findings that male and female representatives have similar attitudes about the importance of a diverse array of political issues and the importance of different parts of the political process but are not always able to translate these priorities into legislative action. I argue that marginalization in Latin America results from the male-dominated legislative institution that has long-standing norms that privilege men (Marx 1992; Rodríguez 2003; Franceschet 2005). The masculine values and norms of the legislative environment are one of many factors that intervene in the translation of preferences to behavior and can result in marginalization of women. In some cases, marginalization is a result of overt or covert discrimination by men who believe that women are less qualified, incapable of leading, or otherwise poorly suited for the job. In many cases, however, it results from the fact that the male-dominated legislative environment has norms, values, and networks that exclude women, intentionally or unintentionally (Marx 1992; Rodríguez 2003; Franceschet 2005). Because women are not fully integrated into the political system or integrated into traditional political networks, women are overlooked by male representatives and male leaders who seek political allies in their legislative work (Rodríguez 2003). When the male majority looks for candidates to nominate for chamber president, they look within their traditional legislative networks and find men. When important committee seats need to be filled or important bills need to be sponsored, male representatives turn to those who have been influential in their informal legislative networks and find men. When men seek cosponsors for bills on the economy, foreign affairs, and the public sphere, more generally, they think of the men with whom they have long worked on these issues. The prevalence of masculine values and norms in Latin American legislatures creates an environment that breeds marginalization of women. Although male and female representatives enter Latin American legislatures with similar issue preferences and priorities for legislative activities, the empirical study in this book shows that male bias in the legislature can intervene and marginalize women into more traditionally female areas of legislative work and into activities that afford women less political power.

Marginalization of women is most evident in Argentina. Despite having similar political preferences to men, female representatives in Argentina are more likely to sponsor legislation traditionally in women's domain, specifically education bills (and health to a lesser extent), and are less likely to sponsor bills traditionally in men's domain, such as the economy and fiscal affairs. They are also more likely to sit on committees and hold committee leadership positions along traditional gender lines. Women are more likely to be on education and health committees and are less likely to sit on economics, budget, agriculture, and foreign affairs committees. They also have never served as president of any committee that deals with issues of the budget, economics, or foreign affairs. Finally, no woman has ever served as president of the Chamber of Deputies, and only four women have served as vice president since 1983.

Marginalization is less evident in Costa Rica, where female deputies have had greater success translating the priority they place on nonwomen-specific constituencies into bill sponsorship behavior but have struggled to achieve full representation on a diverse array of committees and in chamber leadership. Specifically, women in Costa Rica have been more likely to sit on the social committee and less likely to sit on the budget committee. Although they have served as vice president and secretary of many different committees, they too are less likely to serve as president of men's domain committees, particularly the very powerful budget committee in which no woman has ever been president. Women have been elected to chamber leadership posts as secretary and vice president, but only two women have served as president of the chamber between 1974 and 2006.

Finally, this type of marginalization has been weakest, though not nonexistent, in Colombia, where female representatives have been relatively successful representing a wide range of political issues and constituents, though less so in the Senate than in the Chamber of Representatives. The only gender differences in bill sponsorship appeared in the Colombian Senate, where female senators individually sponsor health bills more often than men and agriculture and foreign affairs bills less often than men. In general, female representatives in the Chamber of Representatives and the Senate have achieved proportional representation on both women's domain and men's domain committees. Yet, they still lack access to committee leadership positions. No women had served as president of the economics committee, budget committee, or foreign affairs committee in the Chamber of Representatives through 2006, and in the Senate, the only committee that has had a female president is the social committee. Colombia also lags in electing women to the chamber presidency. Only two women served in that post in the Chamber of Representatives between 1974 and 2006 and only one in the Senate.

These statistical findings are also supported by anecdotal evidence from women in the three legislatures and related research. Interviews with female representatives, conversations with leaders of women's groups, and reports written by female leaders and activists in Argentina, Colombia, and Costa Rica underscore that discrimination against women persists in legislatures despite greater gender equality in society, the election of more women, and pressure from women's groups both inside and outside the countries. Women frequently noted the presence of a *machista* culture in the legislature that they deal with on a daily basis. As Piedad Córdoba (2002, 5) of Colombia described it,

> Although the procedural rules of the Colombian Congress are themselves neutral, the cultural norms on which they are based give them a macho bias. There is no other explanations for the fact that women who garner some of the highest vote totals have not been elected as president of the House, president of the Senate, or chairperson of a congressional committee, but men who are elected to Congress with minimal vote totals are elected to such positions. This macho bias explains the systematic refusal of Congress to approve the creation of committees to oversee the international commitments to eliminate discrimination against women, or to monitor the gender component of development plans, without offering any explanation.

Female representatives also face discrimination due to the fact that they are not integrated into existing political networks and due to informal norms by which decision making takes place. They often noted the difficulty of working in an environment in which meetings and floor debates run until late hours of the night, men gather after hours to discuss politics, internal documents addressed to female representatives still start with *Señor Diputado*, and women are held to different standards than men (Augsburger 2006). Evidence of self-imposed discrimination also exists. Women sometimes exhibited a lack of confidence in their own abilities to be leaders or to work in certain policy areas, and consequently, they defer to men who are more assertive and more confident about their abilities to lead and to legislate. Summing this nicely, Piedad Córdoba asserted, "With a few exceptions, the notion continues to weigh in [men's] minds that politics is a matter for men, and they see women members of Congress as immersed in a world that is not their own" (2002, 5).

The role of discrimination or marginalization of women in Latin American politics has been highlighted in other research on the region as well (Marx 1992; Rivera-Cira 1993; Rodríguez 2003; Franceschet 2005; Heath et al. 2005). For example, Rodríguez (2003) reported that female legislators in Mexico see marginalization of women as a significant problem and one that is evidenced by the fact that women have not gained access to areas of legislative work that are traditionally male-dominated. She noted that "most respondents were convinced that gender segregation within the political sphere is pervasive, and that proof of this lies in the fact that so many female officeholders are denied the opportunity to work in traditionally 'masculine' areas" (138).

Marginalization of women has also been prevalent in Latin American political parties. Marx (1992), for example, found that significant numbers of activists in the UCR party in Argentina in the 1980s were women, but their presence among the party base did not translate into a presence of women in party leadership. She argued that women in the party faced an environment dominated by masculine norms, values, hidden rules, and structures that were used to discriminate against women (24). Although the women that she surveyed did not see open or intentional discrimination against women in the party, they did think that women faced unnecessary obstacles getting into decision making positions in the party. Susan Franceschet (2005) also found marginalization of women in Chilean political parties. She argued that Chilean parties have a male-dominated environment with "cultural and discursive practices" that are inhospitable to women and that this deters women from getting actively involved in parties (Franceschet 2005, 90). Because parties often look for candidates from within the party, women get overlooked as candidates for congressional elections, which leads to women's low levels of representativeness in Chile's National Congress.

In Latin America, more generally, Rivera-Cira's (1993) survey of women in legislatures in the early 1990s found that the few women who had been elected to legislatures had little impact on the legislative process. She suggested that unequal access to political resources was a key factor. Women in office must deal with "lack of technical assistance; scarce support for their initiatives by some of their male colleagues, political parties, and other women; scarce access to positions of decision-making in the Congress and in political parties and, possibly, a stronger and more constant critique of them than male parliamentarians are subjected to" (Rivera-Cira 1993, 61). The Chilean representatives that Rivera-Cira interviewed underscored the problem of women's marginalization. For example, a Chilean deputy noted, "I have the impression that although no one dares to publicly doubt the intellectual capacity of women, private doubts persist. Men still today are surprised when they find an intelligent, prepared, and hard-working woman. There is a lack of confidence among men in the political capacity of women." (Rivera-Cira 1993, 37–38). A Chilean senator was quoted as saying that "the men impose their own rules, establish nighttime meetings and all of them conspire against the participation of women. . . . There is an enormous lack of confidence in our intellectual capacity, and the most serious, our character. They believe that we will break down. The men possess a lot of machista prejudices, such as that women are temperamental" (Rivera-Cira 1993, 37).

This book provides an empirical study of the extent to which one kind of marginalization of women exists in Latin American legislatures and finds that many of the findings of previous scholars are supported. Discrimination against women by the gendered legislative environment and marginalization of women in this male-dominated atmosphere is a fixture in many aspects of politics and in many different Latin American countries. It does, however, vary in pervasiveness across countries.

The Mediating Role of Formal Representation

To what extent are the differences in women's marginalization across countries a result of electoral institutions that create strong political parties or encourage affirmative action for women? There is some evidence that formal representation does mediate substantive representation and that the incentives that electoral rules provide to strengthen the power of parties and party leaders over representatives in office exacerbates marginalization of women. Gender differences in legislative behavior are strongest when electoral rules give male party leaders significant power over the actions of legislators—as in Argentina—and they are weakest in Colombia's personalistic electoral system. Yet, the case of Costa Rica complicates the comparison because it too is a party-centered system, but it exhibits less marginalization of women than Argentina did. Thus, although this study offers some evidence to support the theory that electoral rules that provide incentives for legislators to be responsive to their party or their local district may facilitate women's marginalization, the evidence is not conclusive. It instead underscores the need for additional research on how formal representation mediates substantive representation (Macaulay 2006).

The study also finds little support for the hypothesis that the adoption of gender quotas leads to greater marginalization of women. First, a cross-national comparison shows that Argentina, which has had gender quotas since 1991, does exhibit the most marginalization of women, but Costa Rica, which has had quotas since 1996, has less. Second, in the longitudinal analyses that were conducted (for bill sponsorship, committees, and leadership), marginalization of women generally existed both before and after the adoption of quotas in Argentina and Costa Rica. Women have been underrepresented in chamber and committee leadership in both periods and have exhibited similar bill sponsorship patterns in the pre- and postquota period in Costa Rica. In terms of committee assignments, greater marginalization of women has existed since the adoption of quotas in Argentina, but in Costa Rica, it has been weaker since 1998. Thus, the findings offer no consistent evidence that the adoption of quotas has exacerbated women's marginalization in bill sponsorship, committee assignments, or leadership. The impact that quotas have on the legislative process needs significantly more empirical attention, but thus far, few findings from this book or existing research support the concern of quota critics that quotas hurt women's substantive representation (Xydias 2007; Devlin and Elgie 2008; Zetterberg 2008; see, however, Franceschet and Piscopo 2008).

Symbolic Representation

Finally, this book shows that formal, descriptive, and substantive representation affect symbolic representation of women *and men* in Latin America. Although the citizenry's overall satisfaction with democracy and trust in the legislature and government have declined over time in Latin America to near-record lows, citizens in Latin American countries that use more proportional electoral rules, have more women in the legislature, and pass women's issue policies are more satisfied with democracy, perceive less corruption, and are more trusting of the legislature and government than citizens in countries with lower levels of women's formal, descriptive, and substantive representation. These findings are similar for both women and men, suggesting that citizens respond not only to the benefits of incorporating women into politics but of making government more generally diverse, representative, and inclusive.

The findings for symbolic representation have important implications because a significant amount of gender and politics research argues that the inclusion of women is necessary to improve the quality of representative democracy. Democracy is "rule by the people," and given that women are half of the population throughout the world, representation of women is a fundamental aspect of democracy (Phillips 1995; Williams 1998; Young 2000). This study offers empirical evidence that women's formal, descriptive, and substantive representation can strengthen representative democracy. The use of more proportional electoral rules, the election of women, and the passage of women's policies influence the way citizens feel about their government and improves their image of representative democracy. Electing women to national legislatures is good for representative democracy not only because descriptive representation implies that women as half of the population *should* be represented in the legislature, but because electing women leads to greater representation of female constituents and women's issues and improves citizens' perceptions of their democracy.

Summary

This book has shown that the four forms of women's representation are linked together in Latin America, much as I theorized in chapter 1. Formal representation leads to more descriptive representation of women, both of which affect substantive representation. All three influence symbolic representation of both women and men, making Latin American citizens more supportive of their representative democracies. At the same time, this study reveals the practical implications of this. Women are getting elected in large numbers in many countries, such as Argentina and Costa Rica, and are successfully bringing greater legislative attention to women's equality issues. The presence of women in office also improves citizen perceptions of government, along with proportional electoral rules and passing women's issue policies. At the same time, however, women are not being fully integrated into legislatures. Women face marginalization from the male-dominated legislative environment that prevents them from getting into positions of political leadership, and in some countries, pushes them into work on social issues while keeping them out of work on economics, fiscal affairs, and foreign affairs issues. As a result, female legislators in some Latin American countries are not able to fully represent their constituents.

Implications for Research on Women's Representation

The empirical study in this book focused on Latin America. However, the theory and findings of the book have important implications for research on women and politics more broadly. First, this book underscores that looking at the concept of representation through its multiple dimensions is necessary to get a full picture of women's representation. Doing so avoids inaccurate explanations such as concluding that women are represented simply because 40% of the legislature is female or concluding that they are not represented because only 10% of the legislature is female. It shows that women may be underrepresented in one aspect of representation but can be more represented in others. In Latin America, for example, descriptive representation of women is higher in Argentina and Costa Rica than it is in Colombia. Substantive representation, however, has greater gender equality in Colombia than in Argentina and Costa Rica. To accurately interpret the nature of women's representation in other regions of the world, a comprehensive view of representation is needed.

This study of women's representation also underscores the need to consider the diversity that underlies the concept of *substantive representation* (Celis 2008; Franceschet and Piscopo 2008). Substantive representation refers to both political issues and legislative activities. It also encompasses the political attitudes of legislators, their legislative behavior, and the extent to which those attitudes translate into comparable behavior (Wangnerud 2000b; Dodson 2001; Childs 2004; Lovenduski 2005; Schwindt-Bayer 2006). Substantive representation is not only about policymaking but also includes other important aspects of the legislative process including committees, leadership, and home-style activities (Eulau and Karps 1977; Fenno 1978; Childs 2004). Finally, substantive representation involves the way in which representatives respond to female constituents and women's equality issues *and* the extent to which female representatives are able to function as representatives of all constituents, not just women (Dahlerup 1988; Thomas 1994; Carroll 2002; Lovenduski 2005; Grey 2006). This study of women's representation in Latin America illustrates the importance of considering the multifaceted nature of substantive representation. If this research had looked just at legislators' home-style activities or legislative debates, it would conclude that women are able to represent other constituents just as men are. By studying these activities alongside bill sponsorship, committee assignments, and leadership, however, I show that women are in fact marginalized in some of their legislative activities. Alternatively, if this research examined only representation of women and women's issues, it could draw conclusions only about the extent to which women represent women rather than about how effectively they represent issues that are not women-specific. A comprehensive conceptualization of substantive representation that emphasizes the diversity of ways in which representatives "act for" their constituents produces a much clearer and more complete picture of women's representation.

Finally, the multidimensional and integrative view of the concept of representation highlights a dimension of women's representation that is often overlooked—formal representation. Recent research emphasizes that political institutions are gendered and can mediate women's representation (Duerst-Lahti and Kelly 1995; Hawkesworth 2003). Yet, few studies have considered formal representation when studying women's representation. The comprehensive theory of representation offers a mechanism for incorporating institutions into this research through formal representation. As this study of Latin America shows, electoral institutions can play a role in explaining descriptive, substantive, and symbolic representation of women in Latin America. Gender quotas and districts with larger magnitudes help more women get elected to national legislatures, and proportional electoral rules improve citizen affect toward government. The way in which electoral rules provide incentives for party-centric behavior over personalistic behavior also are likely to make marginalization of women easier in legislative politics. The link between formal and substantive representation, in particular, needs much more attention, but this study underscores that formal representation is a key mechanism for explaining the nature of women's representation and why it varies across legislative chambers.

Conclusion

The causes and consequences of the election of women to Latin American legislatures in recent years are many. Among the primary causes are the widespread adoption of gender quotas throughout the region and the use of proportional electoral rules with large electoral districts. Thus, formal rules play a key role in explaining variation in descriptive representation of women in Latin America. Among the positive consequences of women's election to office are female legislators' representation of women and women's rights, their ability to represent constituents other than women in some legislative activities, and the positive feelings that their representation generates among women and men in society. The election of women to Latin American legislatures still has one persistent drawback, however. Women are winning seats but not gaining political power in all legislatures. They have not held important chamber or committee leadership positions with any regularity and, in some countries, are marginalized in the type of legislative work that they do. Marginalization of women hinders women's ability to represent their constituents effectively. Until Latin America's gendered legislatures begin to value women in office as equal and important political players, women will not attain real political power. Women's representation will continue to be incomplete.

Appendix A

Data Collection

Bill, Committee, and Leadership Data

I collected the data on bills legislators initiated from several sources in each country. In Argentina, bill data were available through the Chamber of Deputies website: http://www.diputados.gov.ar. In Costa Rica, the Legislative Assembly Archive maintains records from which I created a list of all bills initiated during the two congresses. In Colombia, I obtained records of bills from the Congress's *Oficina de la Secretaria* and the congressional archive. The data on committee assignments of legislators in Argentina and Colombia came from archival records in the three countries and were supplemented with data collected by Crisp et al. (2004). Finally, congressional records also supplied the data on which legislators held chamber leadership positions and committee leadership posts.

Survey of Legislators

For this project, I designed a 30-question survey instrument that taps into representatives' views of constituencies, policy priorities, debate participation, home style, and background information. When possible, I modeled questions after those in other women's representation surveys (Dodson and Carroll 1991; Thomas

1992; Reingold 2000). I also formulated questions specifically for this project to address issues that have not been examined in other studies.

The survey was conducted in Costa Rica in October of 2001 and in Colombia and Argentina during the summer of 2002. For Costa Rica and Colombia, legislators were in their last year of a 4-year term, allowing them to have gained considerable experience as representatives even if this was their first term in office. Argentine deputies were more than half finished with the 2001–2003 congressional session. Argentine deputies are elected to 4-year terms, but half of the deputies are reelected every 2 years, creating 2-year congresses. In all countries, the survey was either filled out in the presence of the legislator or, if legislators spent very little time in their offices, it was given to the legislator's staff with instructions for the legislator, not assistants, to complete it.

Response rates for the survey varied across the three countries. Overall, I surveyed 292 legislators—176 in Colombia, 50 in Costa Rica, and 68 in Argentina. Colombia and Costa Rica had very high response rates, 67% and 88% respectively, in part because I had access to the legislative office buildings and was able to visit offices regularly, explain the project directly to many legislators, and collect the surveys personally. The Argentine response rate was lower, 37%, but still large enough for analysis. In Argentina, I could not gain access to the legislative offices and instead hired staffers from the two major political parties to distribute and collect the survey. They were able to survey legislators only from the two major parties. Fortunately, the two largest parties (PJ and UCR) hold 182 of the 257 seats (71%), which is well over a majority of seats. All of the calculations and information in the chapters that analyze the survey results are based on the 182 seats held by the two major parties. Thus, the calculation of the response rate is somewhat inflated because it is the percent surveyed as a function of the number of legislators in the two large parties. When generalizing findings to the Argentine Chamber of Deputies as a whole, I am actually generalizing to the two main party blocs only.

Because of the small number of women in Costa Rica and Colombia, I tried to get as many female respondents as possible, making it likely that women would be overrepresented as respondents. Of the 34 women in the Colombian Congress, I surveyed 26 of them. In Costa Rica, I surveyed 10 of the 11 women in the Assembly. Fortunately, the overall response rates for these two countries were high enough that the proportion of women surveyed is not significantly different from the proportion of women in each of the legislatures. Summary table A.1 shows the representativeness of survey respondents compared to the population of legislators in each congress. In Colombia, women comprised 13% of the Chamber of Deputies and the Senate in the 1998–2002 congress, and the proportion of women in the survey sample was 14% for the Chamber and 16% for the Senate. In Costa Rica, women were 19% of the Legislative Assembly in 1998–2002 and my survey sample is 20% women. Overall, the sample is highly representative of the population.

TABLE A.1. Survey Representativeness

	Sample		Population	
	n	%	*n*	%
Argentine Chamber of Deputies				
Gender				
Men	46	68	128	70
Women	22	32	54	30
Total	*68*		*182*	
Party				
UCR	32	47	67	37
PJ	36	53	115	63
Total	*68*		*182*	
Colombian Chamber of Representatives				
Gender				
Men	90	86	139	87
Women	15	14	21	13
Total	*105*		*160*	
Party				
Liberals	59	56	85	53
Conservatives	26	25	37	23
Small parties	20	19	38	24
Total	*105*		*160*	
Colombian Senate				
Gender				
Men	58	84	88	87
Women	11	16	13	13
Total	*69*		*101*	
Party				
Liberals	35	51	52	51
Conservatives	15	22	19	19
Small parties	19	28	30	30
Total	*69*		*101*	
Costa Rican Legislative Assembly				
Gender				
Men	40	80	46	81
Women	10	20	11	19
Total	*50*		*57*	
Party				
PLN	19	38	23	40
PUSC	25	50	27	48
Small parties	6	12	7	12
Total	*50*		*57*	

Appendix B

Survey Questionnaire

Legislators were given a copy of the survey and a cover letter that described the purpose of the survey. Both were translated into Spanish prior to distribution. Below are the questions included in the survey questionnaire.

Instructions: Please mark with an "X" the response that you prefer.

1. Please indicate the importance of the following organizations and interest groups to your legislative work:

	Very Important	*Important*	*Moderately Important*	*Somewhat Important*	*Not at all Important*
Political party	○	○	○	○	○
Business associations	○	○	○	○	○
Labor unions	○	○	○	○	○
Neighborhood groups	○	○	○	○	○
Women's organizations	○	○	○	○	○
Minority organizations	○	○	○	○	○
Religious groups	○	○	○	○	○
Environmental groups	○	○	○	○	○
Other: ________________	○	○	○	○	○

2. Please indicate the importance of the following geographic regions to your legislative work:

	Very Important	*Important*	*Moderately Important*	*Somewhat Important*	*Not at all Important*
Entire nation	○	○	○	○	○
Province/department	○	○	○	○	○
County (Costa Rica only)	○	○	○	○	○
City/local district	○	○	○	○	○

3. Please indicate the importance of the following constituencies to your legislative work:

	Very Important	*Important*	*Moderately Important*	*Somewhat Important*	*Not at all Important*
Minorities	○	○	○	○	○
The Poor	○	○	○	○	○
Women	○	○	○	○	○
Environmentalists	○	○	○	○	○
Business owners	○	○	○	○	○
Blue-collar workers	○	○	○	○	○
Professionals	○	○	○	○	○
Farmers	○	○	○	○	○
Fishermen	○	○	○	○	○
Other:________________	○	○	○	○	○

4. Please rate the importance of the following aspects of your job:

	Very Important	*Important*	*Moderately Important*	*Somewhat Important*	*Not at all Important*
Helping people in the district who have personal problems with government	○	○	○	○	○
Making sure my constituents get their fair share of government funds and projects	○	○	○	○	○
Initiating bills	○	○	○	○	○
Working in committee	○	○	○	○	○
Giving public speeches or making public appearances	○	○	○	○	○
Representing the program of your political party	○	○	○	○	○

5. In an average **week** (when it is not an election period), how many **hours** do you spend on constituent casework and meeting with constituents? _____________

6. What **percentage** of the casework or time spent meeting with constituents is on behalf of:
women _____ men _____

7. What are the three most common casework requests that you receive from constituents?
a. ____________________________
b. ____________________________
c. ____________________________

8. How frequently do you work with constituents on the following concerns:

	Very Frequently	*Frequently*	*Some-times*	*Rarely*	*Never*
Health	○	○	○	○	○
Education	○	○	○	○	○
Poverty	○	○	○	○	○
Environment	○	○	○	○	○
Taxes	○	○	○	○	○
Women's issues	○	○	○	○	○
Legal problems	○	○	○	○	○
Employment	○	○	○	○	○

9. In an average **week**, how frequently do you speak:

	Very Frequently	*Frequently*	*Sometimes*	*Rarely*	*Never*
During floor debates?	○	○	○	○	○
During committee hearings?	○	○	○	○	○

10. During your term, how frequently do you speak on the floor of the chamber in support of the following types of legislation?

	Very Frequently	*Frequently*	*Sometimes*	*Rarely*	*Never*
Health	○	○	○	○	○
Education	○	○	○	○	○
Women's rights	○	○	○	○	○
Worker's rights	○	○	○	○	○
The economy	○	○	○	○	○
Agriculture	○	○	○	○	○
Other:_______________	○	○	○	○	○

11. In an average **month** (not an election period), how often do you:

	Very Frequently	*Frequently*	*Sometimes*	*Rarely*	*Never*
Visit your district	○	○	○	○	○
Give public speeches (outside of the congress)	○	○	○	○	○
Make public presentations	○	○	○	○	○
Speak with the press	○	○	○	○	○
Attend public events in your district	○	○	○	○	○

12. How many staff members do you have? ______

13. Do you see yourself as a role model for any of the following groups?

	Yes	*No*
Youth	○	○
University students	○	○
Women	○	○
Minorities	○	○

14. How frequently do you participate in activities (rallies, celebrations, conferences, etc.) sponsored by the following groups?

	Very Frequently	*Frequently*	*Sometimes*	*Rarely*	*Never*
Professional organizations	○	○	○	○	○
Women's organizations	○	○	○	○	○
Environmental groups	○	○	○	○	○
Agricultural groups	○	○	○	○	○
Unions	○	○	○	○	○
Other:_______________	○	○	○	○	○

15. How frequently do you do the following activities because they are **symbolic gestures** that increase your constituents' trust and confidence in government:

	Very Frequently	*Frequently*	*Sometimes*	*Rarely*	*Never*
Initiate bills	○	○	○	○	○
Sit on a committee	○	○	○	○	○
Meet with constituents or work on casework for constituents	○	○	○	○	○
Speak on the floor of the chamber	○	○	○	○	○
Give public speeches or make public appearances	○	○	○	○	○
Attend meetings or activities of interest groups	○	○	○	○	○

16. Please indicate the priority of the following policy areas to your legislative work:

	Very High Priority	*High Priority*	*Moderate Priority*	*Low Priority*	*Very Low Priority*
Health	○	○	○	○	○
Agriculture	○	○	○	○	○
Environment	○	○	○	○	○
Inflation	○	○	○	○	○
Education	○	○	○	○	○
Employment	○	○	○	○	○
Equal rights for women	○	○	○	○	○
Equal rights for minorities	○	○	○	○	○
Industrial and commercial development	○	○	○	○	○
Political violence	○	○	○	○	○
The economy	○	○	○	○	○
Crime	○	○	○	○	○
Affordable housing	○	○	○	○	○
Poverty	○	○	○	○	○
Children and family issues	○	○	○	○	○

17. On which committee do you serve? ______________________________

18. Did you request to be on this committee?

○ Yes ○ No

If no, which committee would you have preferred? ______________________________

19. To which political party do you belong? ________________

20. From which district were you elected? ________________

21. What is your gender? ○ Male ○ Female

22. For how many terms have you served as a deputy? ______________

23. Do you plan to run for reelection in the future?

○ Yes

○ No

24. What was your primary occupation prior to getting elected?
- ○ Educator ○ Lawyer
- ○ Business ○ Homemaker
- ○ Politician ○ Other: ____________________

25. What was the highest level of education you received?
- ○ Primary school degree
- ○ High school degree
- ○ University degree
- ○ Master's degree
- ○ Doctorate

26. What is your age? _____

27. Are you married?
- ○ Yes
- ○ No

28. How many children do you have? ____________

29. What other *elected* political offices have you held?

30. What *appointed* political positions have you had?

31. Do you have aspirations for higher offices?
- ○ Yes ○ No

If yes, which offices?

Thank you for your participation.

Appendix C

Variable Coding for Survey Analyses

All data come from the survey of legislators unless otherwise noted. See appendix B for questionnaire.

Variable	Description
Gender	0 = man; 1 = woman
Ideology	5-point ordinal scale from left to right based on self-reported political party affiliation (Alcántara 2006; Coppedge 1997; Rosas 2005)
Age	Continuous variable measuring legislator's self-reported age
Marital status	0 = single, divorced, or widowed; 1 = married
Education level	5-point ordinal scale for highest level of education completed (primary school, secondary school, university degree, master's degree, doctoral degree)
Occupation	Whether legislator had a prior career in a traditional feeder occupation for politics, specifically, business or law (0 = no; 1 = yes)
Legislative experience	Number of terms legislator has served in office including the current term
Prior political experience	Whether legislator previously held an elected or appointed political office (0 = no; 1 = yes)
Political ambition	Whether legislator aspires to higher office or reelection (0 = no; 1 = yes)
Urban district	Coding of legislator's electoral district as urban (1) or rural (0). Urban districts have population densities higher than the country average. Rural districts have population densities lower than the country average.
Constituency priority	Measure of the degree of priority that legislators place on relevant constituencies (women, farmers, educators, etc.). Five-point ordinal scale from lowest (coded "1") to highest (coded "5") priority. This variable is relevant for analyses only on certain home-style activities discussed in chapter 6.

Appendix D

Committees in Argentina, Colombia, and Costa Rica

Argentina Chamber of Deputies

1. Constitutional Issues
2. General Legislation
3. Foreign Relations
4. Budget and Treasury
5. Education
6. Science and Technology
7. Culture
8. Justice
9. Social Security
10. Social Assistance and Public Health
11. Family, Women, Children, and Adolescents
12. Elderly
13. Penal Code Legislation
14. Worker's Rights Legislation
15. Defense
16. Public Works
17. Agriculture and Ranching
18. Finance
19. Industry
20. Commerce

21. Energy and Combustibles
22. Communication and Information
23. Transportation
24. Economics and Regional Development
25. Municipal Issues
26. Maritime Issues, Fishing, and Ports
27. Housing
28. Petitions, Powers, and Rules
29. Justice
30. Natural Resources and Conservation of Human Environment
31. Tourism
32. Economy
33. Mining
34. Drug Addiction
35. Analysis and Security of Compliance with Tributary Norms
36. Population
37. Sports
38. Human Rights and Guarantees
39. Cooperation with NGOs
40. Mercosur

Colombian Chamber of Representatives and Senate

Committee 1—Constitutional

Assigned bills dealing with constitutional reform, statuary laws, territory organization, regulation of organizational control, administrative contracts, notary and registrar, structure and organization of central administration, legislative rights and guarantees, peace politics and strategies, intellectual propriety, and ethnic issues.

Committee 2—Foreign Relations

Assigned bills dealing with international politics, national defense and public police, diplomacy, public treaties, external commerce, economic integration, ports, relations with international organizations, nongovernmental diplomacy, border issues, nationality, foreigners, migration, honors and public monuments, military service, free zones, and commerce.

Committee 3—Economics

Assigned bills dealing with treasury and public credit, taxes (tax exemptions), monetary regimen, banking, monopolies, loans, stock market, economic regulation, national planning, and financial activity.

Committee 4—Budget

Assigned bills dealing with budget laws, fiscal finances, national well-being, regulation of industry, patents and copyrights, creation, elimination, reform, and organization of national public establishments, quantity and price control, and administrative contracts.

Committee 5—Agriculture

Assigned bills dealing with farming/agriculture law, ecology, environment and natural resources, land tenure, maritime issues, mining and energy, and autonomous regional corporations.

Committee 6—Communications and Other Issues

Assigned bills dealing with communications, tariffs, public calamities, public functions and services, scientific and technological investigation, information and digital communication, airspace, public works and transportation, tourism, education, and culture.

Committee 7—Social Affairs

Assigned bills dealing with public employees, unions, social security, loan funds, civil service, recreation, sports, health, community organizations, housing, women, and family issues.

Costa Rican Legislative Assembly

Government and Administration

Assigned bills dealing with governing, public security, foreign relations, transportation, communication, and municipalities.

Economics

Assigned bills dealing with the economy, commerce, industry, common market, and integration.

Treasury

Assigned bills dealing with the national budget and treasury issues.

Social Issues

Assigned bills dealing with work, social security, education, social protection, and health.

Judicial Issues

Assigned bills dealing with justice, civil rights, penal issues, commercial issues, electoral issues, organization of the judicial branch, and all legal issues.

Agriculture, Fishing, and Natural Resources (created in 1982)

Assigned bills dealing with agriculture, ranching, energy, and natural resources.

Notes

Chapter 1

1. Cuba has the largest representation of women in its legislature—43% of its national assembly is female. Cuba is not democratic, however.

2. Political parties in some Latin American countries also have adopted voluntary party quotas that equal or surpass the national quota requirements (Bruhn 2003; Gray 2003; Macaulay 2006; International IDEA 2009).

3. Nepal constitutionalized a 5% gender quota in 1990, but being a nondemocratic monarchy, it was far less notable than Argentina's change to its electoral law.

4. Venezuela's quota was adopted in 1997. It applied to the 1998 election but was not included in the new 1999 constitution.

5. Mexico had national quota recommendations as part of its electoral law beginning in 1994, but it was only in 2000 that the *recommendation* became an enforceable *requirement* (Reynoso 2008).

6. See Dahlerup (2006b) for a set of excellent case studies on the different types of quotas adopted throughout the world.

7. Although not expressly an *activity* of representing, the preferences of representatives translate into the behaviors they display linking them to other aspects of process representation. Comparing the representatives' preferences with their behavior is crucial to testing the theory of marginalization of women.

8. These categories are not all-inclusive. Some political issues do not fall into any of these categories. These categories, however, are those that are most relevant to a study of women's representation.

9. Nomenclature for these issues varies widely. Some scholars refer to them as feminist issues (Thomas 1994; Mazur 2002), others have called them strategic gender issues (Molyneux 1985) or women-friendly policies (Beckwith and Cowell-Meyers 2007), and still others refer to them as women's interests (Sapiro 1981). The most common terms are simply women's issues or women's equality issues.

10. Again, scholars vary on terminology here. Some call them feminine issues (Craske 1999), others refer to them as practical gender interests (Molyneux 1985), while still others talk about mothering issues, maternal concerns, or social issues (Schwindt-Bayer 2006).

11. There are numerous examples of important women's equality issues in Latin America. In Argentina, María José Lubertino (2003, 9) writes that some of the most important women's equality issues include "sexual and reproductive rights, economic and social rights . . . sexual exploitation and violence . . . non-punishable abortions being performed in public hospitals in dignified conditions, a gender perspective being incorporated into the national budget, value being attached to unremunerated work by women." In Colombia, concerns with women's equality sometimes focus on the effects of the ongoing civil war, such as violence and forced displacement, or increasing the low numbers of women in congress. In Costa Rica, women's groups have recently been concerned with issues of responsible paternity and intrafamily violence.

12. Phillips (1995) and Williams (1998) make similar arguments about the effect of the "politics of presence" and "self-representation" on substantive representation of historically underrepresented social groups, such as women.

13. Women also may fear repercussions from voters and male party leaders for emphasizing women's issues too much (Childs 2004; Vincent 2004; Macaulay 2006).

14. In fact, theories of women's difference from men have been stronger in Latin America than in the United States and the United Kingdom, where egalitarian views of women and men dominate (Jaquette and Wolchik 1998; Craske 1999; Franceschet 2005). Gender quota debates in Latin America, for example, have often been justified by an argument that female representatives will represent differently than male representatives. These arguments have been less influential in regions where egalitarian views of men and women dominate.

15. Determining whether women's equality leads to transformation of the legislative arena is beyond the scope of this study. However, I would argue that women achieving equality in the legislature is a critical mechanism for them to have a transformative effect on the legislature. By getting into positions of power, gaining access to the full array of committees, and becoming power players in the legislative arena, women have the greatest potential to make real changes in how the legislature operates. The equality can lead to feminizing the legislature into a less masculinized and more gender-neutral (or perhaps feminized) arena.

16. Lovenduski (2005) provides an excellent discussion of the tension between the *difference theory* of women's representation (that women should represent women) and the *equality theory* of representation (that women should be more equal to men and represent an array of constituent groups). She points out that "both bases for

claiming representation are necessary and flawed" (32), that the two sets of expectations provide a difficult challenge for women in office, but that women are expected to do both. As she notes about British MPs, "Women are required to perform a balancing of masculinity and femininity that is so finely tuned that it is a wonder that elected women continue to show up in the House of Commons, let alone stand for re-election" (148–149). Importantly, this does imply something of a double standard for women that men do not have to face. This, however, is normative concern rather than an empirical one.

17. In addition, chapter 3 provides empirical evidence to support this claim in Argentina, Colombia, and Costa Rica.

18. Although this is an institutional argument, it is not formal representation as defined by (Pitkin 1969) because it is not about electoral institutions.

19. In 2008, Rwanda became the first country in the world where women outnumber men in the national legislature.

20. However, Kittilson (2006) shows that the percentage of women in Western European party executive committees has increased over time to just over 30% in the mid-1990s.

21. Of course, similarities in attitudes and differences in behavior are not the only way that marginalization of women occurs. If women and men had different political preferences but similar forms of behavior, then this also would support the marginalization theory. Women could place higher priority on committee service than men and the gendered legislative environment could marginalize women by giving them equal or less participation on committees. I am not arguing that similarities in attitudes and differences in behavior are the *only* way that marginalization takes place, just that it is one way.

22. For example, Macaulay (2006) argues that framing of policy issues as *maternal* concerns in Chile facilitated adoption of women's policies. This view of Chile is corroborated by Franceschet (2005); however, she notes some movement toward an *equality* framing in recent years.

23. Another explanation for change within countries that is asserted by some is the mere passage of time. As time goes by, women's substantive representation may change. The problem with this explanation is that it does not specify what about time matters. Generally, this argument implies that as time goes by women are gaining more equality in society and so may gain more equality in legislative politics or that as time goes by long-standing gendered legislative norms may ease to facilitate women's representation. Consequently, it is not *time* that really matters but the socioeconomic and institutional factors. In this study, I do not account for time per se, but I do emphasize that socioeconomic changes in Latin America over the past thirty years have likely led to a different type of substantive representation today and examine how institutional change (adopting quotas or changing electoral rules) may mediate substantive representation.

24. Although her research emphasizes the effect of parties on women's ability to promote gender or women's equality issues, Macaulay (2006) argues that Brazil's weak

party system has facilitated a "gender equality and equity agenda." The parties, which are largely unideological and uninstitutionalized due in large part to Brazil's highly personalistic electoral rules, have allowed women to promote a gender equality agenda. She contrasts the case of Brazil with Chile, where strong political parties have minimized women's political participation.

25. This, of course, assumes that these positions are controlled by men. If, as is rarely the case but increasingly may become so, women begin to attain these positions of power with regularity, then institutions may become a tool by which women can achieve greater legislative power than they would otherwise hold. As women increasingly get into positions of power, it will be important to examine just whether this occurs.

26. Specifically, we (Schwindt-Bayer and Mishler 2005) measure substantive representation as policy responsiveness and create an index of women's policies that measures gender equality in political rights, gender equality in social rights, national maternity leave policy, and gender equality in marriage and divorce laws.

27. The Argentine Senate is not studied because up until 2001, senators were appointed by provincial legislatures rather than directly elected by the populace.

28. The Gender-related Development Index (GDI) and Gender Empowerment Index (GEM) are reported by the United Nations Development Program's Human Development Reports. GDI combines men's and women's differences in life expectancy, literacy, and earned income. GEM is an index combining men's and women's shares of parliamentary seats, shares of technical, professional, and management positions in the workforce, and earned income. Each index is on a scale of 0 to 1, with 1 being the highest level of gender equality.

29. Colombia changed its electoral rules in 2003, tightening slightly the incentives for personal vote seeking, but those rules did not go into effect until 2006 (Rodríguez Raga and Botero 2006). All analyses in this study focus on the pre-2006 period.

Chapter 2

1. Miller (1994, 170) notes that "Uruguay was, in theory, the first of all Western Hemisphere nations to recognize female suffrage: the constitution of 1917 stated that women had the right to vote and hold office at local and national levels. However, the principle of woman suffrage required a two-thirds majority in each of the legislative houses to become law." It was 1932 before the law was approved and suffrage was enacted.

2. Women's workforce participation also may be underestimated because significantly more women than men work in the informal sector, which is not captured by these numbers.

3. Other kinds of socioeconomic changes also have occurred in the region. Craske (1999) reports significant improvement in women's literacy rates, life expectancies, maternal mortality rates, fertility rates, use of contraception, likelihood of being head

of household, and willingness to seek divorces. All of these changes indicate greater independence for women and greater access to economic resources outside of the home, which makes them more qualified and marketable for participation in the public sphere.

4. The number of women in the Honduran Congress increased significantly after the 2005 election when closed-list PR was used for the first time (Taylor-Robinson 2007).

5. Related to enforcement is party compliance. Parties must be willing to comply with quotas for them to have an effect (Htun and Jones 2002; Baldez 2004a; Jones 2005; Krook 2007; Tremblay 2008b; Jones 2009). Compliance is much more difficult to measure cross-nationally, however. While compliance could mediate the success of gender quotas, Jones (2009) notes that "compliance with the quota legislation has been good throughout Latin America, although as is often the case with a myriad of laws in the region, some noncompliance has occurred on occasion and the interpretation of the quota law sometimes has been disputed" (64).

6. Other mediating factors include district or party magnitude (Htun and Jones 2002; Baldez 2004a; Schmidt and Saunders 2004; Jones 2005), the proportion of women on the ballot itself or "effective quota" (Schmidt and Saunders 2004), primary elections (Baldez 2007), candidate selection procedures (Krook 2007, 2009), independent electoral tribunals (Baldez 2004a; Krook 2007), and women's movements (Baldez 2004a).

7. I use the language of *open list* here because it is the most common terminology in the gender and politics literature. It is important to note, however, that many of the Latin American open-list systems are actually variations of open list (e.g., flexible lists) rather than pure open-list systems. Some offer *closed and blocked* lists that allow voters to vote for candidates within a party but not across parties, and some allow voters to choose whether to vote for a party's list as a whole or to vote for specific candidates rather than requiring a candidate-level vote. Most important, they are all preference voting systems, as are pure open-list systems.

8. Paraguay is the only country with an election in 2008 that is included in the dataset.

9. The unbalanced nature of the research design does not bias the statistical results.

10. These chambers include the senates of Argentina, Bolivia, Brazil, Dominican Republic, Mexico (up through 1994), and Venezuela (up until 1999 when the Senate was abolished). Also, I follow Payne (2002) in coding Chile as semi-PR/plurality rather than PR because the binomial system used in both chambers favors the two largest parties, as do plurality rules. From here on, I refer to these systems as plurality. For a more nuanced coding of these electoral rules for recent elections, see table 1 in Jones (2009).

11. I opt for a multiplicative index to measure the strength of gender quotas because it is comparable to an interaction term. The theory is that the three dimensions of quota laws have a combined effect on the election of women, which is

commonly modeled with an interaction term (Schwindt-Bayer 2009). Because I am interested in the combined effect rather than the effect of one dimension given certain values on the other dimensions, I include only the three-way interaction term (i.e., multiplicative index) rather than all of the constituent parts (Palmer and Whitten 2003).

12. The index would be 1 if quota size = 1%, there was no placement mandate, and no enforcement (1 * 1 * 1). The index would be 300 if quota size = 50%, there was a placement mandate, and strong enforcement (50 * 2 * 3). I opt for this index over a categorical coding (e.g., Jones [2009]) because it measures the nuances in quota laws.

13. Of course, Ecuador's open-list electoral system likely weakens this strong quota design. Rather than assuming this into the coding of the quota variable, however, I empirically test the extent to which open list weakens the quota in the statistical models below (model 4 of table 2.3).

14. As discussed earlier, culture also has been found to affect the election of women and this most often plays a role through the religion of a country and attitudes toward gender equality in society. All Latin American countries are dominated by Catholicism, so focusing on Latin America holds religion constant, to a large extent. Attitudes toward gender equality do vary somewhat across countries, but survey data on these attitudes is available only from the late 1990s. The fact that culture is more similar than different across these countries and the fact that the models do control for socioeconomic differences (that are likely to correlate with cultural differences) means that omitting a measure for culture should not bias the results.

15. Including this variable changes interpretation of the results slightly. With a lagged dependent variable, estimates of the effect of the independent variables measure the increase or decrease in the percentage of women in office *since the last election* rather than increases or decreases in the overall level of women's descriptive representation.

16. The table presents unbalanced pooled time-series models with panel-corrected standard errors that account for heteroskedasticity in the panels and a correction for first-order autocorrelation (Beck and Katz 1995b, 1995a). Each panel is a country chamber. I ran, but do not present, first difference models that adjust for nonstationarity in the dependent variable (increasing trend in the election of women over time). The results are similar to what is presented in table 2.3. Although the key independent variables are institutions that do not always change from election to election, Latin American democracies have undergone numerous changes to electoral rules since their transitions to democracy. Quota laws have also changed over time, with some countries adding placement mandates or enforcement mechanisms and others changing the size of the quota. Institutional change over time is more limited than socioeconomic change, for example, but sufficient changes have occurred to justify a time-serial analysis of how institutions affect the election of women.

17. Plurality systems are the excluded, comparison category. The estimated coefficient is the effect of PR or mixed compared to plurality systems.

18. Predicted values of the percentage of the chamber that is female are calculated with CLARIFY holding all covariates other than district magnitude or party magnitude at their mean (King et al. 2000).

19. The level of democracy, measured as the average score of political rights and civil liberties by Freedom House (2008), does not affect the election of women when it is included in the statistical models.

Chapter 3

1. See chapter 2 for specifics.

2. The large number of tables and large number of models in each table needed to present the statistical results prohibits presenting all of the statistical results. Because the key variable is gender, I only present the effect of gender in the models in which it is statistically significant. I use CLARIFY to compute the predicted probabilities holding all variables at the mean or mode (King et al. 2000; Tomz et al. 2001). This predicts the likelihood of responses for the average or modal legislator.

3. Due to minimal variation on some control variables, some models failed to converge when all controls were included. In these cases, the control variables that produced the overdetermined models were excluded. The most common contributors to this problem were marital status and prior political experience because most legislators in some countries were married or had prior experience.

4. This deputy asked to remain anonymous out of concern that her party would not be pleased that she placed them last on her priority list.

5. In Argentina, the gender differences are only borderline statistically significant ($p =. 06$) with all controls included in the model, but become highly significant if legislators' prior office holding experience is excluded. Female representatives in Argentina are less likely to have held prior office than are men, and this partly explains some of the gender differences in how legislators view women's groups. Female deputies in Argentina are entering the legislature with less political experience and perhaps more experience working directly on behalf of women and women's groups instead.

Chapter 4

1. Unfortunately, the fact that primary sponsors are not distinguished from secondary sponsors in Colombia and Costa Rica makes it impossible to test empirically whether the gender of the primary sponsor affects who else signs onto a bill. Thus, the analyses in this chapter are limited to testing whether women are more likely to cosponsor, in general, than men.

2. For Argentina, I use the last year in a 2-year congress instead of the full congress because of the large number of bills initiated during a congress and in an effort to keep the number of bills comparable across countries.

3. Previous research often refers to the other issue areas as gender neutral because few gender differences are theorized to occur.

4. In all three countries, each bill can be signed by more than one legislator. Thus when referring to bills initiated by a legislator, some of the bills are also initiated by

other legislators. In other words, initiation of a bill by one legislator is not mutually exclusive from the initiation of a bill by another legislator. All three legislatures in this study permit cosponsorship of legislation (i.e., more than one legislator can introduce a bill). In Colombia and Costa Rica, bills do not specify a primary initiator and each cosigner is equally responsible for the bill. In Argentina, a primary initiator is specified but cosigners are permitted as well. Therefore, when I code a legislator as initiating a bill in a policy area it is not necessarily that he or she was the only sponsor.

5. I tested alternative specifications of the dependent variable including a dichotomous measure of whether or not the legislator sponsored at least one bill in the issue area and a continuous measure of the priority that legislators place on different types of bills measured as the percentage of the bills a legislator sponsors that fall into each thematic area. These specifications yield comparable results.

6. The total possible number of legislators is 514 in Argentina (257 * 2), 322 in the Colombian Chamber of Representatives (161 * 2), 204 in the Colombian Senate (102 * 2), and 114 in Costa Rica (57 * 2). The total number of legislators and the number who sponsored bills are not the same in Argentina and Colombia for several reasons. First, some legislators never sponsor a bill during their time in office, perhaps due to having other responsibilities (e.g., chamber president). Second, some legislators serve only a short time in office. In Colombia, for example, it is not uncommon for an elected representative or senator to renounce his or her seat after the election, only to be replaced by a substitute for whom I had no information.

7. For individually sponsored bills, legislators in Argentina sponsored between 0 and 40 bills (median = 6), and legislators in Costa Rica sponsored between 0 and 107 bills (median = 19). The 107 was an outlier—the second largest number of cosponsored bills for a legislator was 52. In Colombia, legislators in the House of Representatives sponsored between 0 and 29 bills (median = 6) whereas the range was 0 to 55 in the Senate (median = 10). For cosponsored bills, legislators in Argentina cosponsored between 0 and 87 bills (median = 20) and they cosponsored between 6 and 68 in Costa Rica (median = 35). In Colombia, representatives sponsored between 0 and 39 bills (median = 8) and senators sponsored between 0 and 34 bills (median = 10).

8. Models that exclude the three outliers—legislators who sponsored 102, 124, and 148 bills—are comparable to those presented throughout this chapter.

9. Members of both chambers can and often do sponsor bills in the other chamber. I calculate the number of bills that legislators in Colombia sponsor regardless of which chamber the bill was initiated in. Because of this, the sum of the bills that legislators sponsor does not equal the number of bills sponsored in any one chamber.

10. Age, education, and occupation are not in the bill initiation models because archival data on legislators' backgrounds are scant in Colombia and Costa Rica.

11. In Argentina, the Peronist Party (PJ) was the largest party in all three terms studied in this chapter, holding from 45% to 49% of the seats. In both chambers and congressional terms in Colombia, the Liberals were the largest party and held a majority in all congresses except 1998–2002 in the Senate, where they held 48% of the seats. In Costa Rica, the National Liberation Party (PLN) and United Social Christian Party

(PUSC) alternated as the largest party, with the PLN holding 49% of seats in 1994–1998 and the PUSC with 51% of the seats in 1998–2002.

12. On the whole, legislators in Latin America do not exhibit long seniority patterns. The longest serving deputies in Argentina were in their fourth term, and only four deputies served that long. In Colombia, one legislator was in his eighth, 4-year term, but most were in their first or second term. In Costa Rica, 88% of deputies were in their first term. Term limits in Costa Rica that prohibit immediate reelection deter many legislators from seeking additional terms after sitting out for 4 years. Average term length is 2.7 for Argentine deputies, 1.8 for Colombian senators and representatives, and 1.2 terms for Costa Rican deputies.

13. In Colombia, a floor vote determines who sits on the seven permanent committees for the duration of the 4-year congress and each legislator gets one assignment. In Costa Rica, the chamber president makes assignments to the six permanent committees annually. I code legislators as sitting on a relevant committee if he or she did so in any of the 4 years of the congress. The Argentine Chamber has 45 committees, and party leaders assign legislators to multiple committees for a 2-year term. If any of the legislator's committee assignments deal with bills in the thematic area, then I code that legislator as sitting on the relevant committee.

14. For all of the analyses, the dependent variable is a count variable—the number of bills a legislator sponsors. This requires the use of negative binomial regression for the statistical models (Long 1997). Negative binomial models adjust for the problem of overdispersion in the models driven by many more legislators sponsoring small numbers of bills compared to larger numbers of bills. The *alpha*, or overdispersion parameter, is included in the tables. The closer to zero the parameter estimate is, the less of a problem overdispersion is in the data.

15. The predicted value estimates here and in the rest of the chapter are for legislators with mean ideology, mean number of terms in office, and who is from an urban district, not in the plurality party, not the chamber president, and holds a seat in the second year/congress under study. In other words, the estimates hold continuous variables at their mean and dichotomous variables at their mode. I use CLARIFY to calculate the predicted values (King et al. 2000; Tomz et al. 2001).

16. The smaller number of cosponsored bills likely gets overwhelmed by the individually sponsored bills in the combined models.

17. The estimate for gender is borderline significant (p =. 09) but the substantive effect is very small—six bills for women and eight bills for men. And, it emerges only in cosponsorship, which is the smaller subset of bills in the Colombian Senate.

18. In the previous section, it was possible to interpret the statistical results in terms of the number of bills that legislators are estimated to sponsor because wide variation existed across the number of bills. When examining bill sponsorship in issue areas in which only a small number of bills are sponsored, interpreting the results as the number of bills legislators sponsor makes little sense—the estimates will be a fraction between 0 and 1. Instead, it is more appropriate to interpret the results in terms of the incidence rate ratio (exp[B] and the rate at which men or women sponsor more

or fewer bills) or the predicted probability that a legislator will sponsor one or more bills (Long 1997). Consequently, in this section and the next, I interpret the results this way instead.

19. The main component of the Sexual and Reproductive Health Law is the creation of a national reproductive health program that will work on many fronts including the prevention of sexually transmitted diseases and breast/genital cancer, providing information on sexually transmitted diseases and contraceptive use, bringing contraceptives to public hospitals, offering programs on family planning, and promoting sex education in schools.

20. There was no survey question about speaking in committee on different types of issues. Thus, it is impossible to analyze gender differences in committee participation on specific issues.

21. Another reason that women may speak more often in committee debates is that they may be more likely to sit on committees dominated by other women and, consequently, be more comfortable speaking up. Unfortunately, the number of observations is too small for analysis once it is disaggregated by committee assignments.

Chapter 5

1. Ironically, her success also earned her some blatantly sexist media coverage. In a story on her election, the newspaper *El Tiempo* found it imperative to highlight her fitness regime: "Like the majority of women, Blum is vain. Rarely does she interrupt her daily exercise routine on the treadmill and elliptical trainer. It doesn't matter that the floor debate extends into the middle of the night, her cardiovascular routine is inescapable. She is also rigorous with her diet: only vegetable soup and a lot of protein. Cakes, chocolates, and cookies, her weakness, are prohibited" (Quién es La Primera Presidenta del Senado 2005).

2. I present the raw numbers of women in chamber leadership to analyze how gender affects chamber leadership because the number of women in leadership posts is too small for statistical analysis. Data come from legislative archive records on chamber leadership.

3. A secretary general also is part of the leadership, but he or she is not a member of the congress and serves for a 4-year renewable term.

4. Although legislators can be reelected to these positions, reelection is rare.

5. I thank Brian Crisp, Mark Jones, Brad Jones, and Michelle Taylor-Robinson for sharing some of the committee assignment data with me.

6. Dolan and Ford (1997) and Friedman (1996) find some changes in women's access to committees over time in U.S. states and the U.S. Congress. Dolan and Ford (1997) report that women in the 1970s and 1980s were overrepresented on social issue committees and underrepresented on appropriations, finance, and industry and commerce committees in U.S. states. But they find women's underrepresentation on finance and business issue committees to decrease in the early 1990s. Friedman (1996) reports that women in Congress had gained access to

prestigious congressional committees by 1992, as a result of an array of socioeconomic and political changes in the United States.

7. Argentina, Colombia, and Costa Rica have standing committees and special committees. Standing committees are the primary policy committees and are the committees that are clearly defined in congressional rules and on which all legislators must serve. Special committees can be organized by the legislature at any point in time during a congress and deal with a range of issues from government oversight to ethics complaints to reporting on societal problems to special policy considerations. In this book, I focus only on the standing committees in the three legislatures.

8. Both the Colombian Chamber of Representatives and Senate have had seven committees since 1974. The Costa Rican Legislative Assembly had five committees from 1974 to 1982, when it created its sixth committee, the agriculture committee.

9. The number of committees in the Argentine Chamber of Deputies has grown from 27 in 1983 to 45 today.

10. This classification of important and powerful committees is not my own but is how the legislative environment has come to view committees. Some scholars may criticize this classification for furthering the view the women's issues are less important in the legislative chamber. However, for an empirical study of women's access to committees, it is useful to examine whether women are getting represented on what the male-dominated environment considers to be the most important committees. I would argue that by getting on these committees (and on women's issue committees) women have greater opportunity to transform the masculinized committee system as a whole.

11. These additional responsibilities include investigative work on social problems, quality of life issues for women, and human rights concerns, reviewing existing legislation to be sure it complies with international treaties on women's rights, and being a watchdog for any government agency in its actions toward women and women's issues.

12. Unfortunately, records of legislators' committee preferences are not systematically kept by all political parties, making it impossible to conduct an analysis of whether representatives' assignments match their preferences. This type of analysis, however, does not always provide an accurate picture of representatives' preferences for committees because the preferred committees they formally list often reflect what they expect they will receive. Examining attitudes toward issues, as I do in this book, may give a clearer picture of legislators' committee preferences because they are not clouded by informal committee negotiations with parties and pressure from male legislators.

13. Literacy rates and unemployment do correlate statistically with the urbanness or ruralness of electoral districts in Argentina, Colombia, and Costa Rica.

14. Committees in Costa Rica are reappointed annually, but legislators can be reappointed to the same committee each year.

15. The statistical models use the legislator as the unit of analysis. Because legislators are in the dataset more than once for each congress in which they were a member, I cluster the standard errors around the legislator. I also include congress dummy variables. These ensure that the findings are not biased by committee assignments in one

particular congressional session. To facilitate interpretation, I do not include the dummy variables in tables 5.3–5.6.

16. I measure committee assignments as the assignment a legislator received when he or she was first assigned. Therefore, I do not include legislators who swapped assignments midterm or otherwise changed their assignment (except Costa Rica, as noted below). This is particularly important for Colombia, where legislators are often replaced by their *suplentes* at some point during the term, which would significantly complicate any analysis of committee assignments in Colombia. I ignore the *suplentes* and focus strictly on the assignments that the *principales* receive in the first few days of the new congress. This is facilitated by the fact that committee rules require that legislators sit on only one committee for the entire 4-year congress. Because Costa Rican legislators are appointed for a 1-year stint within each 4-year congress, I measure whether or not a legislator sits on a committee at any time during the 4-year congress to make the measure of Costa Rica committee assignments comparable to the other countries. In Argentina, legislators sit on a committee for the entire 2-year congress. However, they can sit on more than one committee at a time and multiple committees fall under each category of committee. To account for this, I consider a legislator as sitting on a committee in a particular category if he or she is on at least one of the committees under consideration regardless of the other committee assignments he or she might have.

17. I use CLARIFY with STATA to compute predicted probabilities for the effect of gender holding the continuous control variables at their mean and the dichotomous control variables at their mode (King et al. 2000; Tomz et al. 2001)

18. The effect of gender on the likelihood that women sit on women's issue committees, however, is positive and statistically significant in both the pre- and postquota periods.

19. Models that measure the dependent variable as the percentage of the 4-year term that a legislator sat on any given committee yield comparable results.

20. The government committee is responsible for foreign affairs, but it also handles policy related to general government administration, transportation, communication, and municipalities.

21. Dolan and Ford (1997) do show that women's access to committee leadership posts has increased from the 1970s to early 1990s. They argue that it is not due to women's increasing presence in legislatures but to their increased seniority.

22. I present bivariate cross-tabulations rather than multivariate models to analyze gender's effect on different types of committee leadership positions because of the small numbers (or entire absence) of women in many of these positions. Multivariate analyses would be possible only for a couple of committees and with only limited control variables.

23. The annual turnover in leadership in Colombia and Costa Rica, however, means that this analysis still includes 12 and 16 leadership terms in Colombia and Costa Rica, respectively.

24. These statistics were generated by combining the leaderships of women's committees, social committees, economic committees, budget committees, agriculture committees, and foreign affairs committees.

25. A multivariate statistical analysis that tests the effect of a legislator's gender on all types of committee leadership positions combined together and controlling for other influences on leadership, such as political experience, being in the plurality party, the number of committees a legislator serves on, and having prior committee leadership experience underscores this (models not shown). Because so many committees have never had a female president, it is impossible to examine the different types of leadership posts. However, models explaining whether a legislator has served in any leadership post on the different types of committees reveal findings similar to those that emerge from the bivariate statistics. In Argentina, women are more likely than men to serve in the leadership of women's issue committees and are less likely to hold leadership posts on economics committees and foreign affairs committees. In Colombia, no gender differences exist in attainment of leadership posts, in general, but these models obscure the absence of women from committee presidencies. In Costa Rica, women are more likely to be leaders of social committees than men, they are more likely to be secretaries of budget committees, and they are more likely to be leaders of the government committee. I do not present these models because they do not illustrate the differences between the types of leadership positions (presidents versus vice presidents and secretaries), which is a critical dimension for examining gender and committee leadership. Instead, I use them as additional support for the findings.

26. Data on who held the leadership posts on the Family, Women, Children, and Adolescents Committee were missing for the 1983–1985 congress.

27. Women's overrepresentation in the presidency of the "foreign affairs" committee in Costa Rica is, in part, due to the fact that the committee that handles foreign affairs is officially the Government Committee and spends more time dealing with issues of administration, communication, and municipal governments than foreign affairs.

Chapter 6

1. The reference to Washington occurs because Fenno's conceptualization emerged from his study of the U.S. Congress, and he wanted to emphasize the distinction between work that legislators do in Washington, DC, from the work they do at home in their districts. I use the more general phrase *explanation of legislative behavior* in this chapter.

2. The survey does not ask any questions that elucidate whether constituency service is legislator initiated or constituent initiated, but it does allow a more general analysis of whether female legislators do more home style activities on behalf of women and women's concerns.

3. Another factor that is particularly important in single member district systems is the electoral margin of victory (Cain et al. 1983; Richardson and Freeman 1995; Studlar and McAllister 1996; Wood and Young 1997; Ingall and Crisp 2001; Heitshusen et al. 2005). Representatives in competitive districts may benefit more from allocating resources to the district, doing constituency service, or explaining their legislative work to constituents than those in "safe seats." However, the security of a legislator's seat is more difficult to measure in multimember districts and closed-list PR

systems. Consequently, I do not control for margin of victory in this chapter's models.

4. All predicted probabilities in this chapter are generated using CLARIFY and holding continuous variables at their mean and dichotomous variables at their mode (King et al. 2000; Tomz et al. 2001).

5. I use ordered probit models with robust standard errors to estimate the effect of gender and the control variables on the frequency of visiting the district. This is the most appropriate statistical model given that the dependent variable is an ordinal scale from 1 to 5. The control variables in this model include ideology, age, marital status, education, occupation, number of terms served, prior appointed or elected office-holding experience, political ambition, whether the legislator represents an urban district, and the priority that legislators place on the electoral district.

6. This analysis also uses ordered probit models with robust standard errors. The dependent variable is again an ordinal scale of increasing frequency of attending public events in one's district that ranges from 1 to 5. It uses the same control variables as the "visiting the district" models (see previous note).

7. These models were ordered probit models with robust standard errors. Control variables include ideology, age, marital status, education, occupation, number of terms served, prior appointed or elected office-holding experience, political ambition, whether the legislator represents an urban district, and the priority that legislators place on the group under study (professionals, environmentalists, farmers, or labor unions).

8. The figures in this paragraph are simply the mean number of hours that legislators in each country claimed to spend on constituency service (regardless of gender). The survey asked respondents to provide an estimated average number of hours per week that they spend on casework or constituency service (see appendix B for specific question wording).

9. One hundred thirty-four hours per week on constituency service is unusually high, and only three of the legislators surveyed reported spending more than 80 hours a week on constituency service—one at 84 hours, one at 96 hours, and one at 134 hours. With these relative outliers excluded, the mean for the Colombian Chamber of Representatives is still higher than the other countries at 22 hours per week spent on constituency service.

10. Table 6.2 reports negative binomial regression models that are more appropriate estimators for count data, such as the number of hours spent on constituency service. They adjust for the common problem of overdispersion in count data. Overdispersion is evident in these models from the nonzero alpha and significant likelihood ratio tests (not reported) comparing Poisson and negative binomial estimates for all four models. Negative binomial estimates are not intuitively interpretable, so I discuss predicted probabilities calculated as noted in note 4.

11. It is not, however, the priority placed on women as a constituency that depresses the effect of the gender of the legislator. Even with the variable measuring views of female constituents excluded from the model, gender is still statistically insignificant.

12. This variable is excluded from the Argentina model for statistical reasons—including the fact that it does not allow the model to converge.

13. The survey specifically asked how often legislators do casework on eight different types of issues: health, education, poverty, environment, taxes, legal issues, employment, and women's issues. This paragraph describes the statistical models that analyze the role of gender in how frequently legislators claimed to do casework in these areas. The models are ordered probit models with robust standard errors because the dependent variable is an ordered scale from 1 (never) to 5 (very frequently). These models controlled for ideology, age, marital status, highest level of education completed, legislative experience, prior political experience, whether they plan to seek reelection or higher office, whether they were elected from an urban district, and either the importance they place on constituency service in their legislative work or the importance of the constituency most relevant to the dependent variable.

14. See previous note for details on these statistical models.

15. Table 6.5 presents bivariate cross-tabulations instead of multivariate models. This is because multivariate models are impossible for three of the four countries where there is minimal to no variation in whether women view themselves as role models. In Argentina, where a multivariate model can be analyzed, women are still significantly more likely to see themselves as role models than are men ($p =. 06$). The model with control variables, however, is not a significantly better estimate than the simple bivariate model—the Wald chi-square for the multivariate model is small and does not reach statistical significance.

16. Again, these 12 models are not shown due to space constraints. The results described in this section are from ordered probit models with robust standard errors with controls for ideology, age, marital status, education, occupation, number of terms served, prior appointed or elected office-holding experience, political ambition, whether the legislator represents an urban district, and the priority that legislators place on giving public speeches or making public appearances.

Chapter 7

1. Argentina, the Dominican Republic, Ecuador, and Honduras are not included in this chapter because they lack data on at least one of two key variables. Argentina was not included in the 2006 Americas Barometer. Data on the passage of women's policies were not available for the Dominican Republic, Ecuador, or Honduras.

2. An alternative source of data is the *Latinobarometro*. The benefit of the *Latinobarometro* is that it has annual data since 1996 (LAPOP has only been conducting the Americas Barometer annually since 2006). However, access to the full *Latinobarometro* dataset is restricted and expensive. In addition, comparable questions are not always asked on every survey. Given that the key explanatory variables in this study vary by legislative term (approximately 4 years) rather than annually, these time-serial data are unnecessary.

3. The original scale used in the survey was 1 to 4 ("very satisfied" to "very dissatisfied"). I inverted this scale so that "very satisfied" is the highest category.

4. Multilevel data do not necessarily require multilevel modeling. Indeed, multilevel or hierarchical modeling is not required in this study because the data have only two levels, the second-level (country) has a relatively small number of observations with 14, and a likelihood ratio test reveals that allowing for slope-varying coefficients is not necessary (except for the democratic satisfaction model). Instead, I report models that cluster around country to eliminate problems of correlated error terms within countries (Franzese 2005; Primo et al. 2007; Arceneaux and Nickerson 2009). These models lend for easier interpretation while not compromising the validity of the findings. For added robustness, I find that results from hierarchical linear models do not significantly change the conclusions drawn from the clustered models.

5. I measure all of these variables drawing on the lower house of congress only. Creating measures of representation that merge the data from two distinct chambers is of questionable validity, given the distinct nature of electoral rules. In all countries, the lower house is at least as important if not more important to government performance and is the chamber where social representativeness often takes precedent over geographic representativeness. Consequently, I focus on data from this chamber only in the bicameral legislatures—Bolivia, Brazil, Chile, Colombia, Mexico, Paraguay, and Uruguay.

6. See chapter 2 for more details on Latin American quota laws.

7. Data are from Schwindt-Bayer (2008).

8. Data on laws were gathered from government websites in the 14 Latin American countries (primarily the congress websites). I created a coding scheme for determining which laws could be considered *women's policies* and coded the laws accordingly. Women's laws are those that dealt with issues of women's rights, gender equality, divorce (if it opened the process to women), maternity, sexual abuse and harassment, crimes against women (particularly domestic or intrafamily violence), women in the workforce, and reproductive rights. I matched the final coding to lists of women's laws from various women's organizations to ensure reliability of the variable.

9. It is surprising to see Chile having the largest proportion of laws that deal with women's issues because Chile is frequently argued to be one of the least gender equal countries in Latin America (Htun 2003; Franceschet 2005; Macaulay 2006). However, this measure is not meant to capture gender equality in society or political and economic outcomes but how many policies are passed that target women. These policies may be large-scale policies that have substantial impacts on women or much smaller policies with only incremental impacts on women in society. They also include pieces of legislation in which women may only be a small part. In Chile, few large-scale policies passed in this time period but several laws passed that addressed women and women's rights in small ways.

10. The coding of these variables is as follows. Gender is measured as 0 for men and 1 for women. Age is a continuous variable measuring the respondent's self-reported age. Catholic is a measure of whether the respondent reports an affiliation with the

Catholic Church (coded 1) or not (coded 0). In Latin America, the Catholic Church has long had a strong relationship with the state such that citizens who are Catholic may feel better about their system than non-Catholics who may be more critical. The respondent's education level is coded on a 5-point ordinal scale—no education, primary education, secondary education, university education, and graduate education. Education level could affect citizen views of government because more educated citizens are thought to be better able to discern government's actual performance from the bravado that government's might offer. Finally, marital status is coded 0 (not married) and 1 (married).

11. Other possible demographic variables include income, employment status, and political ideology. I do not include these in an effort to keep the models as parsimonious as possible and because some countries included in the 2006 Americas Barometer did not include questions about these things in a manner comparable to the other countries.

12. The political interest question asks, "How much interest do you have in politics: a lot, some, little, or none?" The economic question asks, "How would you describe the country's economic situation? Would you say that it is very good, good, neither good nor bad, bad, or very bad?" For both variables, I invert the original coding such that high responses correspond to positive economic evaluations and levels of political interest whereas low responses correspond to negative evaluations. The economic perceptions variable is coded 1 to 5 ("very bad" to "very good"), and the political interest variable is coded 1 to 4 ("none" to "a lot"). Alternative measures of citizen perceptions of the economic situation ask about how citizens feel about their own economic situation (egocentric view of the economy), how they feel the economy has changed over the past year (retrospective view of the economy), and what they expect from the economy in the next year (prospective views of the economy). I use a question asking about citizens' view of the state of the current economy because the dependent variable is views of the current government.

13. Cross-national studies often include additional controls for the socioeconomic environment in a country or cultural context. I do not include country-level measures of these factors, however, because of the need to preserve degrees of freedom and because the individual-level variables already measure socioeconomics and cultural characteristics.

14. The partial proportional odds model is more appropriate here than a standard ordered logit or probit model because the ordered model violates the parallel lines assumption (Long 1997; Williams 2006). The partial proportional odds model adjusts for this *only for the variables that violate the assumption*, which in this model includes all variables except *married* and *gender quota*. Consequently, the model estimates different parameters for each variable that violates the parallel lines assumption for each response category. The model estimates one parameter for all variables that do not violate the assumption (i.e., the estimate reported in table 7.3 for *married* and *gender quota* is the same across all three response categories).

15. I calculate all predicted probabilities in this chapter following Long and Freese (2005). I calculate predicted probabilities holding continuous variables at their mean and dichotomous variables at their mode.

16. Measuring the gender quota as an index that captures the strength of the quota (as described in chapter 2) is statistically nonsignificant also.

17. I use an ordered probit model to estimate the corruption model because of the ordered nature of the dependent variable. This model does not violate the parallel lines assumption (Long 1997; Williams 2006).

18. The effect is even stronger when the quota variable is measured in terms of the strength of the quota in a country.

19. The number of years that a country has been democratic correlates rather highly with the percentage of the legislature that is female ($r = 0.45$). Omitting either variable, however, does not change the lack of statistical significance in the other.

20. Like corruption, trust in the legislature is modeled with an ordered probit regression. Trust in the legislature has seven points to the ordinal scale ranging from 1 to 7, trust "not at all" to trust "a lot." The number of years that the country has been democratic is not included in the model because it creates a problem of multicollinearity with the percentage of the legislature that is female ($r = 0.45$). When both variables are in the model, neither is statistically significant, although the percentage of the legislature that is female is near-significant ($p = 0.12$). The number of years democratic is not significant even when the percentage of the legislature that is female is excluded from the model. When the number of years democratic is excluded from the model, the percentage of the legislature that is female is strongly significant. I present the results with the number of years democratic excluded to highlight the role played by women's descriptive representation.

21. A measure of quotas based on an index of quota strength is not statistically significant either.

22. The percentage of the legislature that is female remains statistically insignificant when the model excludes the variable measuring the number of years that the country has been democratic.

Chapter 8

1. Importantly, gender differences in the priority that representatives place on women and women's groups were not significant in the Colombian Senate, and women in the Colombian Chamber of Representatives did not prioritize female constituents any differently than men. However, women in both chambers placed high priority on women's issues supporting the conclusion that they represent women in their political attitudes.

2. Except in Argentina, where women are more likely to cosponsor these bills but not individually sponsor them.

3. Recall that a special committee for women's issues does not exist in Colombia, making it impossible to know whether women would represent women's issues by sitting on a women's issue committee.

4. Chapter 3 did find that women in Costa Rica are less likely to prioritize bill sponsorship and women in the Colombian lower house are less likely to view sitting on committees as "very important," but the differences were substantively small. In Costa Rica, this lower priority did translate into behavior to some extent. Women in Costa Rica were less likely to cosponsor bills than men.

5. An important difference emerged on agriculture issues, a category often considered to be "men's domain." In Colombia, women placed higher priority on children and family issues than did men.

References

Aarts, Kees, and Jacques Thomassen. 2008. Satisfaction with Democracy: Do Institutions Matter? *Electoral Studies* 27 (1):5–18.

Abdala, Josefina. 2006. Personal interview, June 27.

Achen, Christopher H. 1978. Measuring Representation. *American Journal of Political Science* 22 (3):475–510.

Aguilar, Virginia. 1999. Personal interview, July 13.

Alcántara, Manuel. 2006. *Datos de Opinión: Élites Parlamentarias Latinoamericanas.* Salamanca, Spain: Instituto Interuniversitario de Iberoamérica de la Universidad de Salamanca.

Almond, Gabriel A., and Sidney Verba. 1963. *The Civic Culture.* Princeton, NJ: Princeton University Press.

Anagnoson, J. Theodore. 1983. Home Style in New Zealand. *Legislative Studies Quarterly* VIII (2):157–175.

Anderson, Christopher J., André Blais, Shaun Bowler, Todd Donovan, and Ola Listhaug. 2005. *Losers' Consent: Elections and Democratic Legitimacy.* New York: Oxford University Press.

Anderson, Christopher J., and Christine Guillory. 1997. Political Institutions and Satisfaction with Democracy: A Cross-National Analysis of Consensus and Majoritarian Systems. *American Political Science Review* 91 (1):66–81.

Anderson, Christopher J., and Yuliya V. Tverdova. 2003. Corruption, Political Allegiances, and Attitudes toward Government in Contemporary Democracies. *American Journal of Political Science* 47 (1):91–109.

Araújo, Clara. 2008. Mujeres y Elecciones Legislativas en Brasil: Las Cuotas y Su (In)Eficacia. In *Mujeres y Política en América Latina*, ed. N. Archenti and M. I. Tula, 87–106. Buenos Aires: Heliasta.

Araújo, Clara, and Ana Isabel García. 2006. Latin America: The Experience and the Impact of Quotas in Latin America. In *Women, Quotas, and Politics*, ed. D. Dahlerup, 83–111. New York: Routledge.

Arceneaux, Kevin, and David W. Nickerson. 2009. Modeling Certainty with Clustered Data: A Comparison of Methods. *Political Analysis* 17 (2):177–190.

Archenti, Nélida, and María Inés Tula. 2008a. Algunas Cuestiones Iniciales sobre las Leyes de Cuotas. In *Mujeres y Política en América Latina*, ed. N. Archenti and M. I. Tula, 9–29. Buenos Aires: Heliasta.

———, eds. 2008b. *Mujeres y Política en América Latina: Sistemas Electorales y Cuotas de Género*. Buenos Aires: Heliasta.

Arnold, Laura W. 2000. Women, Committees and Power in the Senate. Paper read at Women Transforming Congress, April 13–15, Carl Albert Center, University of Oklahoma, Norman, OK.

Atkeson, Lonna Rae. 2003. Not All Cues Are Created Equal: The Conditional Impact of Female Candidates on Political Engagement. *Journal of Politics* 65 (4):1040–1061.

Atkeson, Lonna Rae, and Nancy Carrillo. 2007. More Is Better: The Influence of Collective Female Descriptive Representation on External Efficacy. *Politics & Gender* 3 (1):79–101.

Augsburger, Silvia. 2006. Personal interview, June 29.

Baldez, Lisa. 2002. *Why Women Protest: Women's Movements in Chile*. New York: Cambridge University Press.

———. 2004a. Obedecieron y Cumplieron? The Impact of the Gender Quota Law in Mexico. Paper read at International Congress of the Latin American Studies Association, Las Vegas, NV.

———. 2004b. Elected Bodies: The Gender Quota Law for Legislative Candidates in Mexico. *Legislative Studies Quarterly* 29 (2):231–258.

———. 2007. Primaries vs. Quotas: Gender and Candidate Nominations in Mexico, 2003. *Latin America Politics and Society* 47 (3):69–96.

Banaszak, Lee Ann, Karen Beckwith, and Dieter Rucht, eds. 2003. *Women's Movements Facing the Reconfigured State*. Cambridge: Cambridge University Press.

Banducci, Susan A., Todd Donovan, and Jeffrey A. Karp. 1999. Proportional Representation and Attitudes about Politics: Evidence from New Zealand. *Electoral Studies* 18:533–555.

———. 2004. Minority Representation, Empowerment, and Participation. *Journal of Politics* 66 (2):534–556.

Bartels, Larry M. 1991. Constituency Opinion and Congressional Policy-Making: The Reagan Defense Build-up. *American Political Science Review* 85 (2):457–574.

Bauer, Gretchen, and Hannah E. Britton, eds. 2006. *Women in African Parliaments*. Boulder: Lynne Rienner.

Bayard de Volo, Lorraine. 2001. *Mothers of Heroes and Martyrs: Gender Identity Politics in Nicaragua, 1979–1999*. Baltimore: Johns Hopkins University Press.

Beck, Nathaniel, and Jonathan N. Katz. 1995a. Nuisance vs. Substance: Specifying and Estimating Time-Series Cross-Section Models. *Political Analysis* 6:1–36.

———. 1995b. What to Do (and Not to Do) with Time-Series Cross-Section Data in Comparative Politics. *American Political Science Review* 89:634–647.

Beckwith, Karen. 2005. A Common Language of Gender? *Politics & Gender* 1 (1): 128–137.

Beckwith, Karen, and Kimberly Cowell-Meyers. 2007. Sheer Numbers: Critical Representation Thresholds and Women's Political Representation. *Perspectives on Politics* 5 (3):553–565.

Blair, Diane D., and Jeanie R. Stanley. 1991. Personal Relationships and Legislative Power: Male and Female Perceptions. *Legislative Studies Quarterly* XVI (4):495–507.

Bratton, Kathleen. 2005. Critical Mass Theory Revisited: The Behavior and Success of Token Women in State Legislatures. *Politics & Gender* 1 (1):97–125.

Bratton, Kathleen A. 2002. The Effect of Legislative Diversity on Agenda Setting: Evidence from Six State Legislatures. *American Politics Research* 30 (2):-115–142.

Bratton, Kathleen A., and Leonard P. Ray. 2002. Descriptive Representation, Policy Outcomes, and Municipal Day-Care Coverage in Norway. *American Journal of Political Science* 46 (2):428–437.

Britton, Hannah E. 2008. Challenging Traditional Thinking on Electoral Systems. In *Women and Legislative Representation*, ed. M. Tremblay, 111–122. New York: Palgrave Macmillan.

Broughton, Sharon, and Sonia Palmieri. 1999. Gendered Contributions to Parliamentary Debates: The Case of Euthanasia. *Australian Journal of Political Science* 34 (1):29–45.

Bruhn, Kathleen. 2003. Whores and Lesbians: Political Activism, Party Strategies, and Gender Quotas in Mexico. *Electoral Studies* 22 (2):101–119.

Buck, Vincent J., and Bruce E. Cain. 1990. British MPs in Their Constituencies. *Legislative Studies Quarterly* XV (1):127–143.

Burrell, Barbara. 1997. The Political Leadership of Women and Public Policymaking. *Policy Studies Journal* 25 (4):565–568.

Cain, Bruce E., John A. Ferejohn, and Morris P. Fiorina. 1983. The Constituency Component: A Comparison of Service in Great Britain and the United States. *Comparative Political Studies* 16 (1):67–91.

———. 1987. *The Personal Vote*. Cambridge, MA: Harvard University Press.

Campbell, James E. 1982. Cosponsoring Legislation in the U.S. Congress. *Legislative Studies Quarterly* 7 (3):412–422.

Campbell Barr, Epsy. 2004. Las Mujeres en Las Decisiones Fundamentales: Una Experiencia Desde el PAC. *Revista Parlamentaria* 12 (1):19–30.

Canache, Damarys, and Michael E. Allison. 2005. Perceptions of Political Corruption in Latin American Democracies. *Latin American Politics & Society* 47 (3):91–111.

Carey, John M. 1996. *Term Limits and Legislative Representation*. New York: Cambridge University Press.

Carey, John M., and Matthew Soberg Shugart. 1995. Incentives to Cultivate a Personal Vote. *Electoral Studies* 14 (4):417–439.

Carrió, Elisa M. 2002. The Challenges of Women's Participation in the Legislature: A New Look at Argentina. In *Women in Parliament: Beyond Numbers*, ed. J. Ballington and A. Karam, 164–172. Stockholm, Sweden: International IDEA.

Carroll, Susan J., ed. 2001. *The Impact of Women in Public Office*. Bloomington: Indiana University Press.

———. 2002. Representing Women: Congresswomen's Perceptions of Their Representational Roles. In *Women Transforming Congress*, ed. C. S. Rosenthal, 49–68. Norman: University of Oklahoma Press.

Castles, Francis. 1981. Female Legislative Representation and the Electoral System. *Politics* 1:21–27.

Catalano, Ana. 2008. Women Acting for Women? An Analysis of Gender and Debate Participation in the British House of Commons 2005–2007. *Politics & Gender* 5 (1):45–68.

Caul, Miki. 1999. Women's Representation in Parliament: The Role of Political Parties. *Party Politics* 5 (1):79–98.

———. 2001. Political Parties and the Adoption of Candidate Gender Quotas: A Cross-National Analysis. *Journal of Politics* 63 (4):1214–1229.

Celis, Karen. 2008. Representation in Legislatures: When Representative Acts, Contexts and Women's Interests Become Important. *Representation* 44 (2):111–124.

Celis, Karen, Sarah Childs, Johanna Kantola, and Mona Lena Krook. 2008. Rethinking Women's Substantive Representation. *Representation* 44 (2):99–110.

Chamorro, Isabel. 1999. Personal interview, July 8.

Chaney, Elsa M. 1979. *Supermadre: Women in Politics in Latin America*. Austin: University of Texas Press.

———. 1998. Supermadre Revisited. In *Women's Participation in Mexican Political Life*, ed. V. M. Rodriguez, 78–83. Boulder: Westview Press.

Chaney, Paul. 2006. Critical Mass, Deliberation and the Substantive Representation of Women: Evidence from the UK's Devolution Programme. *Political Studies* 54:691–714.

Chang, Eric C. C., and Yun-han Chu. 2006. Corruption and Trust: Exceptionalism in East Asian Democracies? *Journal of Politics* 68 (2):259–271.

Chappell, Louise. 2006. Comparing Political Institutions: Revealing the Gendered "Logic of Appropriateness." *Politics & Gender* 2 (2):221–263.

Childs, Sarah. 2001. In Their Own Words: New Labour Women and the Substantive Representation of Women. *British Journal of Politics and International Relations* 3 (2):173–190.

———. 2004. *New Labour Women's MPs: Women Representing Women*. New York: Routledge.

———. 2008. *Women and British Party Politics: Descriptive, Substantive, and Symbolic Representation*. London: Routledge.

Childs, Sarah, and Mona Lena Krook. 2006. Should Feminists Give Up on Critical Mass? A Contingent Yes. *Politics & Gender* 2 (4):522–530.

Childs, Sarah, and Julie Withey. 2004. Women Representatives Acting for Women: Sex and the Signing of Early Day Motions in the 1997 British Parliament. *Political Studies* 52:552–564.

CLARIFY: Software for Interpreting and Presenting Statistical Results 2.0. Harvard University, Cambridge, MA.

Clarke, Harold D. 1978. Determinants of Provincial Constituency Service Behaviour: A Multivariate Analysis. *Legislative Studies Quarterly* 3 (4):601–628.

Colombia: Ley Contra Violencia a Mujeres. 2008. *La Jornada*. June 13.

Contreras, Rina. 1999. La Mujer y Una Nueva Dimension de la Actividad Politica. *Revista Parlamentaria* 7 (1):45–59.

Cook, Elizabeth Adell. 1994. Voter Responses to Women Senate Candidates. In *The Year of the Woman: Myths and Realities*, ed. E. A. Cook, S. Thomas, and C. Wilcox, 217–236. Boulder: Westview Press.

Coppedge, Michael. 1997. A Classification of Latin American Political Parties. Kellogg Institute Working Paper 244, University of Notre Dame.

Córdoba Ruiz, Piedad. 2002. Mujeres en el Congreso de Colombia. In *Mujeres en el parlamento: más allá de los números*, ed. M. Méndez-Montalvo and J. Ballington, 239–250. Stockholm: International IDEA.

Costa Benavides, Jimena. 2003. Women's Political Participation in Bolivia: Progress and Obstacles. Paper read at International IDEA Workshop, The Implementation of Quotas: Latin American Experiences, February 23–24, Lima, Peru.

Cox, Gary W. 1997. *Making Votes Count*. New York: Cambridge University Press.

Cox, Gary W., and Mathew D. McCubbins. 2005. *Setting the Agenda: Responsible Party Government in the U.S. House of Representatives*. New York: Cambridge University Press.

Craske, Nikki. 1999. *Women and Politics in Latin America*. New Brunswick, NJ: Rutgers University Press.

———. 2003. Gender, Politics, and Legislation. In *Gender in Latin America*, ed. S. Chant and N. Craske, 19–45. Rutgers: Rutgers University Press.

Creevey, Lucy. 2006. Senegal: Contending with Religious Constraints. In *Women in African Parliaments*, ed. G. Bauer and H. E. Britton, 215–245. Boulder: Lynne Rienner.

Crisp, Brian F, and Scott W. Desposato. 2004. Constituency Building in Multimember Districts: Collusion or Conflict? *Journal of Politics* 66 (1):136–156.

Crisp, Brian F., Maria C. Escobar-Lemmon, Bradford S. Jones, Mark P. Jones, and Michelle M. Taylor-Robinson. 2004. Vote-Seeking Incentives and Legislative Representation in Six Presidential Democracies. *Journal of Politics* 66 (3):823–846.

Crowley, Jocelyn Elise. 2004. When Tokens Matter. *Legislative Studies Quarterly* 29 (1):109–136.

Curtin, Jennifer. 2008. Gendering Parliamentary Representation: A Mixed System Producing Mixed Results. In *Women and Legislative Representation*, ed. M. Tremblay, 191–202. New York: Palgrave Macmillan.

Dahlerup, Drude. 1988. From a Small to a Large Minority: Women in Scandinavian Politics. *Scandinavian Political Studies* 11 (4):275–297.

Dahlerup, Drude. 2006a. The Story of the Theory of Critical Mass. *Politics & Gender* 2 (4):511–522.

———, ed. 2006b. *Women, Politics, and Quotas*. New York: Routledge.

Dahlerup, Drude, and Lenita Freidenvall. 2005. Quotas as a "Fast Track" to Equal Representation for Women. *International Feminist Journal of Politics* 7 (1):26–48.

Dalton, Russell J. 1996. *Citizen Politics: Public Opinion and Political Parties in Advanced Western Democracies*. 2nd ed. Chatham, NJ: Chatham House.

———. 2004. *Democratic Challenges, Democratic Choices: The Erosion of Political Support in Advanced Industrial Democracies*. New York: Oxford University Press.

Darcy, Robert, Susan Welch, and Janet Clark. 1994. *Women, Elections, and Representation*. 2nd ed. Lincoln: University of Nebraska Press.

Davis, Charles L., Roderic Ai Camp, and Kenneth M. Coleman. 2004. The Influence of Party Systems on Citizen's Perceptions of Corruption and Electoral Response in Latin America. *Comparative Political Studies* 37 (6):677–703.

del Campo, Esther, and Óscar Luengo. 2008. El Impacto de los Sistemas Electorales y Las Leyes de Cuotas en los Países Andinos: Las Elecciones Legislativas en Bolivia, Ecuador, y Perú. In *Mujeres y Política en América Latina*, ed. N. Archenti and M. I. Tula, 137–164. Buenos Aires: Heliasta.

Desposato, Scott W., and Barbara Norrander. 2009. The Gender Gap in Latin America: Contextual and Individual Influences on Gender and Political Participation. *British Journal of Political Science* 39 (1):141–162.

Devlin, Claire, and Robert Elgie. 2008. The Effect of Increased Women's Representation in Parliament: The Case of Rwanda. *Parliamentary Affairs* 61 (2):237–254.

Diamond, Irene. 1977. *Sex Roles in the State House*. New Haven: Yale University Press.

Diamond, Irene, and Nancy Hartsock. 1981. Beyond Interests in Politics: A Comment on Virginia Sapiro's "When Are Interests Interesting? The Problem of Political Representation of Women." *American Political Science Review* 75:717–721.

di Tullio, Juliana. 2006. Personal interview, June 27.

Dodson, Debra. 1998. Representing Women's Interests in the U.S. House of Representatives. In *Women and Elective Office: Past, Present, and Future*, ed. S. Thomas and C. Wilcox, 130–149. New York: Oxford University Press.

———. 2001. Acting for Women: Is What Legislators Say, What They Do? In *The Impact of Women in Public Office*, ed. S. J. Carroll, 225–242. Bloomington: Indiana University Press.

———. 2006. *The Impact of Women in Congress*. New York: Oxford University Press.

Dodson, Debra, and Susan J. Carroll. 1991. *Reshaping the Agenda: Women in State Legislatures*. New Brunswick, NJ: Eagleton Institute of Politics.

Dolan, Kathleen, and Lynne E. Ford. 1995. Women in the State Legislatures: Feminist Identity and Legislative Behaviors. *American Politics Quarterly* 23 (1):96–108.

———. 1997. Change and Continuity among Women State Legislators: Evidence from Three Decades. *Political Research Quarterly* 50 (1):137–151.

Dovi, Suzanne. 2002. Preferable Descriptive Representatives: Will Just Any Woman, Black, or Latino Do? *American Political Science Review* 96 (4):729–744.

———. 2007. Theorizing Women's Representation in the United States. *Politics & Gender* 3 (3):297–319.

Duerst-Lahti, Georgia. 2005. Institutional Gendering: Theoretical Insights into the Environment of Women Officeholders. In *Women and Elective Office*, ed. S. Thomas and C. Wilcox, 230–243. New York: Oxford University Press.

Duerst-Lahti, Georgia, and Rita Mae Kelly, eds. 1995. *Gender Power, Leadership, and Governance.* Ann Arbor: University of Michigan Press.

Duerst-Lahti, Georgia, and Dayna Verstegen. 1995. Making Something of Absence: The "Year of the Woman" and Women's Political Representation. In *Gender Power, Leadership, and Governance*, ed. G. Duerst-Lahti and R. M. Kelly, 213–238. Ann Arbor: University of Michigan Press.

Duverger, Maurice. 1954. *Political Parties.* New York: Wiley.

———. 1955. *The Political Role of Women.* Paris: UNESCO.

Edelman, Murray. 1964. *The Symbolic Uses of Politics.* Chicago: University of Illinois Press.

Engstrom, Richard L. 1987. District Magnitude and the Election of Women to the Irish Dail. *Electoral Studies* 6 (2):123–132.

Esaiasson, Peter. 2000. How Members of Parliament Define their Task. In *Beyond Westminster and Congress: The Nordic Experience*, ed. P. Esaiasson and K. Heidar, 51–82. Columbus: Ohio State University Press.

Escobar-Lemmon, Maria C., and Michelle M. Taylor-Robinson. 2005. Women Ministers in Latin American Government: When, Where, and Why? *American Journal of Political Science* 49 (4):829–844.

Eulau, Heinz, and Paul D. Karps. 1977. The Puzzle of Representation: Specifying Components of Responsiveness. *Legislative Studies Quarterly* II (3):233–254.

Farrell, David M., and Ian McAllister. 2006. Voter Satisfaction and Electoral Systems: Does Preferential Voting in Candidate-Centred Systems Make a Difference? *European Journal of Political Research* 45 (5):723–749.

Fenno, Richard F. 1973. *Congressmen in Committees.* Boston: Little Brown.

———. 1977. U.S. House Members in Their Constituencies: An Exploration. *American Political Science Review* 71:883–917.

———. 1978. *Home Style: House Members in Their Districts.* New York: HarperCollins.

Fournier Vargas, Alicia. 2001. La Comisión Legislativa de las Mujeres: La Construcción de la Democracia Genérica. *Revista Parlamentaria* 9 (2):37–41.

Franceschet, Susan. 2005. *Women and Politics in Chile.* Boulder: Lynne Rienner.

Franceschet, Susan, and Jennifer M. Piscopo. 2008. Gender Quotas and Women's Substantive Representation: Lessons from Argentina. *Politics & Gender* 4 (3):393–425.

Franzese, Robert J. 2005. Empirical Strategies for Various Manifestations of Multilevel Data. *Political Analysis* 13:430–446.

Frechette, Guillaume R., Francois Maniquet, and Massimo Morelli. 2008. Incumbents' Interests and Gender Quotas. *American Journal of Political Science* 52 (4):891–907.

Freedom House. 2008. *Freedom in the World 2008*. Available from http://www.freedomhouse.org.

Friedman, Sally. 1996. House Committee Assignments of Women and Minority Newcomers, 1965–1994. *Legislative Studies Quarterly* 21 (1):73–81.

———. 2000. Gender, Home Style, and Representation: Four Women Members of Congress. Paper read at Women Transforming Congress, April 13–15, Carl Albert Center, University of Oklahoma, Norman, OK.

Frisch, Scott A., and Sean Q. Kelly. 2003. A Place at the Table: Women's Committee Requests and Women's Committee Assignments in the U.S. House. *Women & Politics* 25 (3):1–26.

———. 2006. *Committee Assignment Politics in the U.S. House of Representatives*. Norman: University of Oklahoma Press.

Furlong, Marlea, and Kimberly Riggs. 1996. Women's Participation in National-Level Politics and Government: The Case of Costa Rica. *Women's Studies International Forum* 19 (6):633–643.

Gallagher, Michael, and Paul Mitchell, eds. 2008. *The Politics of Electoral Systems*. New York: Oxford University Press.

Gallup Organization. 2001. *Latin American Women Leadership Study*. Commissioned by the Inter-American Development Bank in collaboration with the Inter-American Dialogue 2001. Retrieved September 2, 2008, from http://www.iadb.org/sds/doc/GallupStudyEnglish.pdf.

García Quesada, Ana Isabel. 2003. Putting the Mandate into Practice: Legal Reform in Costa Rica. Paper read at International IDEA Workshop, The Implementation of Quotas: Latin American Experiences, February 23–24, Lima, Peru.

Gay, Claudine. 2001. The Effect of Black Congressional Representation on Political Participation. *American Political Science Review* 95 (3):589–602.

———. 2002. Spirals of Trust? The Effect of Descriptive Representation on the Relationship between Citizens and Their Government. *American Journal of Political Science* 46 (4):717–733.

Gerring, John, and Strom C. Thacker. 2004. Political Institutions and Corruption: The Role of Unitarism and Parliamentarism. *British Journal of Political Science* 34 (2):295–330.

Goetz, Anne Marie. 2007. Political Cleaners: Women as the New Anti-Corruption Force? *Development & Change* 38 (1):87–105.

Goetz, Anne Marie, and Shireen Hassim, eds. 2003. *No Shortcuts to Power: African Women in Politics and Policy Making*. New York: Zed Books.

Gray, Tricia. 2003. Electoral Gender Quotas: Lessons from Argentina and Chile. *Bulletin of Latin American Research* 22 (1):52–78.

Grey, Sandra. 2006. Numbers and Beyond: The Relevance of Critical Mass in Gender Research. *Politics & Gender* 2 (4):492–502.

Halligan, John, Robert Krause, Robert Williams, and Geoffrey Hawker. 1988. Constituency Service among Sub-National Legislators in Australia and Canada. *Legislative Studies Quarterly* 13 (1):49–63.

Hansen, Susan B. 1997. Talking about Politics: Gender and Contextual Effects on Political Proselytizing. *Journal of Politics* 59 (1):73–103.

Hawkesworth, Mary. 2003. Congressional Enactments of Race-Gender: Toward a Theory of Raced-Gendered Institutions. *American Political Science Review* 97 (4):1214–1229.

Heath, Roseanna M., Leslie A. Schwindt-Bayer, and Michelle M. Taylor-Robinson. 2005. Women on the Sidelines: Women's Representation on Committees in Latin American Legislatures. *American Journal of Political Science* 49 (2):420–436.

Heitshusen, Valerie, Garry Young, and David M. Wood. 1999. Legislative Home Styles in Cross-National Perspective: Resource Allocation and Perceptions of Constituency in Australia, Canada and New Zealand. Paper read at Annual Meeting of the American Political Science Association, Atlanta, GA.

———. 2005. Electoral Context and MP Constituency Focus in Australia, Canada, Ireland, New Zealand, and the United Kingdom. *American Journal of Political Science* 49 (1):32–45.

Hernández, Cinthya 2006. Personal Interview, June 20.

Hibbing, John R., and Samuel C. Patterson. 1994. Public Trust in the New Parliaments of Central and Eastern Europe. *Political Studies* 42 (4):570–592.

Hibbing, John R., and Elizabeth Theiss-Morse. 1995. *Congress as Public Enemy: Public Attitudes toward American Political Institutions*. Cambridge: Cambridge University Press.

High-Pippert, Angela, and John Comer. 1998. Female Empowerment: The Influence of Women Representing Women. *Women & Politics* 19 (4):53–66.

Hinojosa, Magda. 2008. ¿Más Mujeres? Mexico's Mixed-Member Electoral System. In *Women and Legislative Representation*, ed. M. Tremblay, 177–189. New York: Palgrave Macmillan.

Htun, Mala. 2000. Women's Leadership in Latin America: Trends and Challenges. In *Politics Matters: A Dialogue of Women Political Leaders*, 13–26. Washington, DC: Inter-American Development Bank, Inter-American Dialogue, and International Center for Research on Women.

———. 2003. *Sex and the State: Abortion, Divorce, and the Family under Latin American Dictatorships and Democracies*. New York: Cambridge University Press.

Htun, Mala N., and Mark P. Jones. 2002. Engendering the Right to Participate in Decision-Making: Electoral Quotas and Women's Leadership in Latin America. In *Gender and the Politics of Rights and Democracy in Latin America*, ed. N. Craske and M. Molyneux, 32–56. New York: Palgrave Publishers.

Htun, Mala, and Timothy J. Power. 2006. Gender, Parties, and Support for Equal Rights in the Brazilian Congress. *Latin America Politics and Society* 48 (4):83–104.

Huntington, Samuel P. 1991. *The Third Wave: Democratization in the Late Twentieth Century*. Norman: University of Oklahoma Press.

Hurley, Patricia A. 1982. Collective Representation Reappraised. *Legislative Studies Quarterly* 7:199–136.

Ingall, Rachael E., and Brian F. Crisp. 2001. Determinants of Home Style: The Many Incentives for Going Home in Colombia. *Legislative Studies Quarterly* XXVI:487–512.

Inglehart, Ronald. 1999. Postmodernization Erodes Respect for Authority, but Increases Support for Democracy. In *Critical Citizens: Global Support for Democratic Governance*, ed. P. Norris, 236–256. New York: Oxford University Press.

Inglehart, Ronald, and Pippa Norris. 2003. *Rising Tide: Gender Equality and Cultural Change around the World*. New York: Cambridge University Press.

Instituto Social y Político de la Mujer. n.d. Mujeres en Lugares de Decisión. Retrieved November 6, 2008, from http://www.ispm.org.ar/paridad/poder_legis.html

International IDEA and Stockholm University. 2009. Global Database of Quotas for Women. Retrieved June 1, 2009, from http://www.quotaproject.org

IPU (Inter-Parliamentary Union). 1995. *Women in Parliaments, 1945–1995: A World Statistical Survey*. Geneva: Inter-Parliamentary Union.

———. 2006. Women in National Parliaments, as of July 31, 2006. Retrieved September 20, 2006, from www.ipu.org

———. 2008. Women in National Parliaments, as of July 31, 2008. Retrieved September 14, 2008, from www.ipu.org

Jackman, Robert W., and Ross A. Miller. 1996. A Renaissance of Political Culture? *American Journal of Political Science* 40 (3):632–659.

Jaquette, Jane S., ed. 1994. *The Women's Movement in Latin America: Participation and Democracy*. 2nd ed. Boulder: Lynne Rienner.

Jaquette, Jane S., and Sharon L. Wolchik, eds. 1998. *Women and Democracy*. Baltimore: Johns Hopkins University Press.

Jiménez Polanco, Jacqueline. 2008. La Representación Política de las Mujeres en la República Dominicana: Obstáculos y Potencialidades. In *Mujeres y Política en América Latina*, ed. N. Archenti and M. I. Tula, 165–190. Buenos Aires: Heliasta.

Johnson, Marilyn, and Susan J. Carroll. 1978. *Profile of Women Holding Office II*. New Brunswick, NJ: Center for the American Woman in Congress.

Jones, Mark P. 1996. Increasing Women's Representation via Gender Quotas: The Argentine Ley de Cupos. *Women & Politics* 16 (4):75–96.

———. 1997. Legislator Gender and Legislator Policy Priorities in the Argentine Chamber of Deputies and the United States House of Representatives. *Policy Studies Journal* 25 (4):613–629.

———. 1998. Gender Quotas, Electoral Laws, and the Election of Women. *Comparative Political Studies* 31 (1):3–21.

———. 2004a. The Recruitment and Selection of Legislative Candidates in Argentina. Paper read at Pathways to Power: Political Recruitment and Democracy in Latin America, April 3–4, 2004, Winston-Salem, NC.

———. 2004b. Quota Legislation and the Election of Women: Learning from the Costa Rican Experience. *Journal of Politics* 66 (4):1203–1223.

———. 2005. The Desirability of Gender Quotas: Considering Context and Design. *Politics & Gender* 1 (4):645–652.

———. 2009. Gender Quotas, Electoral Laws, and the Election of Women: Evidence from the Latin American Vanguard. *Comparative Political Studies* 42 (1): 56–81.

Jones, Mark P., and Patricio Navia. 1999. Assessing the Effectiveness of Gender Quotas in Open-List Proportional Representation Electoral Systems. *Social Science Quarterly* 80 (2):341–355.

Jones, Mark P., Sebastian Saiegh, Pablo T. Spiller, and Mariano Tommasi. 2002. Amateur Legislators—Professional Politicians: The Consequences of Party-Centered Electoral Rules in a Federal System. *American Journal of Political Science* 46 (3):656–669.

Kampwirth, Karen. 1998. Feminism, Antifeminism, and Electoral Politics in Postwar Nicaragua and El Salvador. *Political Science Quarterly* 113 (2):259–279.

Karp, Jeffrey A., and Susan A. Banducci. 2008. When Politics Is Not Just a Man's Game: Women's Representation and Political Engagement. *Electoral Studies* 27 (1):105–115.

Kathlene, Lyn. 1994. Power and Influence in State Legislative Policymaking: The Interaction of Gender and Position in Committee Hearing Debates. *American Political Science Review* 88 (3):560–576.

———. 1995. Position Power versus Gender Power: Who Holds the Floor? In *Gender Power, Leadership, and Governance*, ed. G. Duerst-Lahti and R. M. Kelly, 167–193. Ann Arbor: University of Michigan Press.

———. 1998. In a Different Voice: Women and the Policy Process. In *Women and Elective Office: Past, Present and Future*, ed. S. Thomas and C. Wilcox, 188–202. New York: Oxford University Press.

Kenworthy, Lane, and Melissa Malami. 1999. Gender Inequality in Political Representation: A Worldwide Comparative Analysis. *Social Forces* 78 (1):235–269.

Kessler, Daniel, and Keith Krehbiel. 1996. Dynamics of Cosponsorship. *American Political Science Review* 90 (3):555–566.

King, Gary, Michael Tomz, and Jason Wittenberg. 2000. Making the Most of Statistical Analyses: Improving Interpretation and Presentation. *American Journal of Political Science* 44 (2):347–361.

Kittilson, Miki. 2006. *Challenging Parties, Changing Parliaments*. Columbus: Ohio State University Press.

Kittilson, Miki Caul. 2005. In Support of Gender Quotas: Setting New Standards, Bringing Visible Gains. *Politics & Gender* 1 (4):638–644.

———. 2008. Representing Women: The Adoption of Family Leave in Comparative Perspective. *Journal of Politics* 70 (2):323–334.

———. 2010. Comparing Gender, Institutions and Political Behavior: Toward an Integrated Theoretical Framework. *Perspectives on Politics* 8 (1):217–222.

Kittilson, Miki Caul, and Leslie A. Schwindt-Bayer. 2008. Gender, Institutions and Political Engagement: A Comparative Perspective. Paper read at Annual Meeting of the American Political Science Association, August 28–31, Boston.

Kline, Harvey F. 1977. Committee Membership Turnover in the Colombian National Congress, 1958–1974. *Legislative Studies Quarterly* 2 (1):29–43.

Klingemann, Hans-Dieter. 1999. Mapping Political Support in the 1990s: A Global Analysis. In *Critical Citizens: Global Support for Democratic Governance*, ed. P. Norris, 31–56. New York: Oxford University Press.

Koger, Gregory. 2003. Position Taking and Cosponsorship in the U.S. House. *Legislative Studies Quarterly* 28 (2):225–246.

Kostadinova, Tatiana. 2007. Ethnic and Women's Representation under Mixed Election Systems. *Electoral Studies* 26:418–431.

Krehbiel, Keith. 1995. Cosponsors and Wafflers from A to Z. *American Journal of Political Science* 39 (4):906–923.

Krehbiel, Keith, Kenneth A. Shepsle, and Barry R. Weingast. 1987. Why Are Congressional Committees Powerful? *American Political Science Review* 81 (3):929–945.

Krook, Mona Lena. 2004. Gender Quotas as a Global Phenomenon: Actors and Strategies in Quota Adoption. *European Political Science* 3 (3):59–65.

———. 2005. Politicizing Representation: Campaigns for Candidate Gender Quotas Worldwide. Ph.D. Dissertation, Department of Political Science, Columbia University.

———. 2006. Reforming Representation: The Diffusion of Candidate Gender Quotas Worldwide. *Politics & Gender* 2 (3):303–327.

———. 2007. Candidate Gender Quotas: A Framework for Analysis. *European Journal of Political Research* 46:367–394.

———. 2009. *Quotas for Women in Politics: Gender and Candidate Selection Reform Worldwide.* New York: Oxford University Press.

Kunovich, Sheri, and Pamela Paxton. 2005. Pathways to Power: The Role of Political Parties in Women's National Political Representation. *American Journal of Sociology* 111 (2):505–552.

Lagos, Marta. 2001. Between Stability and Crisis in Latin America. *Journal of Democracy* 12 (1):137–145.

Latinobarómetro. 2004. *Informe Resumen: Una Década de Mediciones*. Santiago de Chile: Corporación Latinobarómetro.

Lawless, Jennifer L. 2004. Politics of Presence? Congresswomen and Symbolic Representation. *Political Research Quarterly* 57 (1):81–99.

Leader, Shelah Gilbert. 1977. The Policy Impact of Elected Women Officials. In *The Impact of the Electoral Process*, ed. J. Cooper and L. Maisels, 265–284. Beverly Hills: Sage.

Levi, Margaret, and Laura Stoker. 2000. Political Trust and Trustworthiness. *Annual Review of Political Science* 3 (1):475–507.

Lijphart, Arend. 1999. *Patterns of Democracy: Government Forms and Performance in Thirty-Six Countries.* New Haven: Yale University Press.

Lindgren, Karl-Oskar, Magdalena Inkinen, and Sten Widmalm. 2009. Who Knows Best What the People Want: Women or Men? A Study of Political Representation in India. *Comparative Political Studies* 42 (1):31–55.

Little, Thomas H., Dana Dunn, and Rebecca E. Deen. 2001. A View from the Top: Gender Differences in Legislative Priorities among State Legislative Leaders. *Women & Politics* 22 (4):29–50.

Long, J. Scott. 1997. *Regression Models for Categorical and Limited Dependent Variables.* Thousand Oaks, CA: Sage.

Long, J. Scott, and Jeremy Freese. 2005. *Regression Models for Categorical Outcomes Using Stata.* College Station, TX: Stata Press.

Longman, Timothy. 2006. Rwanda: Achieving Equality or Serving an Authoritarian State? In *Women in African Parliaments*, ed. G. Bauer and H. E. Britton, 133–150. Boulder: Lynne Rienner.

Lovenduski, Joni. 2005. *Feminizing Politics.* Cambridge: Polity.

Lovenduski, Joni, and Pippa Norris. 2003. Westminster Women: The Politics of Presence. *Political Studies* 51 (1):84–102.

Lubertino, María José. 2003. Pioneering Quotas: The Argentine Experience and Beyond. Paper read at International IDEA Workshop, The Implementation of Quotas: Latin American Experiences, February 23–24, Lima, Peru.

Luciak, Ilja A. 2005. Party and State in Cuba: Gender Equality in Political Decision Making. *Politics & Gender* 1 (2):241–264.

Macaulay, Fiona. 2006. *Gender Politics in Brazil and Chile: The Role of Parties in National and Local Policymaking.* New York: Palgrave Macmillan.

Mackay, Fiona. 2008. "Thick" Conceptions of Substantive Representation: Women, Gender, and Political Institutions. *Representation* 44 (2):125–140.

Mansbridge, Jane. 1999. Should Blacks Represent Blacks and Women Represent Women? A Contingent "Yes." *Journal of Politics* 61 (3):628–657.

———. 2003. Rethinking Representation. *American Political Science Review* 97 (4):515–528.

———. 2005. Quota Problems: Combating the Dangers of Essentialism. *Politics & Gender* 1 (4):622–638.

Mansbridge, Jane, and Shauna L. Shames. 2008. Toward a Theory of Backlash: Dynamic Resistance and the Central Role of Power. *Politics & Gender* 4 (4):623–633.

Marsh, Michael, and Bernhard Wessels. 1997. Territorial Representation. *European Journal of Political Research* 32:227–241.

Marx, Jutta. 1992. *Mujeres y Partidos Políticos.* Buenos Aires: Editorial Legasa.

Marx, Jutta, Jutta Borner, and Mariana Caminotti. 2007. *Las Legisladoras: Cupos de Género y Política en Argentina y Brasil.* Buenos Aires: Siglo XXI Editora Iberoamericana.

Matland, Richard E. 1993. Institutional Variables Affecting Female Representation in National Legislatures: The Case of Norway. *Journal of Politics* 55 (3):737–755.

———. 1994. Putting Scandinavian Equality to the Test: An Experimental Evaluation of Gender Stereotyping of Political Candidates in a Sample of Norwegian Voters. *British Journal of Political Science* 24:273–292.

———. 1998. Women's Representation in National Legislatures: Developed and Developing Countries. *Legislative Studies Quarterly* 23 (1):109–125.

———. 2006. Electoral Quotas: Frequency and Effectiveness. In *Women, Quotas, and Politics*, ed. D. Dahlerup, 275–292. New York: Routledge.

Matland, Richard E., and Deborah Dwight Brown. 1992. District Magnitude's Effect on Female Representation in U.S. State Legislatures. *Legislative Studies Quarterly* 17 (4):469–492.

Matland, Richard E., and Donley T. Studlar. 1996. The Contagion of Women Candidates in SMD and PR Electoral Systems: Canada and Norway. *Journal of Politics* 58 (3):707–733.

Matland, Richard E., and Michelle M. Taylor. 1997. Electoral System Effects on Women's Representation: Theoretical Arguments and Evidence from Costa Rica. *Comparative Political Studies* 30 (2):186–210.

Matthews, Donald R. 1960. *U.S. Senators and Their World*. Chapel Hill: University of North Carolina Press.

Mazur, Amy. 2002. *Theorizing Feminist Policy*. Oxford: Oxford University Press.

McAllister, Ian, and Donley T. Studlar. 1992. Gender and Representation among Legislative Candidates in Australia. *Comparative Political Studies* 25 (3):388–411.

Miguel, Luis F. 2008. Political Representation and Gender in Brazil: Quotas for Women and Their Impact. *Bulletin of Latin American Research* 27 (2):197–214.

Miller, Arthur, and Ola Listhaug. 1999. Political Performance and Institutional Trust. In *Critical Citizens: Global Support for Democratic Governance* ed. P. Norris, 204–216. New York: Oxford University Press.

Miller, Francesca. 1994. The Suffrage Movement in Latin America. In *Confronting Change, Challenging Tradition: Women in Latin American History*, ed. G. M. Yeager, 157–176. Wilmington: Scholarly Resources Inc.

Miller, Warren E., and Donald Stokes. 1963. Constituency Influence in Congress. *American Political Science Review* 57:45–56.

Mishler, William, and Richard Rose. 1997. Trust, Distrust and Skepticism: Popular Evaluations of Civil and Political Institutions in Post-Communist Societies. *Journal of Politics* 59 (2):418–451.

———. 2001. What Are the Origins of Political Trust? Testing Institutional and Cultural Theories in Post-Communist Societies. *Comparative Political Studies* 34 (1):30–63.

Molyneux, Maxine. 1985. Mobilization without Emancipation? Women's Interests, State, and Revolution in Nicaragua. *Feminist Studies* 11 (2):227–254.

Morgan, Jana, Rosario Espinal, and Jonathan Hartlyn. 2008. Gender Politics in the Dominican Republic: Advances for Women, Ambivalence from Men. *Politics & Gender* 4 (1):35–63.

Morgenstern, Scott. 2002. Towards a Model of Latin American Legislatures. In *Legislative Politics in Latin America*, ed. S. Morgenstern and B. Nacif, 1–22. New York: Cambridge University Press.

Morgenstern, Scott, and Benito Nacif, eds. 2002. *Legislative Politics in Latin America*. New York: Cambridge University Press.

Moser, Robert G. 2001. The Effects of Electoral Systems on Women's Representation in Post-Communist States. *Electoral Studies* 20:353–369.

Mustapic, Ana Maria. 2002. Oscillating Relations: President and Congress in Argentina. In *Legislative Politics in Latin America*, ed. S. Morgenstern and B. Nacif, 23–47. Cambridge: Cambridge University Press.

Norrander, Barbara. 1999. The Evolution of the Gender Gap. *Public Opinion Quarterly* 63 (4):566–577.

Norris, Pippa. 1985. Women's Legislative Participation in Western Europe. *West European Politics* 8 (4):90–101.

———. 1996. Women Politicians: Transforming Westminster? In *Women in Politics*, ed. J. Lovenduski and P. Norris, 91–104. New York: Oxford University Press.

———. 1999. Institutional Explanations for Political Support. In *Critical Citizens: Global Support for Democratic Governance*, ed. P. Norris, 217–235. New York: Oxford University Press.

Norris, Pippa, and Mark Franklin. 1997. Social Representation. *European Journal of Political Research* 32:185–210.

Norris, Pippa, Elizabeth Vallance, and Joni Lovenduski. 1992. Do Candidates Make a Difference? Gender, Race, Ideology, and Incumbency. *Parliamentary Affairs* 45 (4):496–517.

North, Douglass C. 1990. *Institutions, Institutional Change and Economic Performance*. New York: Cambridge University Press.

Norton, Noelle. 1995. Women, It's Not Enough to Be Elected: Committee Position Makes a Difference. In *Gender Power, Leadership, and Governance*, ed. G. Duerst-Lahti and R. M. Kelly, 115–140. Ann Arbor: University of Michigan Press.

Nye, Joseph S., Philip D. Zelikow, and David C. King, eds. 1997. *Why People Don't Trust Government*. Cambridge: Harvard University Press.

Oakes, Ann, and Elizabeth Almquist. 1993. Women in National Legislatures: A Cross-National Test of Macrostructural Gender Theories. *Population Research and Policy Review* 12 (1):71–81.

O'Regan, Valerie R. 2000. *Gender Matters: Female Policymakers' Influence in Industrialized Nations*. Westport, CT: Praeger.

Pachón Buitrago, Mónica. 2003. Explaining the Performance of the Colombian Congress: Electoral and Legislative Rules and Interactions with the Executive. Paper read at International Congress of the Latin American Studies Association, March 27–29, 2003, Dallas, TX.

Palmer, Harvey D., and Guy D. Whitten. 2003. Questionable Analyses with No Theoretical Innovation: A Response to Royed, Leyden and Borrelli. *British Journal of Political Science* 33 (1):139–149.

Paxton, Pamela. 1997. Women in National Legislatures: A Cross-National Analysis. *Social Science Research* 26:442–464.

Paxton, Pamela, and Melanie M. Hughes. 2007. *Women, Politics, and Power: A Global Perspective*. Los Angeles: Pine Forge Press.

Payne, J. Mark, Daniel Zovatto G., Fernando Carrillo Florez, and Andres Allamand Zavala. 2002. *Democracies in Development: Politics and Reform in Latin America*. Washington, DC: Inter-American Development Bank.

Peterson, V. Spike, and Anne Sisson Runyan. 1999. *Global Gender Issues*. 2nd ed. Boulder: Westview Press.

Phillips, Anne. 1995. *The Politics of Presence*. Oxford: Clarendon Press.

Picado, Sonia. 1999. Personal interview, July 1.

Pitkin, Hanna. 1967. *The Concept of Representation*. Berkeley: University of California Press.

———. 1969. The Concept of Representation. In *Representation*, ed. H. Pitkin, 1–23. New York: Atherton Press.

Poggione, Sarah. 2004. Exploring Gender Differences in State Legislators' Policy Preferences. *Political Research Quarterly* 57 (2):305–314.

Powell, G. Bingham. 2000. *Elections as Instruments of Democracy*. New Haven: Yale University Press.

Prewitt, Kenneth, and Heinz Eulau. 1969. Political Matrix and Political Representation: Prolegomenon to a New Departure from an Old Problem. *American Political Science Review* 63:427–441.

Primo, David M., Matthew L. Jacobsmeier, and Jeffrey Milyo. 2007. Estimating the Impact of State Policies and Institutions with Mixed-Level Data. *State Politics and Policy Quarterly* 7 (4):446–459.

Przeworski, Adam, Susan C. Stokes, and Bernard Manin, eds. 1999. *Democracy, Accountability, and Representation*. New York: Cambridge University Press.

Przeworski, Adam, and Henry Teune. 1970. *The Logic of Comparative Social Inquiry*. New York: Wiley-Interscience.

Putnam, Robert D. 1993. *Making Democracy Work: Civic Traditions in Modern Italy*. Princeton: Princeton University Press.

Quién es La Primera Presidenta del Senado. 2005. *El Tiempo*. July 24.

Ragsdale, Lyn. 1984. The Politics of Presidential Speechmaking, 1949–1980. *American Political Science Review* 78 (4):971–984.

Randall, Vicky, and Ailbhe Smyth. 1987. Bishops and Bailiwicks: Obstacles to Women's Political Participation in Ireland. *Economic and Social Review* 18 (3):189–214.

Reingold, Beth. 1992. Concepts of Representation among Female and Male State Legislators. *Legislative Studies Quarterly* XVII (4):509–537.

———. 2000. *Representing Women: Sex, Gender, and Legislative Behavior in Arizona and California*. Chapel Hill: University of North Carolina Press.

Reingold, Beth, and Jessica Harrell. Forthcoming. The Impact of Descriptive Representation on Women's Political Engagement. *Political Research Quarterly*.

Reynolds, Andrew. 1999. Women in the Legislatures and Executives of the World: Knocking at the Highest Glass Ceiling. *World Politics* 51 (4):547–572.

Reynoso, Diego. 2008. El Exiguo Impacto de Las Leyes de Cuotas en México. In *Mujeres y Política en América Latina*, ed. N. Archenti and M. I. Tula, 87–106. Buenos Aires: Heliasta.

Richardson, Lilliard E., Jr., and Patricia K. Freeman. 1995. Gender Differences in Constituency Service among State Legislators. *Political Research Quarterly* 48 (1):169–179.

Ríos Tobar, Marcela. 2008a. Seizing a Window of Opportunity: The Election of President Bachelet in Chile. *Politics & Gender* 4 (3):509–519.

———, ed. 2008b. *Mujer y Política: El Impacto de las Cuotas de Género en América Latina*. Santiago, Chile: FLACSO-Chile.

Rivera-Cira, Tirza. 1993. "Las Mujeres en los Parlamentos Latinoamericanos." Valparaíso, Chile: Centro de Estudios y Asistencia Legislativa–Universidad Católica de Valparaíso.

Rodríguez, Victoria E. 2003. *Women in Contemporary Mexican Politics*. Austin: University of Texas Press.

Rodríguez Raga, Juan Carlos, and Felipe Botero. 2006. Ordenando el Caos: Elecciones Legislativas y Reforma Electoral en Colombia. *Revista de Ciencia Política* 26 (1):138–151.

Rosas, Guillermo. 2005. The Ideological Organization of Latin American Legislative Parties: An Empirical Analysis of Elite Policy Preferences. *Comparative Political Studies* 38 (7):824–849.

Rose-Ackerman, Susan. 1999. *Corruption and Government: Causes, Consequences, and Reform*. Cambridge: Cambridge University Press.

Rosenthal, Cindy Simon. 1997. A View of Their Own: Women's Committee Leadership Styles and State Legislatures. *Policy Studies Journal* 25 (4):585–600.

———. 1998. *When Women Lead: Integrative Leadership in State Legislatures*. New York: Oxford University Press.

———, ed. 2002. *Women Transforming Congress*. Norman: University of Oklahoma Press.

———. 2005. Women Leading Legislatures: Getting There and Getting Things Done. In *Women and Elected Office: Past, Present, and Future*, ed. S. Thomas and C. Wilcox, 197–212. New York: Oxford University Press.

Rosso, Graciela. 2006. Personal Interview, June 26.

Rule, Wilma. 1981. Why Women Don't Run: The Critical Contextual Factors in Women's Legislative Recruitment. *Western Political Quarterly* 34:60–77.

———. 1987. Electoral Systems, Contextual Factors and Women's Opportunity for Election to Parliament in Twenty-Three Democracies. *Western Political Quarterly* 40 (3):477–498.

———. 1994. Parliaments of, by, and for the People: Except for Women? In *Electoral Systems in Comparative Perspective: Their Impact on Women and Minorities*, ed. J. Zimmerman and W. Rule, 15–30. Westport, CT: Greenwood Press.

Saint-Germain, Michelle A. 1989. Does Their Difference Make a Difference? The Impact of Women on Public Policy in the Arizona Legislature. *Social Science Quarterly* 70:956–968.

Saint-Germain, Michelle A., and Cynthia Chavez Metoyer. 2008. *Women Legislators in Central America: Politics, Democracy, and Policy*. Austin: University of Texas Press.

Saint-Germain, Michelle A., and Martha I. Morgan. 1991. Equality: Costa Rican Women Demand the "Real Thing." *Women & Politics* 11 (3):23–77.

Samuels, David J. 2004. Presidentialism and Accountability for the Economy in Comparative Perspective. *American Political Science Review* 98 (3):425–436.

Samuels, David J., and Matthew Soberg Shugart. 2003. Presidentialism, Elections, and Representation. *Journal of Theoretical Politics* 15 (1):33–60.

Sanbonmatsu, Kira. 2003. Gender-Related Political Knowledge and the Descriptive Representation of Women. *Political Behavior* 25 (4):367–388.

———. 2008. Gender Backlash in American Politics? *Politics & Gender* 4 (4):634–641.

Sapag, Luz María. 2006. Personal Interview, June 16.

Sapiro, Virginia. 1981. When Are Interests Interesting? The Problem of Political Representation of Women. *American Political Science Review* 75 (3):701–716.

Sapiro, Virginia, and Pamela Johnston Conover. 1997. The Variable Gender Basis of Electoral Politics: Gender and Context in the 1992 U.S. Election. *British Journal of Political Science* 27 (4):497–523.

Sawer, Marian, and Marian Simms. 1984. *A Woman's Place: Women and Politics in Australia*. Sydney: George Allen & Unwin.

Schirmer, Jennifer. 1993. The Seeking of Truth and the Gendering of Consciousness: The Comadres of El Salvador and the CONAVIGUA Widows of Guatemala. In *Viva: Women and Popular Protest in Latin America*, ed. S. Radcliffe and S. Westwood, 30–64. London: Routledge.

Schmidt, Gregory D. 2003. The Implementation of Gender Quotas in Peru: Legal Reform, Discourses and Impacts. Paper read at International IDEA Workshop, The Implementation of Quotas: Latin American Experiences, February 23–24, Lima, Peru.

Schmidt, Gregory D. 2008a. The Election of Women in List PR Systems: Testing the Conventional Wisdom. *Electoral Studies* 28:190–203.

———. 2008b. Success under Open List PR: The Election of Women to Congress. In *Women and Legislative Representation: Electoral Systems, Political Parties, and Sex Quotas*, ed. M. Tremblay, 161–172. New York: Palgrave Macmillan.

Schmidt, Gregory D., and Kyle L. Saunders. 2004. Effective Quotas, Relative Party Magnitude, and the Success of Female Candidates: Peruvian Municipal Elections in Comparative Perspective. *Comparative Political Studies* 37 (6):704–724.

Schwindt-Bayer, Leslie A. 2003. Legislative Representation in Latin America: A Comparative Study of Descriptive, Substantive, and Symbolic Representation of

Women. Doctoral Dissertation, Department of Political Science, University of Arizona, Tucson, AZ.
———. 2005. The Incumbency Disadvantage and Women's Election to Legislative Office. *Electoral Studies* 24 (2):227–244.
———. 2006. Still Supermadres? Gender and the Policy Priorities of Latin American Legislators. *American Journal of Political Science* 50 (3):570–585.
———. 2008. Women and Power in the Americas: A Report Card. In *Women in the Americas: Paths to Political Power*: Inter-American Development Bank, Inter-American Dialogue, League of Women Voters.
———. 2009. Making Quotas Work: The Effect of Gender Quota Laws on the Election of Women. *Legislative Studies Quarterly* 34 (1):5–28.
Schwindt-Bayer, Leslie A., Michael Malecki, and Brian F Crisp. Forthcoming. Candidate Gender and Electoral Success in Single Transferable Vote Systems. *British Journal of Political Science.*
Schwindt-Bayer, Leslie A., and William Mishler. 2005. An Integrated Model of Women's Representation. *Journal of Politics* 67 (2):407–428.
Seligson, Mitchell A. 2002. The Impact of Corruption on Regime Legitimacy: A Comparative Study of Four Latin American Countries. *Journal of Politics* 64 (2):408–433.
———. 2006. The Measurement and Impact of Corruption Victimization: Survey Evidence from Latin America. *World Development* 34 (2):381–404.
Shepsle, Kenneth A., and Barry R. Weingast. 1987. The Institutional Foundations of Committee Power. *American Political Science Review* 81 (1):85–104.
Shugart, Matthew Soberg, and John M. Carey. 1992. *Presidents and Assemblies: Constitutional Design and Electoral Dynamics.* New York: Cambridge University Press.
Skard, Torild, and Elina Haavio-Mannila. 1985. Women in Parliament. In *Unfinished Democracy: Women in Nordic Politics*, ed. E. Haavio-Mannila, 51–80. New York: Pergamon Press.
Squires, Judith. 2007. *The New Politics of Inequality.* Basingstoke: Palgrave Macmillan.
Stevenson, Linda S. 1999. Gender Politics in the Mexican Democratization Process: Electing Women and Legislating Sex Crimes and Affirmative Action, 1988–97. In *Toward Mexico's Democratization: Parties, Campaigns, Elections, and Public Opinion*, ed. J. I. Domínguez and A. Poiré, 57–87. New York: Routledge.
Stockemer, Daniel. 2008. Women's Representation: A Comparison between Europe and the Americas. *Politics* 28 (2):65–73.
Studlar, Donley T., and Ian McAllister. 1991. Political Recruitment to the Australian Legislature: Toward an Explanation of Women's Electoral Disadvantages. *Western Political Quarterly* 44 (2):467–485.
———. 1996. Constituency Activity and Representational Roles among Australian Legislators. *The Journal of Politics* 58 (1):69–90.
Studlar, Donley T., and Susan Welch. 1991. Does District Magnitude Matter? Women Candidates in London Local Elections. *Western Political Quarterly* 44 (2):457–467.

Swers, Michele L. 1998. Are Women More Likely to Vote for Women's Issue Bills than Their Male Colleagues? *Legislative Studies Quarterly* XXIII (3):435–448.

———. 2001. Research on Women in Legislatures: What Have We Learned, Where Are We Going? *Women & Politics* 23 (1–2):167–185.

———. 2002. *The Difference Women Make: the Policy Impact of Women in Congress.* Chicago: University of Chicago Press.

———. 2005. Connecting Descriptive and Substantive Representation: An Analysis of Sex Differences in Cosponsorship Activity. *Legislative Studies Quarterly* 30 (3):407–433.

Taagepera, Rein, and Matthew Soberg Shugart. 1989. *Seats and Votes: The Effects and Determinants of Electoral Systems.* New Haven: Yale University Press.

Tate, Alicia. 2006. Personal Interview, June 23.

Tavits, Margit. 2007. Clarity of Responsibility and Corruption. *American Journal of Political Science* 51 (1):218–229.

Taylor, Michelle M. 1992. Formal versus Informal Incentive Structures and Legislator Behavior: Evidence from Costa Rica. *Journal of Politics* 54 (4):1055–1073.

Taylor-Robinson, Michelle M. 2002. The Effect of Party Candidate Selection Procedures and National Electoral Rules on the President's Ability to Achieve His Legislative Agenda: The Case of Costa Rica. Paper read at UNT Conference on Parties and Elections in New Democracies, Dallas, TX.

———. 2007. Presidential and Congressional Elections in Honduras, November 2005. *Electoral Studies* 26:507–533.

Taylor-Robinson, Michelle M., and Roseanna M. Heath. 2003. Do Women Legislators Have Different Policy Priorities than Their Male Colleagues? A Critical Case Test. *Women & Politics* 24 (4):77–101.

Thomas, Sue. 1991. The Impact of Women on State Legislative Policies. *Journal of Politics* 53 (4):958–976.

Thomas, Sue. 1992. The Effects of Race and Gender on Constituency Service. *Western Political Quarterly* 45:169–180.

———. 1994. *How Women Legislate.* New York: Oxford University Press.

———. 2008. "Backlash" and Its Utility to Political Scientists. *Politics & Gender* 4 (4):615–622.

Thomas, Sue, and Susan Welch. 1991. The Impact of Gender on Activities and Priorities of State Legislators. *Western Political Quarterly* 44 (2):445–456.

Thomas, Sue, and Clyde Wilcox, eds. 2005. *Women and Elective Office: Past, Present, and Future.* 2nd ed. New York: Oxford University Press.

Tomz, Michael, Jason Wittenberg, and Gary King. 2001. CLARIFY: Software for Interpreting and Presenting Statistical Results 2.0. Harvard University, Cambridge, MA.

Towns, Ann. 2003. Understanding the Effects of Larger Ratios of Women in National Legislatures: Proportions and Gender Differentiation in Sweden and Norway. *Women & Politics* 25 (1/2):1–29.

Treisman, Daniel. 2000. The Causes of Corruption: A Cross-National Study. *Journal of Public Economics* 76 (3):399–457.

Tremblay, Manon. 2003. Women's Representational Role in Australia and Canada: The Impact of Political Context. *Australian Journal of Political Science* 38 (2):215–239.

———. 2006. The Substantive Representation of Women and PR: Some Reflections on the Role of Surrogate Representation and Critical Mass. *Politics & Gender* 2 (4):502–511.

———. 2007. Democracy, Representation, and Women: A Comparative Analysis. *Democratization* 14 (4):533–553.

———. 2008a. Conclusion. In *Women and Legislative Representation*, ed. M. Tremblay, 233–247. New York: Palgrave Macmillan.

———, ed. 2008b. *Women and Legislative Representation: Electoral Systems, Political Parties, and Sex Quotas*. New York: Palgrave Macmillan.

Tremblay, Manon, and Réjean Pelletier. 2000. More Feminists or More Women? Descriptive and Substantive Representation of Women in the 1997 Canadian Federal Elections. *International Political Science Review* 21 (4):381–405.

Tripp, Aili Mari. 2006. Uganda: Agents of Change for Women's Advancement? In *Women in African Parliaments*, ed. G. Bauer and H. E. Britton, 111–132. Boulder: Lynne Rienner.

Tripp, Aili, and Alice Kang. 2008. The Global Impact of Quotas: On the Fast Track to Increased Female Legislative Representation. *Comparative Political Studies* 41 (3):338–361.

Ulbig, Stacy G. 2007. Gendering Municipal Government: Female Descriptive Representation and Feelings of Political Trust. *Social Science Quarterly* 88 (5):1106–1123.

UNDP. 2008. Human Development Report, 2007–2008. New York: United Nations Development Program.

Venegas, Ismael. 2000a. Alianza Femenina en el Congreso. *La Nación*, February 19, 2000.

———. 2000b. Crece Lucha por Jefaturas. *La Nación*, January 1, 2000.

Villalobos, Sonia. 1999. Personal interview, July 7.

Vincent, Louise. 2004. Quotas: Changing the Way Things Look without Changing the Way Things Are. *Journal of Legislative Studies* 10 (1):71–96.

Walsh, Katherine Cramer. 2002. Enlarging Representation: Women Bringing Marginalized Perspectives to Floor Debate in the House of Representatives. In *Women Transforming Congress*, ed. C. S. Rosenthal, 370–396. Norman: University of Oklahoma Press.

Wangnerud, Lena. 2000a. Testing the Politics of Presence: Women's Representation in the Swedish Riksdag. *Scandinavian Political Studies* 23 (1):67–91.

———. 2000b. Representing Women. In *Beyond Westminster and Congress: The Nordic Experience*, ed. P. Esaiasson and K. Heidar, 132–154. Columbus: Ohio State University Press.

Waylen, Georgina. 2007. *Engendering Transitions: Women's Mobilization, Institutions, and Gender Outcomes*. New York: Oxford University Press.

———. 2008. Enhancing the Substantive Representation of Women: Lessons from Transitions to Democracy. *Parliamentary Affairs* 61 (3):518–534.

Weissberg, Robert. 1978. Collective vs. Dyadic Representation in Congress. *American Political Science Review* 72:535–547.

Welch, Susan. 1985. Are Women More Liberal than Men in the U.S. Congress? *Legislative Studies Quarterly* 10 (1):125–134.

Welch, Susan, and Donley T. Studlar. 1990. Multimember Districts and the Representation of Women. *Journal of Politics* 52 (2):391–412.

Weldon, S. Laurel. 2002a. Beyond Bodies: Institutional Sources of Representation for Women in Democratic Policymaking. *Journal of Politics* 64 (4):1153–1174.

———. 2002b. *Protest, Policy, and the Problem of Violence against Women: A Cross-National Comparison*. Pittsburgh: University of Pittsburgh Press.

———. 2006. The Structure of Intersectionality: A Comparative Politics of Gender. *Politics & Gender* 2 (2):235–248.

Weyland, Kurt. 1996. Neopopulism and Neoliberalism in Latin America. *Studies in Comparative International Development* 31 (3):3–31.

Williams, Melissa S. 1998. *Voice, Trust, and Memory: Marginalized Groups and the Failings of Liberal Representation*. Princeton: Princeton University Press.

Williams, Richard. 2006. Generalized ordered logit/partial proportional-odds models for ordinal dependent variables. *Stata Journal* 6 (1):58–82.

Wilson, Rick K., and Cheryl D. Young. 1997. Cosponsorship in the U.S. Congress. *Legislative Studies Quarterly* 22 (1):25–43.

Wolbrecht, Christina. 2002. Female Legislators and the Women's Rights Agenda: From Feminine Mystique to Feminist Era. In *Women Transforming Congress*, ed. C. S. Rosenthal, 170–197. Norman: University of Oklahoma Press.

Wolbrecht, Christina, and David E. Campbell. 2007. Leading by Example: Female Members of Parliament as Political Role Models. *American Journal of Political Science* 51 (4):921–939.

Women in Development Network. 1995. Statistics—Latin America and Caribbean. Retrieved July 12, 2009, from http://www.focusintl.com/statr4a4.htm#002

Wood, David M., and Garry Young. 1997. Comparing Constituency Activity by Junior Legislators in Great Britain and Ireland. *Legislative Studies Quarterly* 22 (2): 217–232.

World Bank. 2007. *World Development Indicators* [CD-ROM]. Washington, DC: World Bank.

Xydias, Christina. 2007. Women Representing Women: Examining the Effects of Gender Quotas. Paper read at Annual Meeting of the American Political Science Association, August 30, Chicago, IL.

Yoon, Mi Yung. 2004. Explaining Women's Legislative Representation in Sub-Saharan Africa. *Legislative Studies Quarterly* 29 (3):447–468.

Young, Iris Marion. 1990. *Justice and the Politics of Difference*. Princeton: Princeton University Press.

———. 2000. *Inclusion and Democracy*. New York: Oxford University Press.

Zambrano, Laura. 1998. Participación y Representación Feminina en el Congreso. In *Elecciones y Democracia en Colombia, 1997–1998*, ed. A. M. Bejerano and A. Davilá, 255–284. Bogotá: Universidad de los Andes.

Zeigler, L. Harmon, M. Kent Jennings, and G.W. Peak. 1974. *Governing American Schools*. North Scituate, MA: Duxbury Press.

Zetterberg, Pär. 2008. The Downside of Gender Quotas? Institutional Constraints on Women in Mexican State Legislatures. *Parliamentary Affairs* 61 (3):442–460.

———. 2009. Do Gender Quotas Foster Women's Political Engagement? Lessons from Latin America. *Political Research Quarterly* 62 (4):715–730.

Index